Wolfe

The Career of General James Wolfe
from Culloden to Quebec

By the same author and published by Spellmount Publishers:

1745: A Military History of the Last Jacobite Rising

All the King's Armies:
A Military History of the English Civil War 1642–1651

WOLFE

THE CAREER OF
GENERAL JAMES WOLFE
FROM CULLODEN TO QUEBEC

by

Stuart Reid

SPELLMOUNT
Staplehurst

British Library Cataloguing in Publication Data:
A catalogue record for this book is available
from the British Library

Copyright © Stuart Reid 2000

ISBN 1-86227-084-8

First published in the UK in 2000 by
Spellmount Limited
The Old Rectory
Staplehurst
Kent TN12 0AZ

Tel: 01580 893730
Fax: 01580 893731
E-mail: enquiries@spellmount.com
Website: www.spellmount.com

1 3 5 7 9 8 6 4 2

The right of Stuart Reid to be identified
as the author of this work has been asserted by him
in accordance with the Copyright, Designs
and Patents Act 1988

Typeset in Palatino by MATS, Southend-on-Sea, Essex
Printed in Great Britain by
TJ International Ltd, Padstow, Cornwall

Contents

For my son Stuart,
who may be destined to be a great man
and fit for a cap

List of Maps

Preface

"I reckon it a very great misfortune to this country," wrote James Wolfe to his mother, "that I, your son, who have, I know, but a very modest capacity, and some degree of diligence a little above the ordinary run, should be thought, as I generally am, one of the best officers of my rank in the service. I am not at all vain of the distinction. The comparison would do a man of genius very little honour, and does not illustrate me, by any means; and the consequence will be very fatal to me in the end, for as I rise in rank people will expect some considerable performances, and I shall be induced, in support of an ill-got reputation, to be lavish of my life, and shall probably meet that fate which is the ordinary effect of such conduct."

Wolfe did indeed meet his fate on the Plains of Abraham, in winning Canada for the British Empire. By any standard this was a considerable performance for a thirty-two year-old major general and consequently he has not lacked for biographers. However, with some notable exceptions it would be fair to say that most have treated his life merely as a hasty preface to the events of 1759 and that rather more attention has been paid over the years to that famous victory than to just why James Wolfe was granted the opportunity to become the Hero of Quebec in the first place.

In order to fully appreciate *that* it is also necessary to examine the British Army of the mid-18th century. Otherwise it is quite impossible to adequately do justice to a man reckoned "one of the best officers . . . in the service" or to consider whether his reputation was "ill-got" without having a proper understanding of that service. Consequently this book is as much about the Georgian army and its officers and men as it is about James Wolfe, for it would be quite invidious to speak of one without the other.

Rather than dwelling upon the many quirks of Wolfe's character and his relationships with his parents, his brother and the women in his life, therefore, as biographers are commonly wont to do, I have endeavoured here to establish the mechanics of how he actually attained his promotions, and what strings were pulled on his behalf, by whom and why; what his duties were and how well he discharged them; what was the tactical thinking of his day and how did he work within its constraints and go on to develop his own, ultimately very influential, ideas about infantry combat.

ix

Inevitably, it has to be confessed at the outset that this study centres very closely on the infantry to the almost total exclusion of other arms, for although Wolfe once expressed a whimsical desire to ride with the cavalry in Germany, almost his whole career was spent in the infantry. Indeed it is perhaps rather fitting that he should have begun it marching on his own two feet into Germany and ended it, even as a major general, commanding on foot at Quebec.

It would be invidious too to neglect those who have contributed in some way to the writing of this book, including the staff of the Public Record Office at Kew, and Newcastle upon Tyne City Libraries. As to individuals the chief amongst them is undoubtedly Dr. John Houlding, whose *Fit for Service: The Training of the British Army 1715-1795* has been a constant inspiration for some years now, and whose personal encouragement and unfailing advice has led to me now writing a rather better book than might otherwise have been the case. Needless to say he bears no responsibility for any shortcomings, and nor does Lorraine McCann who undertook the arduous task of editing the manuscript and correcting my atrocious punctuation. However I would also be failing in my duty if I neglected to mention my wife Susan, who kept me fed and watered, put up with me when I grew impossible and diplomatically took my son off at critical moments.

Stuart Reid
North Shields, 2000

Technical Notes

Regiments at this period were commonly identified by the name of their colonel, but obviously this changed as commanding officers were successively promoted or translated to glory, and during the 1740s numbers were allocated according to their supposed seniority, largely one suspects in order to ease the task of the War Office clerks trying to keep track of them. Although the numbers did not assume an official primacy over the names until 1751 and both continued to be used interchangeably for some time afterwards, they are used here from the outset in order to avoid confusion. Thus, for example when Wolfe joined the 12th Foot in 1742, it was still being referred to both in official documents and in everyday speech as Duroure's Regiment, having until a few months before been known as Whetham's Regiment and three years later becoming Skelton's. For the sake of clarity, therefore, it is primarily referred to in the text as the 12th Foot.

A peculiarity which will be noticed is the designation of some units such as Ligonier's Regiment as the 59th/48th Foot. This is because their numbers changed for one reason or another. When first raised in January 1741 this particular regiment was numbered as the 59th, but when Oglethorpe's 42nd and the ten regiments of Marines were disbanded in 1748, it survived to serve under Wolfe as the 48th. Similarly another of Wolfe's regiments at Quebec, the 78th Highlanders, started off as the 63rd before being pushed *down* the list of seniority when a number of new units were brought into the line.

Another change made for the better at about the same time concerned the calendar. Until 2 September 1752 Great Britain and her colonies still followed the old Julian calendar and thus lagged temporally behind the rest of Europe by eleven days. Just to further confuse matters the New Year was also reckoned in England and the English colonies to commence on Lady Day – 25 March – although the Scots had long since very sensibly adopted 1 January to the purpose. This present study follows the amiable convention of accepting all dates as they are written save for commencing each year on 1 January in order to avoid puzzling and confusing both author and readers with the clumsy rendering of certain dates as, say, 2 January 1726/1727 or converting them from "old-style" into "new-style" and back again - especially when there might be some uncertainty as to whether they were dated correctly in the first place. When serving on the Continent in the 1740s James Wolfe appears to have employed both styles indiscriminately so we should not trouble ourselves on this particular score either.

Nor is there much justification for laboriously converting sums of money expended in the 18th century into their modern "equivalents". Due to the intervening effects of inflation and some equally dramatic alterations in the relative values of certain items - such as the humble loaf of bread - conversions of this kind are quite meaningless. However, as the currency itself has also changed it may be as well to explain that in the 18th century precise sums of money were expressed in pounds, shillings and pence - usually rendered as £.s.d. In both Great Britain and Ireland there were twenty shillings in the pound and twelve pence or pennies in the shilling, although the pound itself was only a notional denomination and for cash transactions golden guinea pieces worth £1 1s were used. Even more confusingly, the quite separate Irish exchequer's currency traded at a slightly different rate of exchange than English sterling, with the latter being worth £1 1s 8d Irish in 1749. This irritating mismatch then necessitated complex adjustments whenever a regiment passed from the Irish to the British Establishment or vice versa.

Weights and measures were similarly idiosyncratic but from a military point of view, in the British service at least, we need only consider the imperial pound (454gms), usually expressed as lb. At this period cannon were classified not according to calibre but by the weight of shot which they threw. Thus cannon were commonly classed as 1½lbrs, 3lbrs and so on upwards. Firearms were similarly, if slightly more obscurely, categorised. Most of the British Army's firelocks were of what was termed common musket bore, or 14 bore; that is fourteen bullets of the requisite size could be cast from the single pound of lead which had represented the ordinary musketeer's ammunition scale in the 17th century. Carbines, by contrast, were 16 bore and it is worth mentioning that while the term carbine is now applied to short-barrelled weapons, in the 18th century it merely denoted the bore and not the length of the barrel.

Hot Stuff

Come each death-doing dog, who dares venture his neck,
Come follow the hero, that goes to Quebec;
Jump aboard of the transport, and loose every sail,
Pay your debts at the tavern, by giving leg bail;
And ye that love fighting, shall soon have enough;
For Wolfe commands us boys, we will give them Hot Stuff!

Up the river St. Lawrence, our troops shall advance,
To the Grenadiers' March, we shall teach them to dance;
Cape Breton we've taken, and next we shall try,
At their capitol to give them, another black eye;
Vaudreuil tis in vain, you pretend to look gruff,
For those who are coming know how to give you Hot Stuff!

With powder in his periwig, and snuff in his nose,
Monsewer will come down, our descent to oppose;
And the Indians will come, but the light infantry,
Will soon oblige them to take to a tree;
For such rascals as these, may we fear our rebuff?
Advance Grenadiers, and let fly your Hot Stuff!

When the Forty-seventh Regiment is dashing ashore,
And bullets are whistling, and cannon do roar;
Says Montcalm, "Those are Shirley's, I know their lapels."
"You lie" says Ned Botwood, "for we are with Lascelles,"
"Though our clothing has changed, yet we scorn the powder-puff,"
"Have at ye, ye bastards, here's give you Hot Stuff!"

With Monckton and Townshend, those brave Brigadiers,
We'll soon have the town, down about their ears;
And when we have done, with their muskets and guns,
If you would Mother Abbess, a word with your nuns;
Each soldier shall enter, the Convent in buff,
And then never fear, we will give them Hot Stuff!

CHAPTER I
The Family Firm
The British Army in the 18th Century

The British Army in which James Wolfe would come to shine so brightly was an institution of no great antiquity. Traditionally its historians have tended to trace its substantive origins in the former Cromwellian forces which formed the nucleus of King Charles II's English Army after the Restoration in 1660, but there is probably a much more convincing case to be made for regarding Dutch William – King William III – as its true founder. The brief reign of James VII and II had seen a considerable, alarming and perhaps unjustified expansion of the armed forces of the Crown in all three kingdoms of Britain, but their dramatic collapse and indeed near total disintegration in the wake of the Dutch invasion in November 1688 meant that William effectively had to start from scratch. For the most part the surviving regiments had to be purged and rebuilt and a whole host of new ones hastily raised. Arguably, therefore, what would become the British Army was born not on Tower Hill in 1660, but in the wake of the first *Mutiny Act* of 28 March 1689[1] and rather fittingly one of the new officers to be commissioned into Sir George St. George's Regiment of Foot was the future Major General James Wolfe's grandfather, Captain Edward Wolfe.

1
Army and State

Strictly speaking, at the very outset of the 18th century the British Army was still made up from three constitutionally quite separate national organisations; the English Army, the Scots Army and the Irish Army, together with their respective administrative structures and Boards of Ordnance. The political Union of the twin kingdoms of Scotland and England in 1707 saw the armies merged a year later into two "Establishments", one for the United Kingdom and the Dominion of Wales, otherwise known as the British Establishment, and an Irish Establishment which remained constitutionally and in all too many other respects practically independent until the Union of 1801.

While it was generally acknowledged that ultimate authority over the

Army rested with the Crown, the preamble to the first and every successive *Mutiny Act* unambiguously declared that "The raising and keeping a standing army within the United Kingdom in time of peace, unless it be with the consent of Parliament, is against law". Despite the considerable rhetoric subsequently devoted to this point by generations of fiercely (or at least noisily) hostile politicians no one seriously expected the Army to be paid off and replaced by an enlarged County Militia. Consequently an uneasy system of dual control grew up. Other than the fact that Parliament paid for the Army and therefore not unnaturally expected to get its money's worth, the precise parameters of that control were ill-defined and to a very large extent depended upon the personality, ability and energy of the individuals and departments concerned.

The King himself obviously enjoyed a certain degree of historical, moral and practical superiority. He was after all the Head of State and the members of the government, of whatever political complexion, were *his* ministers. The most important of them were the relevant Secretaries of State. Since, as Clausewitz was to put it, war was merely the continuation of diplomacy by other means, any strategic decisions on the employment of His Majesty's forces were generally a matter for His Majesty's Government. This normally meant the Prime Minister and the Foreign Secretaries (there were two, one for northern Europe and one for the south), but the Secretary of State for the Colonies was particularly responsible for the deployment and administration of troops in the British West Indies and British North America, as well as the odd toe-hold on the west coast of Africa. His powers were quite extensive and it was a source of considerable annoyance to officers serving in overseas garrisons that they were required to report in the first instance to the Colonial Office rather than to the military authorities at the Horse Guards. The Secretary's remit, however, did not extend to India, where the broad sweep of military operations were supposedly a matter for the commercial gentlemen of the Honourable East India Company.

William III and the Hanoverian kings who followed him took their military responsibilities very seriously indeed. On a day-to-day basis, however, they generally (but not invariably) delegated most of the work to a commander-in-chief; the most notable of whom during James Wolfe's time was King George II's younger son William Augustus, Duke of Cumberland. Broadly speaking, the King and his commander-in-chief enjoyed virtually unfettered authority over all those matters that would later fall under the remit of the Adjutant General's department, including discipline, training and all the minutiae of uniforms and personal equipment. They also very jealously retained the absolute right of appointing and promoting officers, although this was an area of occasional conflict with the political gentlemen who were thus denied what might otherwise have been a near limitless source of patronage.

Below the King came a number of military officials and departments, the most important of which were the Board of General Officers, the Board of Ordnance, various local commanders-in-chief with semi-independent powers, such as the CinC North Britain, and last but by no means least the Secretary at War. The Board of General Officers was simply an advisory body of varying effectiveness and influence, but the Board of Ordnance actually ran a small army within an army, being wholly responsible for the officers and men of the Royal Artillery, as well as the Royal Engineers, and all matters relating to fortifications, and to the provision and transportation of ammunition and a range of military hardware from cannon to camp equipage such as tents and canteens, including guns and gunpowder for the Royal Navy as well.[2]

Finally, those areas of routine administration which in the field would fall to the Quartermaster General and his staff were, for the most part, delegated to the Secretary at War. Originally no more than the King's Military Secretary, he held a military commission as such but was almost invariably a civilian and normally a political one to boot. He and his frighteningly small staff of clerks were responsible for a wide variety of ill-defined functions, including the deployment and quartering of troops both at home and abroad, a positive morass of financial matters and extensive general correspondence with individual officers and with regimental agents. This correspondence inevitably drew them into the ever-contentious question of promotions and appointments, and in an age when civil posts, sinecures and preferments were entirely managed through patronage it was only natural that politicians should wish to extend that patronage to cover military appointments as well.

While it was no doubt very gratifying to occasionally secure a military commission for the son or other near relation of a voter, the real meat of this patronage lay not in individual promotions but in the granting of Letters of Service to raise new regiments, with all the financial perquisites and opportunities for enrichment which came with them. Yet at the best of times this was a highly contentious issue and one in which the Crown jealously guarded its traditional prerogatives. A prudent, or at least circumspect, Secretary at War was expected to refer such appointments to the King and the vital importance of maintaining this Royal prerogative may easily be gauged both from the iniquities of the separate Irish Establishment and rather more dramatically from the utter chaos which ensued during the great recruiting boom of the early 1790s when the politicians at last had the free and unfettered access to the military patronage which they had craved throughout the century.

Many of the regiments raised by William III had been disbanded after the Peace of Rijswyck in 1697 and in 1699 the *Disbanding Act*[3] grudgingly authorised the retention of an English Establishment of just 7,000 officers and men and an Irish one of 12,000. In the following year the chronically impoverished Scots Parliament limited its own military Establishment to just 3,000 soldiers of all ranks, although here at least the cuts were temporarily cushioned by transferring three regiments to the Dutch Army's famous Scots Brigade.[4] Throughout Dutch William's reign the Scots Brigade was closely integrated with his "British" army, but on his death they naturally reverted completely to Dutch control, leaving his successor, Queen Anne, with a total of just 22,000 officers and men in the three kingdoms – some 8,000 short of what William had considered to be the absolute minimum requirement.

Recognising this, in 1702 Queen Anne succeeded in persuading Parliament to sanction the recruitment of additional forces, but this was only accepted on the strict understanding that each augmentation be particularly justified and annually scrutinised. Somehow the Army managed to scrape through the War of the Spanish Succession without the imposition of large-scale redundancies in mid-campaign, but it was sometimes touch and go.[5] Then in 1713 the end of the war provided a welcome opportunity for consolidation. The artificial distinction between the 7,000-strong standing army allowed under the 1699 Act and the subsequent wartime augmentations disappeared along with the ever-contentious Votes of Supply required to authorise them from year to year. Instead, the scope of the annual *Mutiny Act* was broadened to include an estimate of all military expenditure for the coming year which was in turn justified by including an estimate of the gross pay required for individual formations. This measure was important, for while the outbreak of peace was customarily followed by the wholesale disbanding of regiments, it allowed the Army to retain a relatively large number of fully officered but weakly manned regimental cadres which could be expanded again when required for service.

Nevertheless, with spiralling imperial commitments steadily forcing the size of the English (or more properly British) Establishment up from 15,851 officers and men in 1715 to 26,314 in the 1730s, and no fewer than 45,349 immediately after the outbreak of war with Spain in 1739, Parliament continued to look upon the Army with a decidedly jaundiced eye. The unfortunate fact of the matter was that quite apart from the considerable expense which it represented in peacetime, the Army was a profoundly unpopular institution. There was certainly a degree of justification for this distrust and a variety of unfortunate precedents pointing to the dangers of military despotism both on the Continent and much nearer home under the Stuarts of unhappy memory. The awful spectre of Cromwell and the despotic rule of his major generals was also regularly invoked, and the Army vigorously denounced as a potential if not an actual threat to life, liberty and Parliamentary democracy, while the ordinary citizen merely found it an expensive nuisance.

This profound distrust of the Army found expression in a number of areas. One of them was a long-standing custom, formally enshrined in legislation in 1734,[6] that all troops were to be ordered out from any borough in which a Parliamentary election was to take place. It was confidently assumed that there would otherwise be far too great a temptation for them to be used to interfere in the electoral process. On the whole, however, this particular Act really served to emphasise the fact that in political circles the Army was chiefly resented as being an instrument of the Government. Leaving aside its obvious and necessary counter-insurgency role during the Jacobite uprisings which periodically disturbed the first half of the 18th century, the Army was regularly expected to discharge a number of functions which really ought to have been delegated to a properly constituted civilian constabulary. A particularly high profile function was the suppression of riots and "tumults". As the Secretary at War complained in 1732, local authorities "Frequently send to my Office for a military assistance . . . it has always been the practice of my predecessors . . . to give it them, by sending Troops of Horse or Dragoons, or Companies of Foot to their aid and assistance."[7] Since many of these disturbances were politically inspired or at the very least capable of assuming a political complexion, if only in retrospect, it was natural that the Opposition should loudly resent the Army's reluctant role in suppressing them. Their stance, however, would no doubt have been very different were positions reversed, for as Sir Robert Walpole candidly admitted, "there is no maxim more true than that force is necessary for the support of government".

Necessary it may have been, but the combination of these unpopular duties and the hand-to-mouth existence to which it was condemned by the annual ritual of the *Mutiny Act* inevitably affected the Army's operational efficiency. This was equally badly undermined by Parliament's persistent reluctance to sanction the provision of proper barrack facilities. Yet this was not simply a matter of balking at the considerable capital cost which it would have entailed, for occasionally there was no alternative but to come up with the cash and build barracks in certain strategically important locations such as Berwick upon Tweed, or Portsmouth. The real problem was that the wholesale erection of barracks in mainland Britain (Ireland was always a different matter) would have been a politically unacceptable acknowledgement of the Army's permanence.

The consequences of this prejudice will be examined more closely in due course, but the principal effect of pretending that soldiers only required to be temporarily accommodated in licensed premises on the road to wherever glory awaited was to ensure their continued unpopularity amongst the ordinary people who had to house, feed and put up with them, while simultaneously making it very difficult for units to achieve a satisfactory level of training. The widespread dispersal of troops in temporary billets up and down the country meant that not only was it rare for individual battalions to be concentrated, except in the run-up to their annual inspection, but that brigades could only be formed during wartime. Predictably this in turn led to a narrowing of their officers' horizons, and even the Duke of Cumberland, according to an exasperated Wolfe, could only rarely see beyond the confines of a battalion.

Ireland presented its own, worse and even more intractable problems. The 1699 *Disbanding Act* had been extended to that kingdom by all the awful authority of a Royal Proclamation, and so the figure of 12,000 officers and men then laid down as its military establishment, or rather as its garrison, was quite unassailable. While this happy fact was no doubt a great comfort to William III and his successors, it was also a pretty academic point since none of the Lord Lieutenants of Ireland ever evinced the slightest interest in reducing it. Consequently the security of the Irish Establishment, combined with the absence of hostile scrutiny by the ineffectual Dublin Parliament, soon led to it being used by the Crown as an imperial reserve stuffed with a great many stripped down regimental cadres.

It was no longer, of course, a completely independent army in the way that King James's Irish Army had been, or the old Scots one had been before 1708. It is true that the Lord Lieutenant had a general staff in Dublin Castle to rival the Horse Guards in London and his very own Master of the Ordnance. From 1760 there would also be a Royal Irish Artillery, and in time a Royal Irish Wagon Train, but otherwise no infantry or cavalry units were permanently assigned to the Irish Establishment. The four regiments of "Irish" Horse who spent the whole century stationed there might however have been forgiven for thinking otherwise. Instead, regiments were freely transferred from one establishment to the other according to operational need or political and financial expediency, and when a regiment was ordered overseas it normally transferred at once to the British Establishment and was thenceforth paid and maintained by London.[8]

Unfortunately the advantages of possessing this imperial reserve were undermined by the very independence which made it possible. The assignment of units to Ireland and their summoning forth was a matter for the King and the Secretary at War in London. However, for so long as they actually remained on the Irish Establishment, the Lord Lieutenant and his notoriously incompetent staff at Dublin Castle had complete authority over their movements, quartering (normally in barracks), training and employment, and also to a very considerable extent made an even greater cock of exercising the coveted power to appoint and promote officers. Their priorities were also very different. While London looked to the Irish Army principally as a source for operational reinforcements, the Irish staff, when it gave any thought to the matter at all, persisted in employing it first and foremost as a police force and dispersing it up and down the country in little detachments which ultimately were even more destructive to military efficiency and discipline than the *ad hoc* billeting arrangements in England.[9]

It was only too well known, in fact, that in Ireland regiments went to the dogs and perhaps the most trenchant comment upon this can be found in an entry for May 1752 in the orderly book of Halkett's 44th Foot which splenetically declared: "No Officer to appear in the Barrack Yard, on the Parade or any where out of doors, in his Night Cap or Slippers, Nor is it Proper he should Walk about the Town or Village, where he is Quartered, without his Sword."[10]

Had the Irish Army really been a completely separate organisation this chronic inefficiency might not have mattered too much and the prospect of its degenerating into a bucolic local militia might have been viewed with complacency rather than alarm. The trouble was that with most regiments on the British Establishment already fully committed, it was the Irish regiments hastily brought up to strength by equally useless drafts which all too often found themselves first in line to continue diplomacy by other means. In 1755 two "Irish" regiments, Halkett's 44th and Dunbar's 48th, were ordered to North America. Only partially brought up to strength by drafting from other battalions on the Irish Establishment, they were then completed by local recruiting on their arrival in America before marching to disaster on the Monongahela River.

One of the lesser curiosities of this deep-run split between the two establishments was the requirement for regiments to employ the services of London- or Dublin-based agents according to whether they were carried on the British or Irish pay, and to switch those agents as they switched establishments.

In the absence of a fully developed government/military bureaucracy, the regimental agent was the indispensable link between the Secretary at War and the individual unit. His various functions were admirably described in 1798 by the then Deputy Secretary at War as being to "apply for, receive, disburse and account for public money advanced to him under general regulations or by particular orders. He is the ordinary channel of communication between the Regiment and the Public Departments, and is resorted to not only for providing and forwarding of arms, clothing and other regimental supplies, but also in the business, public or private, of the individual officers."

As with so much else to do with the Georgian army, there was a certain ambiguity about the agent's status. Originally he was no more than a personal servant of the regimental colonel; his confidential clerk and man of business. In theory, therefore, each regiment of cavalry or infantry could have employed its own agent. Many did so, but in practise by the middle part of the 18th century the business began to be concentrated in the hands of just a few professionals. What was more, once the agents established permanent offices, formed partnerships and took on clerks of their own, their status altered considerably. They still had to compete for business in something approaching a cut-throat atmosphere, but now they were no longer mere servants but rather the managers of what could be quite extensive client portfolios. "Army" rather than "regimental" agency was becoming big business indeed and by 1790 there were just fourteen agencies operating in London and eight in Dublin, looking after 108 regiments of cavalry and infantry and 36 independent companies, besides the militia.

Undoubtedly the most prominent of this new breed of agent was "Honest Jack" Calcraft, who at the height of the Seven Years War had no fewer than 63 marching regiments, 16 independent companies, two fencible battalions and four regiments of militia on his books. He was, however, by any standards exceptional and in peacetime the average portfolio seems to have been in the region of just three or four regiments.[11]

This process of consolidation and partnership was a natural consequence of the increasing complexity of the agent's job, and indeed the sheer workload involved. Not only was the agent granted power of attorney to deal with all regimental finances, including the procurement and purchase of clothing and equipment, but also, as was noted in 1798, his role inevitably broadened to include looking after the personal and business affairs of the individual officers. Ultimately, as government departments assumed ever more responsibility for Army administration, it was only this personal service which would remain and eventually the more successful agencies such as Cox and Greenwood evolved into private banks.[12]

2
Officers and Gentlemen

The officers themselves were a surprisingly diverse lot, but before examining at them in more detail it is first necessary to look at the nature of the military command structure.

In 1740, when a thirteen-year-old James Wolfe took his first steps towards a military career, the British Army comprised an indeterminate number of general and staff officers, four grossly over-officered and generally useless independent troops of Horse Guards, four reasonably efficient troops of Horse Grenadier Guards, eight regiments of heavy cavalry styled Horse (including the Blues, who at this time still ranked as the 1st Horse), fourteen other regiments of notionally lighter cavalry classed as dragoons – and still equipped and even trained to some extent in their original role as mounted infantry – three large regiments of footguards, 43 "marching" regiments of infantry or foot, and ten newly raised ones of marines, who at this point in time came under the Army's rather than the Admiralty's control. In addition, there were of course the officers of the Royal Engineers and the officers and men of the Royal Artillery who were administered by the Board of Ordnance, a number of sedentary independent companies, and a frighteningly long Half-pay list.

As to the command of this relatively modest host, general officers broadly fell into two categories. First there were those actually promoted to the substantive ranks of major general, lieutenant general, (full) general, field marshal and very occasionally captain general in ascending order of precedence. None of these ranks could be purchased and instead promotion was supposedly governed strictly by seniority. On the face of it this could very easily have led to the upper reaches of the Army being stuffed with aged and incapable officers, unfit to conduct a review, let alone a campaign. However, as there was no fixed establishment of general officers and absolutely no requirement whatsoever to employ them as such, any number could be promoted in a single brevet in order that the most junior of them could be appointed to a particular command.[13]

Secondly, it was also possible to give officers local or temporary rank, in order to serve, for example, either as a brigadier or more properly brigadier general, which at this time was an appointment rather than a substantive rank, or to serve as, in James Wolfe's case, a local general officer only in a particular theatre such as "North America" or the "East Indies".

Less exalted staff officers similarly fell into two categories. The first, which was by no means as rigidly defined as it would become later in the century, was comprised of what might best be described as departmental appointments; that is the quartermaster general (QMG), the adjutant general (AG) and all their respective deputies, assistants and deputy assistants. It should of course be stressed that none of these gentlemen were actually general officers, unless regularly promoted independently of their office, which at this period (if held permanently) could sometimes be purchased just like any other "office of profit under the Crown".

The QMG was quite literally responsible for the quartering and movement of troops and any other related matters which he could convincingly contrive to incorporate within his sphere of influence – but not for the supply of foodstuffs and other consumables which were the province of a commissary general, who was ultimately responsible to the Treasury. The AG, on the other hand, was primarily responsible for the drawing up, dissemination and enforcement of rules and regulations, for discipline and for training.

While the QMG and AG at the Horse Guards in Whitehall, and their opposite numbers in Dublin Castle, enjoyed primacy in their respective departments, they also had their temporary counterparts in each field army and overseas station. The appointment of such officers, who normally retained their regimental commissions, was normally at the discretion of the general officer commanding, and the staff establishment of Sir John Cope's little army in 1745 provides a good example of the rather casual way in which they could be assembled. Colonel John Campbell, the Earl of Loudoun, left off raising his 64th Highlanders to serve as Cope's adjutant general, while a Major William Caulfield held the post of quartermaster general, and Major Eaglesfield Griffith, ordinarily the Master Gunner of Edinburgh Castle, acted as commissary general, assisted by Lieutenant Colonel Charles Whitefoord of the 5th Marines, who although on leave at the time had declined a formal appointment either as adjutant general or as an aide de camp, preferring instead to look after the army's transport "without the emoluments attached to posts of official preferment".

The second category of staff officers were appointed equally casually merely on the say-so of the general officers whom they served, and comprised majors of brigade and aides de camp (ADCs). The former, usually a captain, was responsible for the transmission of orders and other administrative tasks connected with the day-to-day management of the brigade to which he was appointed, rather like a QMG and AG rolled into one. The ADC served as his general's personal assistant and secretary. Major generals were allowed one ADC at public expense and lieutenant generals two, but others could be employed as "extra" ADCs if the general cared to support them out of his own pocket. There were in fact no real restrictions at this period as to who could or could not be employed. Most were captains, and usually experienced ones at that, but more senior officers might have a major as their principal ADC or Military Secretary – Major James Mossman of the 55th served in this capacity under Cope in 1745 – but conversely there was little to prevent the employment of a subaltern or even a well-connected civilian!

At a regimental level the internal organisation of the individual units and the number of officers required to run them was also rather more fluid than it would later become. Ordinarily an infantry battalion comprised nine or ten companies, one of which was designated as grenadiers, but if ordered on active service it was augmented by an "additional company" which served as a rudimentary depot, and occasionally by extra service companies as well. Occasionally the establishment restrictions of the *Mutiny Act* were even partially circumvented by the recruiting of complete second battalions for existing regiments. The 1st (or Royal) Regiment permanently maintained two battalions throughout the 18th century, and the 60th (Royal American) Regiment had no less than four, two of which would go with Wolfe to Quebec; but for the most part those second battalions hurriedly raised at the outset of the Seven Years War were re-embodied as regiments in their own right once a subsequent *Mutiny Act* retrospectively authorised them as such. James Wolfe's own 67th Foot, for example, actually began life as 2/20th.

Each of the constituent companies within a battalion was nominally commanded by a captain and up until 27 May 1803, three of those captains also ranked as field officers – that is the colonel, lieutenant colonel and major. In the 1740s and 50s a fair number of colonels actually exercised day-to-day command of their regiments at home or on active service.[14] However, the political and financial importance of the post meant the sale of colonelcies met with determined opposition from the Crown during the 18th century. Instead, colonels were increasingly refused leave to sell and when they subsequently died, whether from old age and infirmity or (much less commonly) on active service, or their regiments otherwise became "vacant", the colonelcy was then given by the King to another tried veteran. Since, by the very nature of things, such worthies were generally either actively employed elsewhere, or had effectively retired, the day-to-day command of the battalion devolved instead on the other field officers.

During peacetime, or at least while in garrison or in quarters, regulations forbade both the lieutenant colonel and major to be absent on leave at the same time, but this tended to be cheerfully interpreted as *carte blanche* for them to take themselves off turn and turn about. Not that the situation was any better in wartime, for then it was equally likely that one or other of them might be serving on the staff, or commanding a detachment or post. Consequently it was common for a battalion to be run by just a single field officer and the adjutant. Another result of the frequent absences of the field officers was that two or sometimes all three of their own companies were actually commanded by junior officers. As early as 1725 Henry Hawley had suggested that the service would benefit from the field officers being deprived of their companies in return for an additional allowance paid to them in lieu of the customary "emoluments" due to them as captains, but the issue was widely regarded as far too sensitive and shuffled off until the advent of the Napoleonic Wars.

The captain himself was in many ways the backbone of the service, for not only did he lead and administer his company, he was also routinely accounted capable of exercising that function independently, and of commanding wings, detachments and even *ad hoc* battalions temporarily assembled from several companies. With surprising frequency he could also be found commanding his own regiment in the absence of the field officers. He was also eligible to be promoted to field rank by brevet, sometimes as a reward for outstanding service but more frequently through his appointment to extra-regimental duties.

Next in order of precedence came the lieutenant. As his title implies he was the second in command of the company, but all too often he acted up in the absence of his captain. This fact was officially recognised as far as the colonel's own company was concerned by conferring the rank of captain-lieutenant on the individual concerned. This was a rather ill-defined appointment ranking between the junior captain and the senior lieutenant. The incumbent was by courtesy styled and socially ranked amongst the other captains, but unfortunately he appears to have stood outside the ordinary channels of promotion and could readily be purchased over by more junior lieutenants. He did at least, however, have the consolation that upon finally achieving promotion, his seniority as a full captain was invariably accounted from the date of his original appointment as captain-lieutenant.

The frequent and sometimes unavoidable absence of the captains was also more or less tacitly acknowledged in wartime by temporarily augmenting the establishment of each company from one lieutenant to two. These additional subalterns should not, however, be confused with 2nd lieutenants. In the majority of infantry regiments the most junior officer was styled an ensign and in the 17th century, when each company had its own colour or ensign, it was his duty to carry it, which was reckoned to be a useful way of keeping him out of trouble while he learned his trade. However, since neither grenadier, fusilier nor marine companies possessed colours they boasted 2nd lieutenants in place of ensigns. Although by Wolfe's time ordinary infantry battalions had just two colours in total, the rank of ensign was retained throughout the 18th century.[15]

The footguards, rather unsurprisingly, had their own slightly different rank structure. The field officers normally ranked (and frequently served) as general officers and the captains were styled "Captain and Lieutenant Colonel", the former being their regimental rank and the latter their Army rank. Lieutenants were similarly ranked as captains in the army and only ensigns were considered on a par, militarily if not socially, with their counterparts in the line.

Turning to the cavalry, regiments were normally organised in six or occasionally eight troops (in place of companies), each of them again commanded by a captain, seconded by a lieutenant and in place of the ensign was a cornet. With the exception of the Blues, who were organised just like any other regiment of horse, the mounted household units boasted an even more arcane rank structure with each individual troop commanded by a colonel, two lieutenant colonels, two majors, four exempts, four brigadiers, four sub-brigadiers and an adjutant.

The adjutant was actually a regimental staff officer who appeared on the establishment of all infantry and cavalry units. As we shall see, it was an important post with particular responsibility for administration and training which was often held by former NCOs, or which could be a fast track to the promotion of keen young officers such as James Wolfe. The appointment was usually considered as being entirely in the gift of the colonel and as an especial favour he was occasionally permitted to sell it, but otherwise it was not purchasable. Normally it was simply an appointment held by a lieutenant or even occasionally by an ensign[16], rather than as a rank in its own right. While unusual, it *was* possible for a man to be appointed as adjutant without holding a company officer's commission, though this normally appears to have been the case with promoted NCOs. Otherwise serving as adjutant did not exempt an officer from his ordinary duties with his company, and in the early 1760s, for example, Lieutenant William Bannatyne, the adjutant of the 13th Foot, was frequently *commanding* his company in the absence of his captain.

The remaining regimental staff officers comprised the surgeon, chaplain, quartermaster and paymaster. The first held his commission by virtue of his professional standing and was accounted to be on a par with the captains when it came to the allocation of billets and allowances. Although every regiment had one on its books, chaplains were rarely to be encountered, especially on foreign postings, and the appointment was generally regarded as little more than a sinecure in the gift of the colonel. The quartermaster, on the other hand, was usually a professional. Each infantry battalion included a commissioned regimental quartermaster and cavalry regiments had one for each troop, but while both appear to have enjoyed comparable rates of pay their status was quite different. In the infantry it was an appointment which originally could be purchased and held by any officer, though the nature of the job meant that it was best handled by an experienced former NCO, and in 1779 George III went so far as to insist that "the proper persons to be recommended for quartermasters are active Sergeants, His Majesty not thinking the office very fit for men of better extraction and consequently very improper for a Captain . . .". Cavalry quartermasters, on the other hand, were merely junior officers ranking below the cornets. Despite holding commissions, they were in fact the equivalent of the modern troop sergeant or troop sergeant major. As such they did not appear in the *Army List* and the rank was abolished entirely in 1809.

Finally the paymaster, prior to 1797, was usually a captain who held the job on a part-time basis, after providing suitable financial securities. Although the colonel was naturally in a position to make strong recommendations, in this at least he was sometimes in the position of first amongst equals for the appointment was traditionally decided by means of a vote amongst all the captains, of whom he was but one.

3
Fit for a Cap

It would probably be fair to say that the 18th-century British Army is popularly held to have been recruited from the very scum of the earth and officered by rich aristocratic dilettantes. There is no doubt of course that a great many officers were indeed aristocrats, or if not titled members of the nobility they were at least drawn from the old landed gentry which amounted to pretty much the same thing, and that at the time there was a fairly broad consensus that this state of affairs was only right and proper. In December 1744, for example, Henry Pelham pompously declared to a receptive audience in Parliament that:

> I have always heard it admitted that our liberties can never be in danger so long as they are entrusted to men of family and fortune, and the reason is obvious as well as unanswerable. The security of property must always depend on the preservation of liberty. Under a despotic government there is neither property nor liberty, for every man's estate as well as his life, depends upon the rapine of an arbitrary sovereign. Has not then a man of fortune more reason to avoid such a melancholy predicament than a man of no estate? Has it not always been with good reason urged that our liberties are in no danger from our standing army because it is commanded by men of the best families and fortunes?[17]

Overall, however, the aristocrats were in fact in the minority in the Army. In his study of the social origins and backgrounds of British Army officers, P.J. Razzell[18] estimated that in 1780 only some 24% of officers were members of the aristocracy, while a further 16% were drawn from the untitled landed gentry. They were, moreover, disproportionately concentrated in the guards and in the more fashionable cavalry regiments. Although Pelham might have taken some comfort from the fact that around 30% of general officers bore inherited titles, his sleep may perhaps have been a little disturbed by the obvious supplementary calculation that the remaining 60% of all officers and – perhaps more worrying still – the remaining 70% of general officers did *not* bear inherited titles.

While the eventual abolition of the purchase system in 1871 is widely hailed as a thoroughly good thing, it actually appears to have had no discernible effect whatsoever on the social composition of the British Army's officers. Or to be more accurate, far from throwing open command of the Army to men of talent rather than breeding, as is generally supposed, it may actually have had the opposite effect.

It was a frequently heard complaint in the Royal Navy of the Napoleonic Wars that, whereas midshipmen had formerly required only to "pass as lieutenants" (i.e. prove themselves to be professionally qualified) in order to reach commissioned rank, by the early 1800s they also had to "pass as gentlemen" as well. Exactly the same thing appears to have happened in the Army and while the snobbish Captain Le Couter of the 104th Foot could smugly record in October 1814 that Major General Sir James Kempt "was pleased to say that He had never seen a mess so like the establishment of a private family of distinction", that of the 39th Foot in the 1740s was a much more robust establishment in which Lieutenant William Dawkin once threatened to cut the Major's throat![19]

By 1830 although the percentage of officers belonging to the titled aristocracy had declined to 21%, the landed gentry's had risen to 32% – exactly double the proportion in 1780. The "upper classes", therefore, had increased their share of commissioned ranks by 25% and now accounted for over half, rather than just 40% of officers as in the previous century.[20] Despite the subsequent abolition of the purchase system in 1871 this situation did not alter to any significant extent before the First World War and it is clear that for much of the 19th century the Army continued to be dominated by precisely that level of society – the aristocracy and landed gentry – who had always been best placed to purchase commissions in the first place. It is at least arguable, therefore, that far from opening up the profession, the abolition of purchase actually served to ensure the continuation of the *status quo* by effectively preventing the middle-classes from buying their way in to the Victorian army in appreciable numbers. This indeed was even one of the arguments advanced in favour of abolition.[21]

By contrast the rather more raffish Georgian army drew its officers from a much wider social base than the Victorian one, and was certainly much more open to promotion from the ranks. In peacetime, with the Army maintained on a reduced establishment and casualties of all kinds at a minimal level, it was only natural that the ability to purchase commissions should be the dominant factor in all appointments and promotions, but in wartime it was a very different matter. Not only was the establishment of officers in existing regiments increased, but a whole host of new ones were raised – during the course of the Seven Years War the establishment rose from 450 cavalry officers and nearly 1,650 infantry officers at the outset to 600 cavalry officers and nearly 4,000 infantry officers by 1763. As it was patently impossible for this sudden demand to be met by a corresponding increase in the birth rate of the nobility and gentry, it naturally followed that the new officers had to be looked for much further afield.

Writing of 1812, but describing a picture which was no doubt equally applicable to earlier conflicts, Le Couter of the 104th Foot was rather sniffy about this, declaring that "In those days of raging wars, all sorts of men obtained Commissions, some without education, some without means, some without either, and many of low birth. It was a Society so vulgar, so drunken, so vicious and so disorderly that, on meeting, One absolutely dreaded who to sit by or who to converse with".[22]

The greater number of 18th-century army officers were drawn from what Razzell rather blandly and quite inadequately characterises as the middle classes. Actually they belonged (if that is the right word) to an ill-defined and socially diverse group of "private gentlemen" – itself a rather elastic term in the 18th century – variously drawn from the lesser landed families and from the families of "respectable" professionals and tradesmen, generally, doctors, clergymen, farmers and the like. Some had money with which to purchase their commissions, or at least sufficient credit to borrow some for the purpose, but all too often they lacked it and although one bitterly referred to himself as "a private Gentleman without the advantage of Birth and friends", they generally relied upon patronage or "interest" rather than wealth to further their careers.

Captain Robert Bannatyne of the East India Company's service spoke for many of them when he declared in 1759: "My father had no great Estate and dying whilst his children were young you May guess whether five of us did not find use for small inheritance."[23] Both Bannatyne's father and stepfather were Scottish clergymen – and neither of them were wealthy. Nevertheless, the latter, Alexander McBean, secured free vacancies for his own son Forbes McBean who entered the Royal Artillery, commanded a battery at Minden in 1759 and died a general, and for two of the Bannatyne brothers, of whom Robert died at the storming of Conjeveram in 1759, and William retired as a lieutenant from the 13th Foot to make a modestly fortunate marriage. This sort of success rate seems to have been fairly typical and goes a long way to explaining why, despite the comparatively low rates of personal pay, a career in the Army was so attractive to the middling sort of people – and to Scots in particular.

While King George's officers were comparatively indifferent to the social origins of their colleagues, one thing which did sometimes exercise them was the apparent predominance of Scotsmen. Although Britain had only officially existed as a unitary state since 1707, the 19th-century fossilisation of individual regimental nationalities was still some way in the future and a quite disproportionate number of officers in the Army at large were Irish or Scots. The overt nationalism of the Jacobite movement which dominated politics and actual events in Scotland during the first half of the 18th century obscures the fact that a surprising number of Scots viewed the Union of 1707 in an extremely positive light and eagerly seized upon the opportunities for advancement which it offered. Two of the more important routes to advancement were the East India Company and the British Army and it has been estimated that by the 1760s something in the region of between and 20 and 30% of all army officers were Scots. Even this is probably an underestimate and the proportion certainly rose much higher during the second half of the century. There was actually a decided feeling in some quarters that by the 1790s the Army was in the grip of something akin to a Scottish mafia and as early as 1747 that ever-contentious Welshman, Lieutenant William Dawkin of the 39th Foot had complained: "I begin to think it damn hard to purchase every Thing when I am equally inclin'd to do my Duty with those who come at preferment at an easier rate, had I been a Scott instead of a Cambrian I should have had a Company long agoe – friends or Foes, I think they prevail."[24]

As it happens, a 1752 return shows just three Scots officers serving in the 39th, which seems to have been something like the average for this period, although other regiments boasted many more. A quite exceptional one-in-three officers serving in Colonel Harry Pulteney's 13th Foot in 1740 appear to have been Scots and twenty years later the proportion was still about one in six.[25] Nor was this particularly unusual. An analysis of the *Army List* for 1794 reveals that at least 845 out of 2,470 officers (excluding regimental colonels) actually serving in 82 battalions of the line can be identified as Scots – or 34.2% of the total, although the true percentage was probably around 40% or even higher. Moreover, only 204 of those officers positively identified as Scots were serving in Highland regiments and just 79 more in other regiments with Scottish connections such as the 1st (or Royal) Regiment. In other words, at least 22.7% – nearly a quarter of all infantry officers – were Scotsmen serving in regiments which a century later would be considered as English or Irish formations.

Even then, their distribution was quite surprising. Only a single battalion (the 8th Foot) appears to have had no Scots officers in 1794, but on the other hand the 19th (Green Howards) had at least nineteen – an astonishing 68% – while the 9th and 57th Foot were scarcely far behind with sixteen and seventeen Scots officers respectively. In all, leaving aside for obvious reasons the Highland regiments, fifteen other battalions boasted between eleven and fifteen Scots officers apiece, thirty-four had between six and ten, and the remaining nineteen battalions had five or only occasionally fewer.

Formidable though these figures are, they still do not tell the whole story, for at least thirty-one regimental colonels, amounting to 40% of the total, were Scots and they appear to have wielded their powers of patronage almost exclusively to the benefit of their fellow countrymen. The fact that General David Graeme had commanded the 19th Foot for upwards of 25 years certainly accounts for the large number of Scotsmen in that particular battalion, but others bid fair to achieve similar results in much less time. Lieutenant General James Grant's 11th Foot certainly had eight Scots officers besides himself in 1794, all gazetted to the battalion since his appointment in 1791, and by 1798 that number had doubled so that Scotsmen accounted for 40% of his officers. Similarly the 8th Foot, which appears to have had no Scots officers at the beginning of 1794, had at least nine by 1798, and all of them had been gazetted since Ralph Dundas took command in July 1794.

Irishmen were equally common and foreigners,[26] usually of French Huguenot descent, also found their way into the British Army in surprising numbers, as did Americans. Some of the latter naturally joined locally raised regular units such as Shirley's and Pepperell's American regiments,[27] but others served on equal terms with their metropolitan colleagues. The well-known fact that the young George Washington, then a Virginia Militia officer possessed of social rather than military qualifications, was refused a regular colonel's commission in the 1750s has long been advanced as evidence that colonial-born officers were unfairly discriminated against, but the reverse can be seen in the not particularly glorious career of Staats Long Morris (1728-1800). A younger son of Lewis Morris of Morrisania, New York, his social standing was comparable with that of the Virginian aristocrat Washington, but unlike him he embarked upon a career in the regular army.

Beginning as a lieutenant in the New York Independent Company in 1748, Morris was a captain lieutenant in 1751 and then a captain in Shirley's American-raised 50th Foot by 1755, before exchanging into the 36th Foot in May 1756. As lieutenant colonel commandant of the 89th Highlanders between 1759 and 1763 he served in the East Indies, including the siege of Pondicherry, before being rewarded with a full colonelcy by brevet on 25 May 1772. He saw no service during the American Revolution, perhaps because his brother Lewis was a signatory to the Declaration of Independence, but nevertheless he was promoted to major general on 29 August 1777, appointed colonel of the 61st Foot on 14 May 1778 and a lieutenant general on 20 November 1782. Subsequently he served on the staff as second in command of Western District from 1793-1796 before being promoted to full general on 3 May 1796 and appointed Governor of Quebec on 15 December 1797. The important point about Morris's career is that having entered the service at the bottom just like everybody else, he eventually rose to full general's rank through a combination of very modest talents, a short but respectable period of active service, and then sheer longevity. It was a wholly unexceptional career, which was neither hampered nor aided in any way by the fact that he was an American.

Another, and increasingly significant, grouping of officers was made up of men who were by any standards professional soldiers, and included amongst them were a surprising number of men promoted from the ranks. Dr. J.A. Houlding has identified over 598 promoted NCOs in the period 1739-1793, which he suggests points to some 3% of the 23,000 new entrants commissioned between those dates. Some of them, such as Terry Molloy, who successfully held Ruthven Barracks against several hundred rebels in 1745, were commissioned in recognition of a dramatic demonstration of their fitness and ability. For the most part, however, they were appointed into newly raised corps not only in order to serve as adjutants but also to provide a leavening of experience amongst the subalterns.[28]

Others were themselves the sons and grandsons of soldiers. Some of them were aristocrats or members of the landed gentry with a family tradition of service in the Army, such as the Campbells, Dalrymples, Greys, Howards, or Pulteneys. Others, including the numerous officers of foreign origin or descent, owed their present position and future prospects solely to the Army and some of this latter group were very frequently the sons of former NCOs or even, in a few cases, private soldiers. For the most part they entered the Army simply because the only real provision which their fathers could make for them was to employ their interest, either to find commissions for them or to advance their subsequent careers. The future Major General James Wolfe was a classic example of the breed.

James's grandfather, Edward Wolfe was turned out of King James' Irish Army during the Earl of Tyrconnell's purge of Protestant officers, but soon afterwards he was re-engaged by Dutch William and commissioned as a captain in Sir George St.George's Regiment of Foot by Queen Anne. His son Edward, James's father, then followed him into the Army, being commissioned as a 2nd lieutenant of marines on 10 March 1702. He subsequently served in the Netherlands under Marlborough and in Scotland during the Jacobite rising of 1715, before being appointed a captain and lieutenant colonel in the 3rd Footguards in 1717. Thereafter his career languished but the family's fortunes revived with the outbreak of war with Spain in 1739. Command of a new regiment of marines followed and in July 1740 Colonel Wolfe was also appointed adjutant general to an expeditionary force of 10,000 men being assembled by Lord Cathcart to take Carthagena des Indes (Colombia). The way was now open for him to launch his own sons' military careers.

4
Patronage, Purchase and Promotion

Ever since the 1720s a prospective subaltern normally had to be aged between sixteen and twenty-one, although the upper limit was routinely waived in the case of commissioned NCOs and rankers, and officers transferring from the militia, or from foreign armies. As to under-aged entrants, these were equally if not more common, although here the position was by no means as straightforward as it might appear. It is above all vitally important to approach the question from an 18th-century perspective, for to Georgian eyes there was nothing remarkable at all about awarding military commissions to teenagers. Higher education was ordinarily reserved for those who were destined to enter the Church, the Law, or medicine and was very largely confined to those narrow subjects.

While legally considered to be infants until the age of twenty-one many, perhaps most, youngsters completed their elementary schooling and began their working lives – or at the very least entered upon apprentice-ships – between the ages of twelve and fifteen. It is no coincidence at all, therefore, that men should so frequently be described as having been "bred up" to a particular trade or calling, whether by land or sea.

In the absence of a formal system of education for prospective officers of either service, the only real way in which to learn their trade was through early "hands on" training – and as was generally agreed, the earlier the better. A Royal Naval Academy was set up at Portsmouth in 1730 in order to provide formal training for a limited number of would-be officers, and a number of privately run military ones also existed during the 18th century. However, the majority of sea officers certainly looked down upon this kind of "book" education as being of considerably less value than practical experience at sea, and it is likely that most Army officers were similarly unimpressed by military "academites". On a narrower basis a proper education was certainly provided for the officers of the Royal Artillery and Royal Engineers at Woolwich, but this reflected the technical nature of their service and it is perhaps worth noting that even when a more universal Royal Military College was opened in 1801 its principal object was to train up staff rather than line officers.

There is no doubting that actual rather than notional children were from time to time commissioned into the Army while still confined to the nursery. John Blakiston, for example, was first commissioned an ensign in the 119th Foot in 1794 – at the age of nine – and transferred on to the Half-pay of Fraser's 71st Highlanders a year later without ever having appeared on a parade ground.[29] Although generally admitted to be undesirable the practice was afforded a certain official sanction by the Crown's occasionally bestowing of free vacancies upon the otherwise destitute orphan children of officers killed in action. However, there is equally little doubt that such cases were as uncommon as they were prominent, and certainly a good deal less common than in the Royal Navy where it was so very much easier to conceal these things. Notoriously there was a widespread custom in that service of fraudulently entering very young children in a ship's books as Captain's servants, or even as able seamen, in order to increase their notional sea-time and so further their eventual career prospects. By contrast, surviving returns indicate that far from being children, the majority of subalterns actually appear to have entered the army between the ages of fourteen and sixteen in peacetime, and that in wartime the average age of new entrants was generally a year or two higher. Even in a random sample of ten regimental inspection reports from 1791, when the Army was supposedly declining in the grip of terminal corruption, the youngest ensigns were aged sixteen and their average age was twenty-one!

It is unsurprising, therefore, that although James Wolfe's father was the colonel of a regiment and could easily have found him a place in it at any time, he had to wait until he was fourteen before securing his first commission.

There were a number of avenues by which an aspiring young hero could take his first steps on the road to glory. Like Wolfe he could, for example, initially go out as a volunteer; that is, he could accompany a regiment at his own expense, carrying a firelock and standing in the ranks but messing with the officers in the hope of picking up a non-purchase vacancy. This happened with surprising frequency. Working from entries in the *London Gazette* Professor Michael Glover reckoned that in the early 1800s as many as 4.5% of newly commissioned subalterns were volunteers. This percentage may have been true of the previous century too, although given the comparative readiness with which commissions were being granted at that particular period it might actually have been even higher!

However the most straightforward, and consequently the commonest, route to a military career at this time was simply to purchase a commission in much the same way as a doctor bought his practice, or indeed any other professional man or public servant bought his "place". While all three of the Georges were vehemently opposed to the purchasing of military commissions, no realistic alternative to this system was to present itself during the 18th century, and if this at first appears surprising, there were in fact quite widespread political as well as professional objections, both inside the service and out, to the abolition or replacement of purchase. In the first place, from the political point of view it was, as we have seen, argued that possession of (or at least the ability to borrow) the required capital ensured that the majority of army officers were men of some substance, who had a real stake in preserving the country and its institutions – a point reiterated with his usual clarity and a certain impatience by the Duke of Wellington in 1833:

> . . . it is promotion by purchase which brings into the service men of fortune and education; men who have some connection with the interests and fortune of the country, besides the commissions which they hold from His Majesty. It is this circumstance which exempts the British army from the character of being a 'mercenary army' and has rendered its employment, for nearly a century and a half, not only not inconsistent with the constitutional privileges of this country, but safe and beneficial.[30]

Politicians never seemed to tire of recalling that the execution of King Charles I and the "arbitrary government" of Oliver Cromwell had been brought about and supported by an army which, in the popular mind at least, was officered by landless commoners. The fact that the same army had subsequently engineered the restoration of the monarchy was merely regarded as further damning evidence of its mercenary nature.

Apart from these constitutional arguments, Army officers themselves also defended purchase for its impartiality, and the check which it placed upon the nepotism and favouritism so rampant in the Georgian navy. Both naval contemporaries and historians invariably contrast the presumed professionalism of the sea service with the supposedly corrupt and inefficient arrangements for promotion on land, but this view is far too one-sided, and it is instructive to compare the two objectively.

A critical fascination with the supposed and actual iniquities of the much-maligned purchase system tends to obscure the all-important point that its function was merely a mechanical one. The Army did not stand apart from 18th-century society but was quite deliberately and intimately bound up with it. Consequently, the primary factor in determining promotions and appointments in military just as in civil life was the active exercise of patronage or "interest", to which the concurrent application of promotion by seniority and hard cash served as an effective set of checks and balances. In the ordinary run of things, interest was not only an essential feature of the system, but was so fundamental as to be taken for granted by all concerned – which may be why it is so little discussed in the literature. Indeed the argument may be taken further, in that the eventual abolition of purchase may in the end have come about because stern Victorian morality had curtailed the benevolent exercise of interest which complemented it, and therefore left purchase as very nearly the sole determining factor in promotions. In 1871 a young Royal Artillery officer named Evelyn Baring actually referred in a memorandum to an apparent unwillingness on the part of contemporary commanding officers to put officers forward for promotion on the grounds of merit, lest it be thought that they were in reality actuated by patronage and nepotism, whilst on the contrary: ". . . as regards the aversion shown by commanding officers to assume responsibility [for making such recommendations], it must be borne in mind that the assumption of such responsibility is one of their most important duties."[31] Such an aversion to exercising their interest would have been quite incomprehensible to their predecessors of a century before!

The requirement for a young man to receive a nomination to a vacant commission whether by purchase or otherwise inevitably required the intervention of a patron who would intercede on his behalf with the regimental colonel, or even with the Secretary at War – or in Ireland with the Lord Lieutenant. The frequently cited Samuel Bagshawe, for instance, owed his first commission in the 30th Foot to the goodness of the 3rd Duke of Devonshire, who by great good fortune happened to be the Lord Lieutenant of Ireland at the time. Samuel owed his intervention to the fact that the Bagshawes were long-standing clients of the powerful Cavendish family, but this kind of influence could still be exercised at several removes. A country parson seeking a commission for his son might take the matter up with the local squire, whose own social credit depended upon his being able to take it up with a still greater man and so on upwards until the desired intervention could be made. It may sound cumbersome but that was just how 18th-century British society was accustomed to working. The process could, of course, be shortened considerably if more or less direct access could be had to the colonel himself, and in this regard serving or retired officers obviously enjoyed a considerable advantage.

Only if such patronage could not be obtained was it necessary to resort to a commission broker, who would undertake to find the desired vacancy – for a price. Commission broking was illegal, as it blatantly contravened a ruling that an officer should have no say in the appointment of his successor, but there is no doubt that it happened. Commissions were valuable commodities and the necessary capital often had to be raised by means of a loan. The guaranteed interest in the form of the officer's personal pay made it a particularly attractive investment, but sometimes that investment required to be realised in a hurry, with or without the approval of the Crown. Consequently some rather shady characters could get involved, and as an army agent, Captain Alexander Wilson, rightly remarked, "those who apply to brokers are commonly a mean sort of people destitute of any other recommendation".[32]

Thus far the process was exactly paralleled in the Royal Navy, where it was indispensably necessary to engage the interest of a captain – the exact equivalent of a regimental colonel in that service. He alone could rate a young man as a midshipman and, as the saying went, "take him on his quarterdeck". There the resemblance ended, on the surface at least, for in order to qualify for *commissioned* rank as a lieutenant it was then necessary for an amphibious young gentleman to produce certificates and other proofs testifying that he had indeed served the necessary sea-time (nominally six years) and that he was competent in the unique skills associated with ship-handling and marine navigation. Just to make sure, he also had to pass what could sometimes be a pretty rigorous *viva* conducted by a board of captains. There is no denying the necessity for this procedure, given the nature of the service, although there is ample (albeit anecdotal) evidence of falsified certificates and uncommonly lenient passing boards. However, once a candidate had successfully passed the board his subsequent career – including his actual appointment to commissioned rank, for passing and promotion were by no means synonymous – depended entirely upon the naked exercise of interest. Without it he would remain a midshipman or at best a master's mate indefinitely, and once he was commissioned all of his subsequent promotions, all the way up to being made "Post" – that is being appointed to the substantive rank of captain – were also dependent upon interest.[33] Even then, although further promotion to Admiral's rank was outwardly governed by the strict application of seniority, in reality promotion to an active command was wholly dependent upon interest, albeit exercised at a very high level.

In the Army, by contrast, although interest was unfailingly exercised at every opportunity it was also generally kept within decent bounds. While each regiment of cavalry or infantry was indisputably and un-ambiguously a part of the British Army, and the colonel only commanded it in both form and actuality at the pleasure of the King, for so long as he did so it was indeed *his* regiment and up to a point he could promote and appoint officers as he pleased. His express consent was also required if an officer wished to exchange into another corps, or to sell out of the service entirely. This could obviously make life difficult for an officer who was not on the best of terms with him. Captain John Peebles of the 42nd Highlanders, for example, spent a very difficult period at the end of 1781 trying to obtain permission to sell his commission and only succeeded after the uncooperative Colonel Stirling returned to Scotland in the New Year.[34]

The regimental colonel was thus blessed with considerable powers of patronage and the opportunities for exercising that interest were greatest when a regiment was newly levied and required to find a complete establishment of officers from scratch. With some few exceptions, all but the ensigns were supposed to be serving or half-pay officers and could normally expect a step in substantive rank on transferring to the new unit. Ordinarily, there were essentially just two limitations upon the colonel's powers. The first was the requirement for him to submit all his recommendations for Royal approval. In practice, if the colonel was in good odour with the King – or with the Lord Lieutenant in Ireland – and the regiment well conducted, his recommendations would be readily accepted and the required commissions would be forthcoming without delay. As a particular mark of favour he might also be permitted occasionally to sell regimental staff appointments, such as the adjutancy. It was not unknown, however, especially if he himself had purchased rather than been appointed to the colonelcy, for recommendations and particularly those to field rank to be overruled and another candidate, sometimes an outsider, preferred. Secondly, and in the long run rather more importantly, he was pretty well obliged to adhere to the "custom of the service" in recommending an officer for promotion or preferment strictly according to regimental seniority. Since it was a well established principle that commissions were not heritable property, and that consequently a dead officer's commissions could not be sold, a death – or a dismissal in consequence of the sentence of a court martial – invariably created a non-purchase vacancy which was claimed as of right by the senior man in the grade below.[35] What was more, as he moved up everyone else gratefully shuffled after him in strict order of seniority until eventually a free vacancy was created for a new ensign or cornet. Even when purchase was involved, seniority still came into play. When a commission was offered for sale it was not simply knocked down to the highest bidder for it was understood that the senior man in the rank below had the right of first refusal. In justice, therefore (if not always in practice), a commission could only be offered to a more junior applicant if the senior one lacked the funds to buy it at the regulated price.

A colonel could certainly recommend that a near relation – or even just a fellow countryman – should be appointed to a vacant ensigncy in his regiment and expect his recommendation to be upheld without any adverse comment. He also, as we have seen, had an unfettered right to approve or disapprove of exchanges; but ordinarily he was obliged to approve and recommend promotions, whether by purchase or not, in accordance with their seniority within the regiment. He could not put a protégé or relation forward for promotion out of his turn without exciting loud protests from those whose established rights might thereby be infringed or overlooked. Men *could* occasionally be promoted out of turn, but only if the circumstances (such as the age or proven incapacity of more senior candidates) warranted. Advancing a popular and particularly deserving officer, or conversely recommending that an incapable one should be passed over was one thing; but for an officer to jump the queue for a non-purchase vacancy in particular merely on the grounds of consanguinity was quite another.

Notwithstanding the widespread application of interest, the claims of seniority therefore played a very considerable part in determining officers' career patterns. It was indeed the sole determining factor in the Royal Artillery, in the Royal Engineers and in the East India Company's service, where, as the authors of one 1794 pamphlet lamented, "We are not generally speaking, men of interest, else we should not have preferred a service in which seniority gives command".[36] It is not difficult to understand why promotion by seniority alone should be considered unsatisfactory and in 1797 the Marquis of Cornwallis complained that ". . . no system for military promotion can so effectually tend to destroy all spirit of energy and attention to discipline, as that of a regular succession of the mass of Officers, according to seniority, from the lowest to the highest, throughout a whole army".[37]

Nevertheless, even here it was still possible for officers to accelerate the process. It was not, for instance, unknown for an officer to privately intimate to his colleagues that a certain sum of money might influence his decision to take early retirement and so clear the way for their own promotion. This practice appears to have been quite common in the East

India Company's service and also occurred from time to time in the equally rigid hierarchy of the Royal Artillery as well. All of those benefiting from the officer's departure were expected to contribute to the pot according to their rank, and although, strictly speaking, the commission was not purchased thereby, the effect was the same.

As to the operation of the official purchase process itself, once his application had been privately accepted by the regimental colonel all that a young gentleman supposedly had to do in order to purchase his first commission was to deposit the regulated price with the relevant regimental agent. He in turn would then submit the applicant's name and any endorsements and testimonials as to his fitness and suitability to the adjutant general's office at the Horse Guards for ultimate approval by the King or his commander-in-chief. Once the initial commission had been obtained, further steps could be purchased in exactly the same manner and in due sequence. Such, at least, was the way in which it was intended to work – but in reality it was a good deal less straightforward.

By way of variation from simply handing the cash over (or under) the agent's counter, an officer might also obtain his commission by recruiting for rank, though this was widely and with some considerable justification looked down upon as a "job". In this case an officer, or occasionally a would-be officer, would engage to raise a specified number of recruits for an independent company, or an augmentation of an existing unit, or even for a whole new regiment in return for the promise of commensurate substantive rank. Ordinarily only a single step could be obtained in this way, but if a new regiment was being raised, such as Montgomerie's 62nd/77th or Fraser's 63rd/78th Highlanders, it could sometimes be a different matter and the opportunities for the exercise of patronage could be quite considerable and well in excess of those usually enjoyed by commanding officers. The customary allowances and bounty monies would be advanced to the hopeful officer and should he succeed in keeping within budget he might well obtain the desired commission for no more than the "horrid drudgery" of supervising the recruiting party. In the way of things, however, the necessary beating orders were usually issued at a time of intense competition for recruits and in order to fight off that competition he might well have to dip into his own pocket in order to supplement the official bounty – or even *in extremis* "buy" his men from a crimp – so that in the end he often gained very little financially and delivered a pretty sorry collection of recruits.[38]

The Crown's close supervision of promotions and appointments throughout most of the 18th century also ensured at least outward observance of the ruling that a commission could only be sold to the next officer in rank. In other words, an officer had to serve successively as an ensign, lieutenant and captain before attaining field rank. It was not, however, necessary to spend a period as captain lieutenant. Since this officer officially ranked as the senior lieutenant, he was entitled to claim a vacant captaincy by seniority; but if it was offered for sale and he was unable to raise the money there was nothing to prevent another lieutenant purchasing over his head.

It was, of course, possible to purchase each rank in turn over an extremely short period if the right vacancies could be identified through an agent or even a broker, but ordinarily the Crown frowned upon this and for the most part promotion rates were fairly slow, particularly at the time when James Wolfe first joined the Army. His father's regiment of marines, which he joined as a 2nd lieutenant on 3 November 1741, had only been raised two years previously, and while all but a handful of the other subalterns were also new entrants, the captains, all taken from the Half-pay or promoted from other corps, had originally joined the army between 1708 and 1732, and had an average of some eighteen years' experience. Edward Wolfe himself had served nearly thirty-nine years – including a period on half-pay – before getting his regiment, and his lieutenant colonel, John Cotterell, was in a similar condition having first been commissioned on 4 July 1716.

Four months later young James exchanged into Colonel Scipio Duroure's 12th Foot, and here his fellow officers must have seemed positively elderly. Duroure himself had received his first commission as far back as December 1705 and did not get his colonelcy until thirty-six years later on 12 August 1741. As for the captains, they were similarly placed, with the eldest entering the army as a 2nd lieutenant on 24 May 1705, two more joining in 1706, another in 1708, and one in 1712, although the most junior, George Stanhope, had entered the service as recently as 1733. Stanhope was evidently well provided with ready cash, for he took only six years to purchase his captaincy, and his colleague Edward Phillips did it in nine. John Cossley and Charles Rainsford, however, took seventeen and twenty-six years respectively which seems altogether more typical, while Matthew Wright and Edmond Harris evidently worked their way up by seniority rather than purchase, taking thirty-one and thirty-two years to succeed to the command of companies. Even more depressingly the captain lieutenant, Sampson Archer, was the oldest of them all, having first been commissioned as long ago as 1704 and only succeeding to that rank by seniority in November 1739.

It was a very similar story with Barrell's 4th Foot, into which Wolfe was promoted as a captain on 23 June 1744. Colonel William Barrell himself had entered the British service as a captain in March 1698 and, like Duroure, received his regiment thirty-six years later, while his own captains had for the most part gained their first commissions between 1705 and 1710 and on average served between fifteen and twenty-five years before attaining command of a company.[39]

This comparatively aged officer corps was the inevitable consequence of the long peace which followed Queen Anne's War, and after 1740 promotion rates were speeded up quite considerably. By 1759 captains were attaining that rank after a much more comfortable average of just ten years' service and majors after seventeen. As we shall shortly see, James Wolfe was to make captain after a mere three years and eight months and major after just five years – but this is a reflection of his exceptional talent rather than the judicious application of hard cash.

Remarkable though it was, in one respect at least Wolfe's career was entirely typical of other high-flyers' in that the swiftness of his promotions was facilitated in part by a willingness to switch from one regiment to another in pursuit of vacancies – in his case from the 1st Marines to the 12th Foot, then the 4th Foot and the 20th, before finally attaining the command of his very own 67th Foot in 1758. Inter-regimental exchanges were also eagerly sought after whenever there was a suggestion that "reductions" were planned. On such occasions it was always the "younger", higher-numbered regiments which were disbanded first and their demise was invariably preceded by a flurry of exchanges as career-minded officers sought to find billets in lower-numbered regiments which might be expected to survive. In either case, officers normally turned to the agent in his legally dubious role as broker. The agent and his clerks represented the respectable or at least acceptable end of the trade since, particularly in those agencies with a large portfolio of regiments, they were best placed to know who was selling and who was actively looking for promotion. Unsurprisingly, therefore, a great many exchanges took place between units handled by the same agency.

Commission prices themselves had supposedly been regulated by an official tariff published on 21 February 1720, in which rates ranged from £9,000 for the colonelcy of a regiment of horse all the way down to a more easily affordable £200 for an ensigncy in a regiment of foot at home, or just £170 if it was serving abroad. This tariff was supposedly linked to pay scales – and this was certainly the method used to determine the revised rates of 1766. The basic premise was that the sum invested in the purchase of the commission would produce an annual dividend for the Treasury equal to the officer's personal pay. Purchase could therefore be defended not only on the grounds that it supposedly ensured that command was reserved to gentlemen, but also on the infinitely more gratifying grounds that it was self-financing. Indeed, since the individual officer concerned could presumably enjoy the same or even a better income by simply sitting at home and investing his capital in stocks rather than a commission, it surely followed that honour alone rather than any thought of pecuniary gain led him to a military career. This notion may have been more optimistic than accurate, but no one can have purchased a commission with a view to making his fortune. This was always a rather sore point with Army officers who were apt to reflect unkindly on their naval colleagues' avaricious pursuit of prize money, and upon the grumbling of the East India Company's officers.

Having laid down this tariff, the Crown then attempted to ensure compliance by insisting that the vendor should play no part in the selection of the purchaser. A Royal Warrant of March 1722 even required the colonel of the regiment to make a written declaration that the promotion was purchased "according to our regulation price and no higher". For the next century and more these declarations would be solemnly if not religiously set down in the colonel's own fair hand, or ultimately on a printed form, but to no avail. Except in wartime, when commissions could more or less be had for the asking, demand always exceeded supply and naturally enough prices rose accordingly. By the middle of the 18th century, although personal pay scales had remained static, a combination of inflation and largely stagnant promotion rates had pushed the asking price of commissions well above the "regulated" tariff. In 1740, at the time when Wolfe was entering the Army, one of the more prominent agents, Captain Alexander Wilson, estimated the going rate for an ensigncy could be as high as £450 – well over double the regulated price and equivalent to over six years' full pay. Even twenty years later Major Robert Preston found it necessary to write to his commanding officer, Colonel Samuel Bagshawe, asking his advice as to the relative value of different commissions and admitting complete confusion as to just what the going rate might be.

> The Officers asked what would be the difference of the Prices from one Rank to another . . . The only foundation I had to go upon, was that a Lieutenancy in a young Regiment was better than an Ensigncy in an old one for that Severall Ensigns in the old went Lieuts into the Young. That I valued an Ensigncy in an old Regtt at £450, The Difference from Lieutenant to Captain Lieutenant at £200 from Captain Lieutenant to Captain at £350, That I valued the Ensigncy [in Bagshawe's "new" 93rd Foot] at £300 and from Ensign to Lieutt at £150." [40]

Elsewhere in the Bagshawe papers is an undated memorandum, which looks very much as if it may be a draft of his reply to Preston, or at least an *aide mémoire* used in preparing it:

> When a Capt has leave to quitt the Service & dispose of his Commission 'tis generally done in this manner, the Lieutenant recommended either gives him his Commission and the difference between the Commissions of a Capt and Lt. or a certain sum of money in which case the Lt. has the disposing of his own Commission which

29

if sold to an Ensign, that Ensign acts in the same way that is gives the Lieutenant his Ensign's Commission and the difference or else a certain Sume & sells the Colours himself, So that the price of a Captain's Commission is either a certain Sum, or is compos'd of the difference between a Lieutenancy and a pair of Colours & the Colours. Now suppose a Company is dispos'd of in this last way & sold for eleven hundred pounds the case stands thus

The difference between the Captains & the L[tt] Commission	600: :
The Diff. between y[e] Lieutenancy & y[e] Colours	100: :
The Colours	400: :

$$£1100: \quad 0: \ 0:''^{41}$$

Although at first sight the process might appear cumbersome, the regimental agent would normally handle the paperwork. Bagshawe's memorandum also provides a helpful illustration of the important point that the agreed purchase price of a particular commission, whether it was regulated or not, normally represented what might best be termed its "absolute value" as an investment, rather than the sum which actually changed hands on each promotion. By the latter part of the 18th century the regulated price of an ensign's commission (as settled by a revised regulation in 1766) had stabilised at £400, irrespective of whether the regiment was serving at home or abroad, and leaving aside the usual minor fees and disbursements to the agent and the clerks at Horse Guards, and anything else which might have been clandestinely agreed, this is exactly what it cost him.[42] However, in order to purchase his next step, an ambitious ensign only had to find an additional £100, which represented the "difference" between the value of his existing commission and the regulated price of £500 for a lieutenancy. Similarly with a captain's commission officially valued at £1,500 a lieutenant who wished to buy his way up had only to find the difference of £1,000.[43] The fact that one or other of an officer's commissions may have been acquired in the course of his career without purchase made little or no difference. The grateful recipient of a free ensigncy still required only £100 to purchase his lieutenancy.

However, when he eventually came to retire an officer might not be permitted to sell those steps which he had not actually paid for. For the most part, provision for an officer's retirement was inextricably linked with purchase. Ordinarily an officer was expected to provide for his own retirement by selling his commissions and purchasing an annuity with the proceeds. If the whole sum was invested it was calculated that an interest rate of just 4% would produce an annual income equivalent to his full regimental pay. This was all very well if each of the steps had been purchased, but otherwise there could be problems.

If we suppose that after having purchased his ensigncy at the regulated price of £400 an officer was fortunate enough to be promoted to lieutenant without purchase, his subsequent advancement to captain still only cost him the £1,000 "difference" between those ranks, and he would normally still expect to receive the full £1,500 for his three commissions when he sold out. This was by no means a right, however, and an ensign who began his career with a free commission could sometimes find himself in a decidedly unhappy position. As we have seen, should he choose to purchase further promotion he only required to pay the easily borrowed "difference" of £100 for the privilege of styling himself a lieutenant and might then rely upon seniority to bring him to a captaincy. In this case, however, he only had an assured right to sell the lieutenancy and therefore had two alternatives. The first was to apply through his colonel for permission to sell his non-purchase commissions as well.[44] Officially this was discouraged since it obviously reduced the number of free vacancies available to new entrants, but on the whole it was widely felt in the service that long service might entitle him to do so, especially if the money provided the necessary incentive for him to retire rather than hang on past his usefulness. The privilege was therefore occasionally granted in exceptional circumstances, but a much commoner alternative was to retire or exchange on to the Half-pay list.

Both the British and Irish Half-pay establishments were made up of phantom regiments and companies, earlier disbanded or "reduced" and only continuing to exist on paper.[45] Half-pay was originally provided for the officers of those regiments because they would clearly be unable to find buyers for their empty commissions. For their part, they were expected to return to full pay if and when required. This actually occurred with surprising frequency since the Government was always anxious to keep the bill as low as possible – justifying the cost of "effective" soldiers was difficult enough – and whenever a new levy was ordered it was piously expected that the prospective colonels would draw as many of their officers as possible from the Half-pay. This also resulted in a two-way traffic. As these officers returned to active duty they left behind them notional vacancies which could later be filled by retiring non-purchase officers. For example, when Lieutenant William Bannatyne, then the adjutant of Pulteney's 13th Foot, retired from the service at the beginning of September 1765, he did so by obtaining an appointment to the Half-pay of Monson's 96th Foot, which had been reduced two years before.

This was a relatively straightforward matter and considered to be well worth the slight additional burden which it placed upon the exchequer, since the retiring officer's transfer to the Half-pay created a vacancy in his original corps when he might otherwise be forced by his financial circumstances to stay on duty long after he had ceased to be fit or even willing for service. It was also a good deal more attractive to his erstwhile colleagues than the alternative, which was for the officer in question to retire upon full pay – as sometimes happened as a particular favour – leaving his successor to enjoy the rank but not the pay.[46]

All in all, therefore, it can be argued that the Georgian officer, and the purchase system that governed his career, was of a piece with 18th-century British society at large. The plum positions typically went to the aristocracy and the landed gentry, not least because they so often served in the Guards and so came more readily to the personal notice of the King, but the greater number of officers, including James Wolfe, were "active stirring men" frequently drawn from the rising middle classes, and if the purchase system ensured that those with money to invest in their careers enjoyed a certain advantage, it was not yet closed to talented but impecunious men from the lower ranks. Throughout the 18th century all three Georges took a close interest in "their" Army and unhesitatingly promoted or at least provided for officers whose ability and services counted for more than their wealth or connections.

NOTES

1. 1 Will & Mary cap.5. So parlous was the state of the English Army in the wake of the invasion that William had to transfer three English regiments from his own army to serve as a politically reliable nucleus. They eventually became the 3rd, 5th and 6th Foot.
2. Ships' gunners also received their warrants from the Board of Ordnance rather than from the Admiralty and the heavy mortars on bomb vessels were actually manned by Royal Artillery personnel during the 18th century.
3. 10 William III cap.1.
4. The Scots Brigade always occupied an ambiguous position in that while it remained an integral part of the Dutch Army it frequently came under British operational control and its officers exchanged freely between the two services during the 1690s. The three regiments transferred from the Scots Army in 1700 replaced the three English ones previously transferred to British pay in 1689. Even after William's death, informal links were maintained and the regiments were permitted to carry on recruiting officers and men in Scotland – though this occasionally led to complaints. In 1746 it was suspected that Dutch officers were enlisting Jacobite fugitives, but usually it was a matter of British recruiting officers protesting about unfair competition. The six regiments also wore red coats and carried British colours throughout the 18th century until their disbandment in the 1780s and even then the surviving Scots officers formed the nucleus of the British Army's "Scotch Brigade" (later the 94th Foot) in 1793.
5. The most dangerous period came in 1712 after Marlborough's replacement by the pro-Jacobite Duke of Ormonde. Military operations were halted and preparations made to reduce the British forces in Flanders, which resulted in a dramatic French recovery culminating in victory over Britain's abandoned Dutch allies at Denain.

6. 8 George II cap.30 *An Act for Quartering Soldiers at Elections.*
7. W. Strickland to Attorney General 19 October 1732, quoted in Clode, *Military Forces of the Crown,* (1869), Vol.II pp621-2.
8. Exceptionally the Irish Parliament agreed to fund 8,000 troops ordered abroad in 1761, at the height of the Seven Years War.
9. For the same reason units assigned to the Irish Establishment were forbidden to recruit in that country. This apparently led to the somewhat bizarre practice of clandestinely shipping Irish recruits across to Stranraer, clapping blue bonnets on their heads and then bringing them back by the next boat as "legitimate" enlistees from Scotland – see "Letters of Captain Nicholas Delacherois" *JSAHR* Vol.LI no.205 p7.
10. Dr. John Houlding "Irish Army Orders" *JSAHR* Vol.LXXII no.290 pp107-117. This order was one of a number inserted in regimental orderly books on the insistence of Lieutenant General the Earl of Rothes, who was evidently unimpressed by what he had discovered on a recent tour of inspection.
11. Even as late as 1790 three of the London-based agents and four of the Dublin agents were looking after just one regiment apiece.
12. In this case Cox and Co.'s Bank, later part of Barclays.
13. This system or practice was precisely paralleled in the Royal Navy where promotion from captain to the rank of admiral was automatically governed by seniority; but whilst those intended to be employed were appointed to one of three flags or squadrons – the red, white or blue – those who were not were merely appointed "Rear Admiral without distinction of squadron," or in the parlance of the service "yellowed", that is made an Admiral of the quite notional Yellow Squadron.
14. There were also a number of officers in the Seven Years War and afterwards styled lieutenant colonel or major commandants. This rank was normally conferred on officers holding temporary commissions by virtue of having raised their own regiments, although the rank was also held by the officers commanding the four constituent battalions of the Royal Americans.
15. At this time there were actually *four* Fusilier regiments: the 7th (Royal), 21st (Royal Scots), 23rd (Royal Welch) and 32nd. When and why the latter were designated as Fusiliers, and for how long, is unknown but the 1740 *Army List* shows all the subalterns to be lieutenants and they were certainly still referred to as Fusiliers in June 1746 (WO4/42).
16. Those holding the rank of Ensign were normally former rankers rather than infants.
17. Coxe, *Pelham Administration* I, pp192-5 quoted in Guy, A.J. *Oeconomy and Discipline: Officership and administration in the British Army 1714-63,* Manchester (1985) p89.
18. Razzell, P.J. "Social origins of officers in the Indian and British home army 1758-1962". *British Journal of Sociology* 14 (1963), pp248-60.
19. Graves, Donald (Ed), *Merry Hearts Make Light Days,* p215.
20. Razzell, op.cit. p254.
21. Bruce, Anthony, *The Purchase System in the British Army 1660-1871,* (1980). Although concentrating upon the events leading up to the abolition of Purchase, this work is indispensable. Harries-Jenkins, Gwyn, *The Army in Victorian Society,* is also useful.
22. Graves, op cit. pp52-53. These somewhat ascerbic remarks were prompted by Le Couter's arrival in a mixed mess at the Newport depot on the Isle of Wight. Since the officers there included those of various foreign and penal corps (and East India Company officers as well) it is hardly surprising that some of them

failed to live up to his elevated social expectations.

23. Letter attached as codicil to his will – Register of Madras Mayoral Court, Vol.61: 7 July 1759.

24. John Rylands Library, Bagshawe MSS 2/2/141, quoted in Hayes, James, "Scottish Officers in the British Army 1714-63", *Scottish Historical Review* XXXVII, 1958, pp25-67. (Dawkin never did get his company, but sold out as a lieutenant two years later.)

25. This particular circumstance would appear to be accounted for by the long periods that the 13th Foot spent in Scotland throughout the 18th century.

26. It should perhaps be pointed out that the Army's crude statistical system took account of a man's birthplace, but not his nationality. A man born to English parents in an overseas garrison such as Gibraltar or Minorca would invariably be accounted a foreigner in official records.

27. Confusingly, both men raised two different regiments in quick succession. Shirley's 65th Foot was disbanded in 1749 and followed by his short-lived 50th, raised in 1754 and disbanded in 1757. Similarly, Pepperell's 66th Foot was disbanded in 1749 only to be followed by his equally short-lived 51st Foot of 1754-1757.

28. Pers. comm. The true proportion of promoted NCOs may actually have been higher still, for Prof. Michael Glover's analysis of *Gazette* entries suggested that by the early 1800s 5.42% of newly commissioned subalterns were ex-NCOs and this was exclusive of the ensigns appointed to Veteran Battalions who were almost invariably drawn from the ranks. A few, presumably "gentlemen rankers", were even commissioned directly from the rank of private although such men are not identified as such in the *Gazette* and consequently it is quite impossible to quantify them. Rather pleasingly, notices of promotions in the *Gazette* before about 1800 invariably described a newly commissioned officer as a "gentleman" whatever his actual background.

29. Blakiston eventually went to the wars in 1801 as a lieutenant of engineers in the East India Company service, and while still drawing half-pay as an officer of the 71st.

30. Bruce, A. *The Purchase System in the British Army 1660-1871*, (1980), p1.

31. Ibid. p85. The absence of interest from the Victorian army is debatable, the infamous "Wolsey Ring" being a notable example, but the context had certainly changed and interest was no longer of use in obtaining a first commission.

32. Ibid. p57. A useful and no doubt typical account of a commission obtained through a broker is to be found in *An Eighteenth-Century Secretary at War: The Papers of William, Viscount Barrington* (ed.) T. Hayter. (1988), pp289-292. A brickmaker named Gillingham paid a certain De Marville 300 guineas besides sundry other minor disbursements to obtain a vacant ensigncy in the 5th Foot for his son. However, the commission in question was actually a free one, which had been obtained as a mark of favour from the King by the Portuguese ambassador. He in turn had solicited it in order to gratify De Marville for some suspiciously innocuous services and was hastily cleared in the subsequent investigation. The transaction was only discovered when the younger Gillingham declared that he had purchased the commission and was therefore entitled to sell it. De Marville, meanwhile, was reportedly still in the business.

33. See N.A.M. Rodger's *The Wooden World* (1986) for a superbly considered and eminently readable account of the Georgian navy.

34. Gruber, Ira (ed), *John Peebles' American War 1776-1782*, (1997). This excellent journal provides an extremely detailed everyday account of life, promotions and appointments in the Georgian army.
35. When an officer was dismissed from the service by the sentence of a court martial it was an invariable rule that he should be replaced by a man brought in from outside the regiment, in order to avoid any suggestion that his erstwhile colleagues had anything to gain from convicting him. In this case, therefore, the free vacancies arose in the other regiment.
36. Callaghan, R. *The East India Company and Army Reform 1783-1798*, (1972), p25.
37. Ibid. p205.
38. In 1757 the Hon. Archibald Montgomerie was granted letters of service to raise a regiment, successively (and confusingly) designated the 62nd Foot, 1st Highland Battalion and eventually the 77th Foot. All of the officers were "raising for rank". On 9 March it was inspected at Nairn and found to be 1,029 strong (WO1/974), but no fewer than 472 of them were promptly rejected by the inspecting general, including every man in the four companies raised by Major Alexander Campbell, and Captains John Sinclair, Alexander McKenzie and Roderick McKenzie.
39. All figures are taken from the 1740 *Army List*, which very helpfully notes officers' first commission dates as well as their present ones. There will no doubt have been some changes in personnel by the time Wolfe joined – Scipio Duroure, for example, was only Lieutenant Colonel of the 12th in 1740 – but the picture is entirely typical of the Army at the outset of the War of the Austrian Succession. See also Dr. J.A. Houlding's analysis of career patterns and promotion rates in *Fit for Service* (1981), pp107-111.
40. Guy, A.J. (ed), *Colonel Samuel Bagshawe and the Army of George II*, (1990), pp240-241.
41. Ibid. p38. Guy tentatively dates this to 1742 rather than 1761.
42. Not surprisingly it is difficult to find documentary evidence of such bargains, but a very good idea of what might be involved can be gained from a letter written in October 1812 by Major Edward Cocks of the 79th Highlanders, who was attempting to buy out Lieutenant Colonel Fulton of that regiment:

"I am to give him £1,500 above the regulation and take on myself the selling of his commissions. There is a doubt whether he will be allowed to sell his Majority. If he cannot the loss falls on him. The sums to be provided therefore are as follows;

To be lodged immediately in the hands of A.Lawrie, Army Agent, Adelphi, London	£900
To be paid under the (?) to a friend of Lt.Col F's as shall be hereafter mentioned:	£1,500
	£2,400
To be paid to Lt.Col F on account of his Company and Lieutenancy	£1,500
To be paid as above in case he is allowed to sell his Majority	£1,100
Total: £2,400	

Of these two latter sums, viz. £1,500 and £1,100, in case he is allowed to sell the Majority I shall only be out until the commissions are filled up, which will be done immediately. The £900 to be lodged with Lawrie is indisposable as the promotion might otherwise not go on.

I expect F will send his resignation the day after tomorrow. I will then write again to you. Should Price be in any difficulty about the sum I think it might be procured from Lord Beauchamp."

It will be noted, of course, that while Cocks was agreeing to pay over the odds for the lieutenant colonel's commission, Fulton was only to receive the regulated "difference" for his other commissions. In the event, Cocks got himself killed before the transaction could take place. The Price who was to find the money was presumably Cocks' banker. Page, Julia, *Intelligence Officer in the Peninsula: Letters and Diaries of Major the Hon. Edward Charles Cocks*, pp200-1.

43. Ward, S.G.P. 'The Letters of Captain Nicholas Delacherois' *JSAHR* LI p12. In an interesting case early in 1770 Lieutenant Nicholas Delacherois of the 9th Foot was keen to purchase his captaincy. In March he appears to have come to a tentative agreement to buy out Captain Denshire for a bargain £1,400, for he only required to find the "difference" of £900 rather than the £1,000 which he would have had to pay if Denshire was selling at the regulated price. Unfortunately he could only raise £200 of this and wrote to his father, asking for a loan. As an alternative he was prepared to settle for the captain-lieutenancy, which was on offer at the regulated price of £800, for which he only required to borrow £100 in order to make up the £300 of "difference" between the value of that rank and his own lieutenancy.

44. Another alternative was to engage a commission broker, take the money and run, but this was clearly fraught with danger.

45. Regiments were placed on the Half-pay of whichever Establishment they were serving at the time of their being reduced, which could lead to some odd situations. The Half-pay officers of the 105th Highlanders, for instance, were paid through the Irish exchequer after being disbanded there in 1763.

46. The worst feature of this practice was that the holder of this particular commission would go on drawing only a lieutenant's pay until such time as the gentleman who had retired died and finally ceased drawing pay as a captain.

CHAPTER II
Military Apprenticeship
Service in Flanders, Germany and Scotland

Britain's dramatic emergence in the course of the 18th century as one of the dominant forces in European and ultimately in world politics is conventionally and to some extent quite rightly ascribed first and foremost to her naval supremacy. The fortuitous existence of the English Channel and the Royal Navy have famously prevented invasion and near certain defeat on a number of occasions, but British seapower also facilitated the growth of an overseas empire. This empire in turn created the unimaginable wealth with which to maintain armies and to subsidise allies on a scale which would have been quite impossible if the exchequer's sole means of support had been its domestic revenues and ordinary import tariffs.

Although the sources of this wealth were naturally very broadly based, there were two areas in particular which quickly stood out as being vitally important to the British economy. One was the extensive trading network beyond the Cape of Good Hope managed by the increasingly powerful East India Company, while the other was the much looser, more diverse and infinitely more vocal confederation of businessmen known as the West India merchants.

Individually, or in partnership with each other, the West India merchants shipped African slaves, raw materials and European luxury goods to the Antilles. In return they took back to Britain high-value cargoes of coffee, rum and above all sugar – which very happily complemented the tea carried from China by the East India Company. Such was the immense value of the so-called triangular trade across the Atlantic that the sugar islands of the Caribbean saw almost continuous warfare throughout the 18th century as Spanish influence in the region declined and British and French interests competed for domination in its place. Indeed the perceived value of the sugar islands may be gauged by the simple fact that when a defeated France was offered the stark choice of having either Canada or her lost Caribbean colonies restored to her as part of the peace settlement at the end of the Seven Years War in 1763, she unhesitatingly plumped for the latter. Similarly, when French intervention in the subsequent American Revolutionary War in 1778 transformed it from a relatively localised colonial rebellion into an international conflict, Britain's first priority immediately changed to the defence of its more lucrative West Indian possessions at the expense of the hitherto winnable struggle for North America.

In the 1730s, however, all of that lay far in the future. Spain's influence might be on the wane but it was still the dominant power, both in the islands and also to some considerable extent along the southern fringes of what would eventually become the United States as well. Over the years British merchants had gradually won significant trading concessions in the region, particularly in the peace settlement at the end of Queen Anne's War in 1713, which spawned the infamous *Asiento* or right to carry slaves to Spanish America. Nevertheless, those ship-owners who took the trouble to obtain the necessary licences in Cadiz were greatly out-numbered by unauthorised interlopers, who were increasingly basing themselves in the British North American colonies. Naturally enough the Spanish authorities did their best to restrict the activities of these interlopers and in 1731 one of them, named Robert Jenkins, famously lost his ear in an unfortunate encounter with the Spanish coastguards off Cuba. This is not the place to discuss the circumstances in which the rather shady Captain Jenkins had his ear amputated – or if, indeed, it was ever cut off in the first place – for it was no more than a very convenient provocation in a much deeper seated political campaign, one in which the West India merchants successfully exerted their very considerable Parliamentary influence to bring about a war aimed at seizing Cuba and so ending Spanish hegemony of the Caribbean once and for all.

1
Going to the Wars

A major war of this nature commonly requires large numbers of soldiers to fight it, far in excess of those employed in peacetime and although the British Government eventually yielded to mercantile pressure in de-claring war on Spain in 1739, it was most unwilling to release more than a handful of regulars for the purpose. As a precautionary measure ten regiments of foot[1] were immediately transferred from the Irish to the British Establishment on 25 June 1739, (the traditional prelude to sending them overseas), but the Prime Minister, Robert Walpole, was obsessed with the notion that if they were indeed to be sent abroad the country would then be left wide open to a Spanish invasion and perhaps a pro-Jacobite rebellion as well. In an abrupt reversal of policy it was suddenly decided to retain the regiments at home and, much to the bemusement of everyone who reckoned to know anything of military matters, newly levied troops were to be shipped to the West Indies instead of supposedly well-trained veterans. On 26 December 1739 a certain Colonel Spottiswood was granted letters of service to raise four infantry battalions in North America, specifically for this purpose. It was a fairly novel and surprisingly sensible idea, and recruitment for the new American Regiment was successfully stimulated by the enticing prospect of land grants in a conquered Cuba. However, the greater part of the Carthagena "reinforcement" allocated to Lord Cathcart in that same month was still to be sent directly from Britain. It would consist of just two old regiments, Colonel Henry Harrison's 15th and Colonel Thomas Wentworth's 24th Foot, and six newly levied regiments of marines.[2]

The final decision to raise these marine regiments had been taken on 3 December 1739. As usual, most of the officers were to come from the Half-pay or from other existing units, and the nucleus for the rank and file was to be formed by drafting 120 corporals from the footguards to serve as sergeants. Fully one third of the private soldiers on their authorised establishments were also to be drafted in from various marching regiments on the British Establishment. The 1st Marines were accordingly allocated men from Whetham's 12th, Peers's 23rd (Royal Welch Fusiliers), and Cavendish's 34th Foot, and the man appointed to command them, with a commission backdated to 17 November, was Lieutenant Colonel Edward Wolfe of the 3rd Footguards.

Edward Wolfe's career at first glance gives no real hint of the talents soon to be displayed by his elder son, James. Indeed, he was to be characterised by one writer as "extremely upright and benevolent", but possessed of "no great force of character". These first appearances, however, are deceptive. Born at York in 1685, he was himself the son of a soldier, an officer in the Royal Regiment of Irish Footguards also named Edward Wolfe. As has already been mentioned, the elder Edward Wolfe was one of the Protestants turned out of the Irish Army by Tyrconnell in King James's time, and subsequently served thirteen years as a captain in Sir George St.George's Regiment of Foot. Beyond these bald facts it is perhaps unwise to go. Beckles Willson and Charles Dalton both follow an extremely dubious genealogy contained in Ferrar's "History of Limerick" to identify this Edward as the son of a Captain George Woulfe – a *Catholic* officer who had helped defend the city against General Ireton in 1650! However, other than an undoubted family connection to the literary Goldsmiths, the Limerick origin is more than a touch tenuous. As Willson himself admitted, there are several omissions and discrepancies in Ferrar's supposed genealogy, while Dalton's book also contains precious little if any documentation to back it up. Instead, given the family's undoubted Yorkshire links – both James's father, and his mother, Henrietta Thompson, were born and married there – it is probable that James's ancestors were not Irish at all, but English. Indeed, on balance it seems likeliest that he was in fact descended from a Lieutenant Colonel Edward Wolfe of Ireton's Regiment, who died at Youghal in 1649.[3]

At any rate, whatever the truth of his ancestry James Wolfe's father, Edward, was first commissioned as an ensign in Viscount Shannon's Marines on 10 March 1702. He next appears as a captain in Sir Richard Temple's Foot, serving in Flanders, and was appointed major of the same regiment on 24 April 1710. Reaching this responsible rank after only eight years' service and at the comparatively youthful age of twenty-four through ability and interest rather than by purchase was a good start which argues for considerable talent and easily bears comparison with his more famous son's similar achievement forty years later. If James was to attain the rank of major at just twenty-two, the advantage only lay in the fact that he joined the Army at the age of fifteen, two years earlier than his father. There can be little doubt, therefore, that James Wolfe's military ambitions were stimulated by a strong desire to emulate his father's early success, and driven at the same time by an equally strong desire to avoid the bitter disappointment which had followed that initial promise.

While Edward Wolfe had risen quickly under the great Duke of Marlborough, military operations in Flanders began to wind down after 1710. Temple's Regiment (by then known as Newton's) was disbanded in the usual brisk massacre of surplus units which followed the formal signing of peace in 1713 and Edward was accordingly placed on the Half-pay. His career momentarily came to a dead stop, and there he might have remained indefinitely but for the fortuitous outbreak of a Jacobite rebellion in 1715. This time service in Scotland was eventually rewarded by promotion to the rank of captain and lieutenant colonel in the 3rd Footguards on 10 July 1717. The appointment notionally restored him to the active list but brought no opportunity for advancement in the long years of peace that lay ahead.

His new duties as a guardsman were far from onerous and to all intents and purposes Edward was unemployed when he married Henrietta Thompson. Unable to afford a London address the Wolfes took a comfortable three-gabled property known as Speirs (now called Quebec House) at Westerham, near Sevenoaks in Kent. However, during the Colonel's absences on duty at Whitehall[4] Mrs Wolfe fell into the habit of temporarily moving up the steep hill to lodge with friends in the rather more modestly proportioned vicarage, and it was there that her first son James was born on 2 January 1727. A second son, Edward, was also born at Westerham almost exactly a year later on 10 January 1728 but in 1737 the family moved to Greenwich. Little information of any real consequence is known of this period, but both boys were evidently sickly. Young Edward would die, probably of tuberculosis, in 1744 and James may well have been suffering from the same disease when he met his death at Quebec in 1759 – though given his hypochondriac nature it is hard to be sure.

If, as seems very likely, the family was living in modest (and perhaps unhealthy) circumstances in Greenwich, then the appointment of Colonel

Wolfe to command the new 1st Marines, with all of the financial perquisites and congenial opportunities for the exercise of interest attached to that happy position, could not have come at a better time. Some provision would very shortly have to be made for the two boys and there must undoubtedly have been a considerable temptation to immediately bestow a 2nd lieutenant's commission on James at least. Doing so, particularly at this moment, would not have excited any comment, but nevertheless the Colonel refrained and his son was not appointed to the original establishment of the 1st Marines at Hilsea Barracks after all. Instead, James remained at home until July of 1740 when his father accepted the post of adjutant general under Lord Cathcart.

When the newly appointed adjutant general travelled down to the Isle of Wight to take up his post, James accompanied him, nominally in the capacity of a volunteer. Some biographers, Beckles Willson amongst them, have represented this first, early step towards a military career as having been taken with his father's active encouragement, and despite his mother's deep misgivings,[5] but it is unlikely that Edward Wolfe's acquiescence was altogether wholehearted – if indeed it was real in the first place. He had declined to bestow a commission on his son in December, and although a suitable vacancy could still no doubt have been found or at least arranged in July, he again passed over the opportunity. The fact that Colonel Wolfe did not exercise his undoubted influence at this stage must surely indicate that while he was perfectly willing to give the boy a taste of military life in camp, he never had any real intention of taking him out to the Caribbean.

If this was indeed the case, James evidently had no inkling of it as his first, excited letter to his mother reveals;[6]

> I received my dearest Mamma's letter on Monday last, but could not answer it then, by reason I was at camp to see the regiments off to go on board[7], and was too late for the post; but am very sorry, dear Mamma, that you doubt my love, which I'm sure is as sincere as ever any son's was to his mother.
>
> Papa and I are just going on board, but I believe shall not sail this fortnight; in which time, if I can get ashore at Portsmouth or any other town, I will certainly write to you, and when we are gone by every ship we meet, because I know it is my duty. Besides, if it is not I would do it out of love, with pleasure . . .

The expected two weeks stretched into two months and more and just before the fleet finally sailed in November, James was put ashore and returned home. His health, we are assured, had been bad, which no doubt provided a convenient excuse, for Colonel Wolfe cannot have anticipated the awful mortality, or indeed the extent of the dissension and ineptitude which would characterise the expedition. He knew, however, that an Atlantic crossing in winter was no place for his son, and so the boy was turned ashore as he had no doubt always intended, and sent back to school for another year. Disappointing though this must have been, it was an important and perhaps even formative episode. It confirmed James in his desire to follow in his father's footsteps, and the time spent on board ship and at Hilsea Barracks with his father's 1st Marines must also have given him a certain insight into both military routines and the sometimes obscure ways of the Royal Navy and its officers.

Having returned home, it was to be more than a year before James finally received a commission as a 2nd lieutenant in the 1st Marines. Moreover, while it was signed by the King on 3 November 1741, the precious document was not actually delivered into James's hands until over a month later, just a few days before his fifteenth birthday. By that time it had become all-too obvious that steps would have be taken to ensure that he was employed elsewhere, for Carthagena had by now revealed itself to be a fever-ridden death trap.

The expedition had in fact got off to a decidedly bad start with the death of its land commander, Lord Cathcart, on 20 December 1740. Although his successor, Thomas Wentworth, was conscientious, methodical and had been a more than competent second-in-command to Cathcart, he lacked the force of character to act with the speed necessary to secure his objectives before the ravages of yellow fever fatally weakened his unacclimatised forces. Yet more disastrously, the fact of his having succeeded Cathcart by accident rather than by appointment fatally undermined his authority *vis-à-vis* the expedition's naval commander, Admiral Vernon. Not only was the Admiral a political opponent of the ministry which had set the expedition in motion in the first place, but his curious notion of combined operations very firmly relegated the army to a supporting or rather a completely subservient role to that of the fleet. Vernon's unwarranted assumption of authority even extended to his refusing to land hundreds of the newly raised American troops since he preferred to keep them on board the ships in order to augment his own weakened crews. This might have perhaps been justified had he been prepared to employ those ships aggressively, but his political opposition was translated into sheer bloody-minded obstruction and deliberate inactivity at every turn. Poor Wentworth was quite incapable of standing up to him and was in consequence reduced to spending more time wrangling with his naval "colleagues" than in actually fighting the Spaniards. By the time he admitted defeat, fully half the expeditionary force had succumbed to disease. Young James was well out of the sorry mess, but his father's dismal accounts of the debacle cannot but have had an influence on his own subsequent involvement in combined operations.

Although duly gazetted to the 1st Marines, James Wolfe was therefore never destined to join the regiment, and instead he exchanged as an ensign into Colonel Scipio Duroure's 12th Foot on 27 March 1742. It is not difficult to divine how this exchange was managed, for the regiment's previous commander, Thomas Whetham, had been married to Edward Wolfe's sister-in-law. Moreover when the 1st Marine Regiment was being raised, about 100 men from the 12th had been drafted into it. When such drafts took place the Colonel who received them was required to settle up with the parent unit for money already expended that year on their clothing, necessaries and equipment, and for any outstanding stoppages on their pay. If he were particularly fortunate he might even have had the opportunity to receive the men in person and reject those who were patently unsuitable – it being a recognised part of the game that the unit being milked would endeavour to pass off its worst men. Colonel Wolfe must inevitably, therefore, have come into contact with both the regimental agent and with Scipio Duroure, who was at that time the regiment's Lieutenant Colonel and so in day-to-day charge of it. Whetham had died at the beginning of August 1741 and so, on balance, is unlikely to have had much involvement in finding a place for James, but access to Duroure and his agent would certainly have been essential in arranging the desired exchange, which now came about at a significant time.

The military operations in the Caribbean, so reluctantly entered into, were now no longer the British Government's first priority, for it had in the meantime become peripherally involved in the War of the Austrian Succession. In October 1740 the Holy Roman Emperor Karl VI died. The imperial throne was an elective one – the presidency of a ramshackle confederation of German states rather than a conventional monarchy – and the incumbent was supposedly chosen on the death of his predecessor by the vote of a number of the more senior princes of the empire, styled "electors". However, just as the electorships were hereditary, so by the 18th century the imperial crown had long since fallen to the inheritance of the Austrian Hapsburgs. Ordinarily their election was only a colourful formality, but Karl VI had the misfortune to leave no male heir, only his twenty-three-year old daughter, Maria Theresa. Recognising that a female candidate could not count upon the automatic support of the electors, Karl had busied himself in engineering the so-called Pragmatic Sanction, which bound them individually to recognise her after his death. Perhaps predictably, he had no sooner breathed his last than it all fell apart. A rival candidate, Karl Albrecht of Bavaria, put himself forward and at the same time the new King of Prussia, Frederick II, took the opportunity to seize the Hapsburg province of Silesia. However, Maria Theresa, the would-be Empress and undoubted Queen of Hungary, still had the Hapsburgs' hereditary lands and a handful of supporters, amongst them Georg, Elector of Hanover, who also happened at one and the same time to be King George

II of Great Britain. Initially Georg was restrained from action by French threats to invade his Electorate. In fact a treaty of neutrality was signed with France, but when a French army led by *Marechal* Belle-Isle marched into Bohemia, it was decided as a precautionary measure to send a British expeditionary force to the Austrian Netherlands – modern-day Belgium.

On 3 May 1742, little more than a month after James Wolfe had been gazetted to the 12th Foot, his regiment was ordered to prepare for service in Flanders. It was to go out, augmented to 815 of all ranks, as part of a formidable force some 17,000 strong and comprising: two troops of the Horse Guards and one of the Horse Grenadier Guards, the 1st (Blues) and Ligonier's 8th Horse, six regiments of Dragoons; Hawley's 1st(Royal), Campbell's 2nd (Royal North British), Honeywood's 3rd, Rich's 4th, Stair's 6th (Iniskilling) and Cope's 7th; three battalions of the Footguards and thirteen marching regiments of foot; Thomas Howard's 3rd (Buffs), Onslow's 8th (King's), Cornwallis's 11th, Duroure's 12th, Pulteney's 13th, Bligh's 20th, Campbell's 21st (Scots Fusiliers), Peers's 23rd (Welch Fusiliers), Bragg's 28th, William Handasyd's 31st, Huske's 32nd, Johnson's 33rd and Ponsonby's 37th. The whole was initially to be commanded by Field Marshal the Earl of Stair, Lieutenant Generals Sir James Campbell, Lord Dunmore and Philip Honeywood, Major Generals Lord Albemarle, Sir John Cope, Henry Hawley, Thomas Howard and John Ligonier, and six brigadiers: Colonels Philip Bragg, Stephen Cornwallis, Lord Effingham, John Huske, Henry Ponsonby and Harry Pulteney.[8]

In the event, Bragg's 28th stayed behind. Like a number of the units earmarked to go, they had only recently been transferred from the Irish Establishment, but being a notoriously inefficient regiment they had failed to augment their numbers to the required strength. The others, a fifteen-year old Ensign James Wolfe amongst them, assembled for the King's inspection at Blackheath and then began embarking at Deptford on 20 May 1742. Some days later they crossed to Ostend and so from there the 12th marched to take up their quarters at Ghent.

The 12th were to stay there for rather longer than they can have at first expected, for although Stair and the expeditionary force had been noisily despatched to Flanders, no one appears to have given very much thought to what they were supposed to do once they arrived. Thus far they were still restrained from acting offensively by that treaty of neutrality. They might serve very well to defend the Austrian Netherlands against a French invasion should the occasion arise, but as yet France was not directly involved in the war. Nor, it seemed, were the British expected in Ghent either, despite their presence having been agreed in advance. For the first two nights of their stay they encamped in the market place and other open spaces, but in time all were accommodated in billets. This was just as well, for they would not move out of them until the following February.

2
The Subaltern Officer

As a newly commissioned subaltern James Wolfe was master of the princely sum of three shillings and eightpence per diem, or rather of the three shillings of it which was accounted as subsistence. He received it as an accumulated sum every two months or so, and as for the arrears, sometimes referred to as clearings, these were commonly credited to his account at the agent's every six months or so after being mulcted of various deductions ranging from 1s in every pound retained by the Paymaster General to 2d in the pound for the agent.[9] Writing in 1768, Captain Thomas Simes reckoned that an ensign's daily expenses for breakfast and dinner, the wine and beer with which to wash them down, and for laundry and sundries – including the services of a "Soldier to dress your hair, shave you &c." – ran to 2s 6d, leaving a bare 6d for any extraordinary expenses.[10] Needless to say the arrears, when he finally fingered them, could scarcely be expected to service the usual loan required to purchase a commission as well as cover the very considerable expenditure on his kit.

There were few hard and fast rules on exactly what kit was needed, though Captain Simes once again provides a pretty fair idea in his *Military Medley*.[11]

A List of Things Necessary for a Young Gentleman to be furnished with upon obtaining his first commission in the Infantry.

A suit of clothes
Two frock suits
Two hats
Two cockades
One pair of leather gloves
Sash and gorget
Fuzee or espontoon[12]   } all Regimental
Sword, sword knot and belt
Two pairs of white spatterdashes
One pair of black tops
One pair of gaiters
One pair of boots[13]

A blue surtout-coat
A portugal cloak
Six white waistcoats[14]
One dozen of stocks
Eighteen pairs of stockings

One black stock
One pair of leather breeches
Six pairs of shoes
Two dozen shirts
Six towels
Three pairs of sheets
Three pillow cases
Six linen night caps

A field bed-stead, a painted canvas bag to hold it, bed curtains, quilt, three blankets, bolster, pillow, one mattress and a palliase. These articles should be carried in a leather valise; a travelling letter-case, to contain pens, ink, paper, wax and wafer; a case of instruments for drawing; and Muller's works on fortification &c. It is also essential that he should have a watch, that he may mark the hour exactly when he sends any report . . .

At first sight it is a quite daunting list. Although a newly commissioned officer such as Wolfe would no doubt already be in possession of a competent number of the more basic items such as the shirts and other linen, Sam Bagshawe estimated the cost of his regimentals alone at £20.00 per anum in about 1749,[15] while in 1788 Ensign MacDonald of 2/1st Royal was billed £20 3s 4d just for the materials for his regimental coat, quite apart from what it cost him to have it made up.[16]

A complete suit of regimentals was by any standards an expensive item and unsurprisingly was little worn except on the most formal of occasions. Instead, for everyday use most officers wore one of the two "frock" suits recommended by Sime. Although rather cheaper – Bagshawe reckoned one to cost him £13 10s even with a few additional pairs of breeches thrown in – these frocks were still of good quality, but plain and undecorated. Normally the lack of decoration also extended to having plain red cuffs instead of regimentally coloured facings, hence occasional references to officers wearing "red clothes".[17] As well as being more practical than the expensively laced regimentals, plain frocks could obviously continue to be worn when an officer exchanged from one corps into another and indeed there was probably no reason why an officer who obtained his commission in wartime should not have made do with a frock suit alone. Even as a major general, Wolfe was in fact to be wearing just such a suit of "red clothes" when he was killed at Quebec in 1759.

The plain blue surtout coats or long greatcoats, also mentioned in Sime's list, were equally popular, especially in foul weather, and although Georgian officers are frequently illustrated as rather popinjay figures, the evidence shows that their actual appearance was normally rather staid and workaday, and altogether more professional than their formal portraits might suggest. It is still a touch disconcerting, however, to find that when young MacDonald of Kinlochmoidart purchased his kit in 1788 he paid £2 10s for a gold-laced hat, but only £1 16s for his sword!

Howsoever these sums might be looked at, the total represented a considerable expense and unsurprisingly, as in Wolfe's case, an officer's initial kit (and often many later items as well) was usually purchased for him by his father or some other relative since there was no official grant for the purpose. Often it was the only real provision which a father could make for his son's future and in a typical example Lieutenant James O'Neill addressed a memorial to the Commander-in-Chief soliciting commissions for his sons, one of whom he had already "fitted out at an inconvenient Expense . . .".[18]

Commissioned rankers obviously faced difficulties of their own, for whatever their varied background at this period officers were accounted gentlemen and expected to conduct themselves accordingly. It seems to have been common, therefore, to immediately send an ex-ranker off "recruiting" for a few months in order to give him the time and opportunity to sort himself out, and perhaps misapply the usual expenses to that purpose. Otherwise he might have to rely upon a loan, which should have been reasonably affordable given that he would not already be committed to servicing a much larger one for the price of his commission. In the very last resort dress regulations, on active service at least, were not so strictly enforced as to preclude his temporarily parading in a sword, sash and greatcoat, as Sergeant Austin of the 73rd did in 1815. The resourcefulness of old soldiers should never be underestimated and both they and other impecunious subalterns regularly augmented or completed their wardrobes with second-hand items purchased cheaply from departing officers, or even more cheaply in the customary auction which followed an officer's death on active service.

Nearly a year of more or less enforced inactivity in a foreign and occasionally openly hostile town could have been a frustrating period for any would-be hero, but in Wolfe's case it was a wholly beneficial one. In some of the larger Continental armies it was considered best practice to send young soldiers to a garrison for six months or a year at the outset of their service in order to accustom them to military life and thoroughly train them up in their chosen trade. Ordinarily the wide dispersion of British units in far-flung billets – or the constant movement from one set of quarters to another – effectively ruled out this kind of intensive training, and the custom of immediately sending newly commissioned subalterns off on recruiting duty, was also hardly calculated to improve their military knowledge. However, the long months spent in Ghent for once provided the opportunity for some thorough training, some flavour of which may be obtained from a letter written by Wolfe in about 1756 to Hugh Lord, a nephew of his old friend William Rickson:[19]

By a letter from my mother, I find you are now an officer in Lord Chas. Hay's Regiment, which I heartily give you joy of, and, as I sincerely wish you success in life, you will give me leave to give you a few hints which may be of use to you in it. The field you are going into is quite new to you, but may be trod very safely, and soon made known to you, if you only get into it by the proper entrance.

I make no doubt but you have entirely laid aside the boy and all boyish amusements, and have considered yourself as a young man going into a manly profession, where you must be answerable for your own conduct; your character in life must be that of a soldier and a gentleman; the first is to be acquired by application and attendance to your duty; the second by adhering most strictly to the dictates of honour, and the rules of good breeding; and be most particular in each of these points when you join your Regiment; if there are any officers' guard mounted, be sure constantly to attend the parade, observe carefully the manner of the officers taking their posts, the exercise of their espontoon, &c.; when the guard is marched off from the parade, attend it to the place of relief, and observe the manner and form of relieving, and when you return to your chamber (which should be as soon as you could, lest what you saw slip out of your memory), consult Bland's *Military Discipline* on that head; this will be the readiest method of learning this part of your duty, which is what you will be the soonest called on to perform. When off duty get a serjt or corporal, whom the adjutant will recommend to you, to teach you the exercise of the firelock, which I beg you to make yourself as much a master of as if you were a simple soldier, the exact and nice knowledge of this will readily bring you to understand all other parts of your duty, make you a proper judge of the performance of the men, and qualify you for the post of an adjutant, and in time many other employments of credit.

When you are posted to your company, take care that the serjeants or corporals constantly bring you the orders; treat those officers with kindness, but keep them at a distance, so will you be beloved and respected by them. Read your orders with attention, and if anything in particular concerns yourself, put it down in your memorandum book, which I would have you constantly in your pocket ready for any remarks. Be sure to attend constantly morning and evening the roll calling of the company; watch carefully the absentees, and enquire into reasons for their being so; and particularly be watchful they do not endeavour to impose on you sham excuses, which they are apt to do with young officers, but will be deterred by a proper severity in detecting them . . .

It was sound advice and more likely than most admonitions of this nature to have been followed by the man who preached them; but it was not all work, as he explained in another letter to his mother:

> You desire to know how I live. I assure you, as to eating, rather too well, considering what we may come to. For drink I don't care much; but there is very good rum and brandy in this place, and cheap, if we have a mind to take a little sneaker now and then at night just to warm us . . .
>
> This place is full of officers, and we never want company. I go to the play once or twice a week, and talk a little with the ladies, who are very civil, and speak French.[20]

It was no doubt meant to be reassuring, and he would not be the first or the last young man to pen a letter solemnly assuring his mother that he was refraining from the consumption of ardent spirits whilst blearily recovering from the previous night's debauch, but somehow it rings true. In a statement of his expenses the ever-frugal Sam Bagshawe reckoned to eat most of his meals in a tavern, but other contemporary diaries[21] indicate that it was probably commoner to form small informal messes, and either employ a caterer or at the very least pool resources. Gentlemen were expected to take wine as a matter of course and their social life was also marked by both formal and informal celebrations. These were in the first instance held on important occasions such as the King's and other royal birthdays, and also on recognised national "holidays" such as St. Andrew's Day (30 November), or St. George's Day (23 April). In between these fixed anniversaries which normally involved large numbers of officers and their guests, there were numerous smaller affairs, dinner parties, dances and the like. Both types of occasion ordinarily called for the conspicuous consumption of food and alcohol, and engendered considerable conviviality, but James, however, may well have been lonely. The majority of the 12th's officers were considerably older than he was and this may have inhibited him from participating as fully as he might otherwise have done in the battalion's social life. At any rate, he mentions none of his fellow subalterns in his surviving correspondence and although a number of old acquaintances turned up at Ghent in due course of time, and were evidently warmly welcomed, they were all of them serving in other regiments.

We do know, on the other hand, that he spent some of his leisure time in learning to play the flute,[22] which was a very popular pastime amongst both military and naval officers of the period. This was no doubt because of its sheer convenience, as it could easily be stowed in the lightest of kits and pulled out at odd moments; but by its nature it was a solitary pastime, and so too was reading. British officers were often prodigious readers. The inventory of his possessions "Sold . . . at Publick Outcry" after Captain

Robert Bannatyne was killed at Conjeveram in 1759 included no fewer than thirty-one titles ranging from the rather dubious sounding *History of Miss Betsey* to a parcel of "6 odd books".[23] It was famously remarked during the American Revolutionary War that whilst British officers stuffed their bags with plays and novels, rebel ones packed copies of Frederick the Great's *Instructions to his Generals*. Captain Bannatyne's collection certainly seems to have contained only two military titles: the widely admired *Reflexions militaires et politiques* by Santa Cruz and the even more obligatory copy of Humphrey Bland's *Treatise of Military Discipline*. Wolfe, on the other hand, similarly enjoyed plays, and on the evidence of his well-known admiration for Grey's *Elegy*, liked poetry as well, but his professional reading was much more extensive. Once again a letter, this time written to Thomas Townshend, a government official whose brother Henry wished to join the army, gives a pretty good idea of Wolfe's tastes and academic accomplishments.[24]

> . . . I do not recollect what it was I recommended to Mr.Cornwallis's nephew: it might be the Comte de Turpin's book[25] which is certainly worth looking into, as it contains a good deal of plain practice. Your brother, no doubt, is master of the Latin and French languages, and has some knowledge of the mathematics; without the last he can never become acquainted with one considerable branch of our business, the construction of fortifications and the attack and defence of places; and I would advise him by all means to give up a year or two of his time now while he is young, if he has not already done it, to the study of mathematics, because it will greatly facilitate his progress in military matters.
>
> As to the books that are fittest for this purpose, he may begin with the *King of Prussia's Regulations for his Horse and Foot*,[26] where the economy and good order of an army in the lower branches are extremely well established. Then there are the *Memoirs* of the Marquis de Santa Cruz,[27] Feuquieres,[28] and Montecucculi;[29] Folard's *Commentaries upon Polybius*;[30] the *Projet de Tactique*; *L'Attaque et la Defense des Places*, par le Marechal de Vauban; *Les Memoires de Goulon*; *L'Ingenieur de Campagne*. Le Sieur Remie[31] for all that concerns artillery. Of the ancients, Vegetius, Caesar, Thucydides, Xenephon's *Life of Cyrus*, and *Retreat of the Ten Thousand Greeks*. I do not mention Polybius, because the Commentaries and the History naturally go together. Of later days, Davila, Guicciardini, Strada, and the *Memoirs of the Duc de Sully*. There is an abundance of military knowledge to be picked out of the lives of Gustavus Adolphus and Charles XII, King of Sweden, and of Zisca the Bohemian; and if a tolerable account could be got of the exploits of Scanderbeg, it would be inestimable; for he excels all the officers, ancient and modern, in the conduct of a

small defensive army. I met with him in the Turkish History, but nowhere else. The *Life of Suetonius* too, contains many fine things in this way. There is a book lately published that I have heard commended, *L'Art de la Guere Pratique*[32] – I suppose it is collected from all the best authors that treat of war; and there is a little volume, entitled *Traite de la Petite Guerre*,[33] that your brother should take in his pocket when he goes upon out-duty and detachment. The Marechal de Puysegur's book, too, is in esteem.[34]

I believe Mr. Townshend will think this catalogue long enough; and if he has patience to read, and desire to apply (as I am persuaded he has), the knowledge contained in them, there is also wherewithal to make him a considerable person in his profession, and of course be very useful and serviceable to his country. In general, the lives of all great commanders, and all good histories of warlike nations, will be instructive, and lead him naturally to endeavour to imitate what he must necessarily approve of . . .

Not all of these books would have been available to Wolfe in 1742 of course but Santa Cruz' *Memoires* were, and appear to have been regarded highly for his insights on the practical aspects of the trade, while Folard is reckoned to have been immensely influential in developing the theoretical aspects, and in particular in attempting to apply Polybius' texts to modern conditions. Interestingly, comprehensive as it appears, there is a notable lack of English-language material in this reading list. This is all the odder, for Wolfe by his own testimony was an indifferent scholar, although he was by no means unusual amongst British officers in taking an intense academic interest in his trade. That he should turn to Vauban while at Ghent for instruction on fortification is hardly surprising since the Frenchman was universally admitted to be the master of this particular science, but while the first of Captain John Muller's treatises on fortification would not appear until 1746[35] it seems seems strange that Wolfe did not think to recommend him to Townsend ten years later. Similarly works by Richard Kane[36] and Lieutenant General Richard Molesworth are as conspicuous by their absence as Humphrey Bland's immensely influential *Treatise of Military Discipline*, first published in 1727 and in the seventh of nine editions by 1753. James had, of course, studied Bland from the outset and in 1752 he referred to the others as "two very accurate writers – [who] have expressed their thoughts in a very pretty, concise discourse, to the great advantage and improvement of those persons for whom they were intended." Perhaps Wolfe deliberately overlooked the available English literature since it was almost exclusively confined to the management and manoeuvring of the battalion. Simply put, even as late as the Napoleonic Wars British military writers, although prolific, seemed to lack the breadth of vision displayed by some of their Continental colleagues.

In the meantime Wolfe's assiduity had not gone unnoticed and although his letters are silent upon the subject, the latter part of his time at Ghent was evidently taken up in training to be an adjutant. As noted in the previous chapter, this appointment was in the colonel's gift and although it could very occasionally be disposed of as a mere sinecure, it was ordinarily a particularly responsible post whose duties were set out with some clarity in a contemporary set of standing orders:[37]

> ADJUTANTS are to see all detachments before they be sent to the parade; that their arms be clean, their ammunition, accoutrements, &c. in good order, and that a serjeant be sent with them to the parade . . .
>
> That they keep an exact journal of the duty of every one in their respective regiments; viz. all detachments, all sick, gone to or returned from the hospital, deserted, discharged, dead, entertained from year to year, discharged, or absent by leave; and that they give in a weekly return every Friday morning to the major of brigade in the usual method, to be given to the general of foot on Saturday morning.
>
> That they always take care to send their sick to the hospital, and take measures for carrying the arms and accoutrements of the sick.
>
> That all the adjutants of the British corps keep an exact list of duty with the majors of brigade; that they may see justice performed, and be able to tell every body when they are near duty, in order to keep in camp, and provide accordingly.
>
> That all adjutants keep constantly to all the rules and forms of discipline and exercise, now used in the British Foot, and on no pretence whatever to change or let fall any of the said customs till farther order.

That Wolfe should be fast-tracked into this important position at such an early age was a signal mark of Scipio Duroure's confidence in the young subaltern. There is no doubt too that it enabled him to "perfect" his knowledge of basic military administration and the "forms of discipline and exercise"; but whether he was wise to do so before youthful ardour had time to be tempered by a measure of maturity is perhaps a different matter altogether, as the coming campaign would demonstrate.

3
High Germanie

In 1741 a Franco-Bavarian offensive down the Danube had initially seemed to threaten Vienna, but at the last moment the French were distracted by a weakly defended Bohemia and, swinging northwards, took Prague by escalade on 26 November. In an age when fortress cities commonly withstood formal sieges of weeks' if not some months' duration this was a notable feat, but it was fatal to Karl Albrecht's imperial ambitions, for it gave the hard-pressed Austrians a vital breathing space. Next year, while Wolfe was learning to be a soldier in Ghent, Maria Theresa's husband, Prince Charles of Lorraine, took advantage of Prussia's temporary withdrawal from the war to commence a counter-attack. Prague was eventually re-taken in December of 1742 and the French under *Marechal* Belle-Isle forced to retire into Bavaria. Under their protection Karl Albrecht spent an uneasy winter in Munich, but a renewed Austrian offensive in the spring then drove him to seek refuge in neutral Frankfurt. The French at first declined to oblige the Austrians with a battle, but the prospect of their now running loose in Germany rather than in far off Bohemia brought the Earl of Stair and the British Army out of their comfortable quarters in Ghent and set them in motion towards the Rhine.

Douroure's regiment initially formed part of a rather small brigade under the newly promoted Lieutenant General John Ligonier;[38] apart from Douroure's 12th it only comprised a composite battalion of grenadiers and Campbell's 2nd Dragoons. Consequently Ensign Wolfe, in his capacity as trainee adjutant of one of the two battalions, must have come into regular contact with Ligonier in the following weeks and thus added one more influential officer to his growing network of useful acquaintances. Leaving Ghent on 17 February, the brigade marched by way of Brussels, Louvain, St. Trond, Maastricht and Aix-la-Chapelle (Aachen) to the army's concentration area near Duren, in Germany, which it reached on 1 March. For Wolfe, despite his on-going training as adjutant, this meant hard marching on his own two feet.[39]

> This is our fifth day's march; we have had very bad weather all the way. I have found by experience that my strength is not so great as I imagined; but, however, I have held out pretty well as yet. To-morrow is a very bad road to Tongres, so if I can I will hire a horse at this place, and march afoot one day and ride the other, all the rest of the journey.
>
> I never come into quarters without aching hips and knees; and I assure you the wisest part of the officers got horses at Ghent, though some would have done it if their circumstances would have allowed it.
>
> We have lived pretty well all the way, but I have already been glad to take a little water out of a soldier's flask, and eat some ammunition bread. I am now quartered at the head man of the Town's house, one of the civilest men I ever met with in my life. The people where I was billeted refused to let me in, so I went to the townhouse and complained, and this gentleman took me and another officer that was with me to his house.

I shall write to my father when we get to the end of our march; I'm glad to hear, with all my heart, that he is well. I'm in the greatest spirits in the world; I have my health pretty well, and I believe I shall be able to hold it out with a little help of a horse . . .

The horse was the thing. Subalterns were allowed £3 15s at the outset of a campaign to purchase a nag or "bat" horse for their baggage, but he was evidently speaking here of a riding horse. The hint was at least partially successful for in a subsequent letter his younger brother Edward, who had just been commissioned into the same regiment, referred to their sharing a horse, although this expedient was not to last long.

The move to Liege had been undertaken in order to link up with some 16,000 Hanoverian troops and a number of Austrian regiments commanded by the Duc d'Aremberg. Once he had picked up the Allies, Stair, hampered by bad weather, worse roads, a seasonal shortage of supplies and the need to disperse his troops in billets every night, slowly moved towards Hochst, near Frankfurt am Main. There he and d'Aremberg hoped to effect a junction with another Austrian army led by Marshal Neipperg, but it took three weeks to throw a bridge across the river and by that time a French army, under *Marechal* Noailles was at Speyer, just 30 miles to the south. Learning of, or at least suspecting, a French attempt to cross the Main at Aschaffenburg, Stair lunged forward and forestalled them only to find his army trapped in the relatively narrow area between the right bank of the Main and the Spessart Hills. French control of the left bank successfully interdicted the passage of supplies downstream from Franconia, and effectively cut the Allies off from their depot at Hanau.

At this unhappy juncture King George and his favourite son, William Augustus, Duke of Cumberland, finally turned up to take command on 19 June. It was a significant moment in Wolfe's career, though the news appears to have made little impression on him when he wrote a long letter to his father on the 21st:[40]

Dear Sir, – Captain Rainsford[41] joined the regiment yesterday; he brought us your letter, and made us both very happy with the good news of yours and my mother's health. We also got a letter from you by the post. Your kindness is better than our best behaviour can deserve, and we are infinitely happy in having so good parents.

My brother is at present very much fatigued with the hard duty he has had for some days past. He was on a party last night, and saw shot fired in earnest, but was in no great danger, because separated from the enemy by the river Mayne. The French are on the other side of that river, about a mile from us. We have now and then small skirmishes with those people. They attacked the other night a party of our men, but were repulsed with the loss of an officer and four or five men killed, and some made prisoners. They desert prodigiously; there were yesterday no less than forty deserters in the camp, that came over in the middle of the day, and brought with them great numbers of horses, for the river is fordable. 'Tis said there are 2000 Austrian Hussars come to us; I fancy they will harass them a little. The Hessians, Pulteney's and Bligh's regiments have not yet joined us, as likewise some Hanoverian horse. I believe we only wait for them to attack our enemy. We shall soon know what we are to do now that our King is come. His Majesty came two days ago. The Duke of Cumberland is declared Major-General.

The Earl of Stair had like to have been hurt by an escort of two squadrons of English and Hanoverian cavalry (when he was reconnoitring the enemy), who retreated with a little too much haste before some squadrons of French hussars, who, upon their retreat fired upon them, and killed a trooper and dragoon of ours. The reason of the retreat, as I heard, was this, – the word being given to a sergeant and twelve men, who were an advanced guard, to go to the right about, the whole did it, thinking they were ordered, and, I fancy, at the odd and unexpected appearance of the hussars out of a wood. However, they were rallied by General Cope, and would have charged the hussars had they been permitted.

Colonel Duroure, who acts as Adjutant General, was thrown from his horse yesterday by a Hanoverian discharging his pistol just by him, and was very much bruised. We are all sorry for it. He has been very good to his ensigns this march; we have had the use of his canteens whenever he thought we had occasion for them. We are now forty miles from Frankfort, which we marched in two days and two nights, with about nine or ten hours' halt, in order to gain a pass that is here, and now in our possession. The men were almost starved in that march. They nor the officers had little more than bread and water to live on, and that very scarce, because they had not the ammunition bread[42] the day it was due. But I believe it could not be helped.

We have left a very fine country to come to the worst I ever saw. I believe it is in the Prince of Hesse's dominions. The King is in a little palace in such a town as I believe he never lived in before. It was ruined by the Hanoverians, and every-thing almost that was in it carried off by them, some time before we came. They and our men now live by marauding. I hope we shall not stay here too long, if we do I don't know how it will be possible to get provisions. The French are burning all the villages on the other side of the Mayne, and we are ravaging the country on this side.

I am now doing, and have done ever since we encamped, the duty of an adjutant. I was afraid when I first undertook it that the fatigue would be too much for me, but now I am used to it, I think it will agree very well with me, at least I hope so. Brigadier Huske inquires often if I have heard from you lately, and desires his compliments to you. He is extremely civil to me, and I am much obliged to him. He has desired his Brigade-Major, Mr. Blakeney,[43] who is a very good man, to instruct me all he can. My brother intends writing very soon. We both join in love and duty to you and my mother . . .

It is an interesting letter both in its style and substance. From a purely biographical point of view it certainly very clearly illustrates the extent to which Wolfe and his father were part of a close-knit network of "old army" acquaintances ranging from Captain Rainsford to Brigadier Huske, and taking in Brigadier Blakeney's nephew on the way. It is also broadly informative to be sure, but only in describing the course of the campaign; other than in the wholly conventional opening and closing passages, it reads rather more like a military report to a superior officer than an affectionate letter to a father from his son. He addresses him as "Dear Sir". Very strictly speaking his father *was* his superior officer, but with a year's service at his back already there was surely no need for the punctilio of a youthful playing at soldiers. At the very least it is more than a touch disappointing that he did not unbend sufficiently to tell his father (and us) very much more about himself than the fact that he was now acting as adjutant to the 12th Foot – why? – and that he was coping with the job better than he had at first expected, though this was just as well for he was now about to go into action for the first time and learn in the process just what an awful gulf existed between book-learning and bloody reality.

Five days after Wolfe wrote the letter, Stair, prodded heavily by the King, issued orders for a retreat westwards to Hanau. Tents were to be struck and wagons loaded under cover of darkness in preparation for moving off at four o'clock on the morning of 27 June. Unfortunately, Noailles anticipated him and as soon as the Allies evacuated Aschaffenburg, he started passing men across the river and into the town. This was at least predictable since no attempt had been made to blow the bridge, and Stair may indeed have been hoping that all of Noailles' forces would seize the opportunity dangled before them and tamely follow in the Allied rear as they steadily fell back on Hanau. Instead, Noailles pushed only 12,000 men into the town, and passed another 30,000 across two pontoon bridges further downstream at Seilenstadt, with orders to dig in around Dettingen and thus completely block the Allied retreat.

Hemmed in on three sides, for the French artillery on the south bank of the Main soon had their range, the Allies deployed to fight for Dettingen. Had the French commander, the Duc de Grammont, done as he was told and dug in to wait for them, it would have been a far stiffer fight than it turned out to be; as it was, Grammont came forward and British soldiers went into a major action for the first time in twenty-eight years. Duroure's regiment was now part of Colonel Harry Pulteney's brigade, standing on the left of the Allied front line, and would lose twenty-nine officers and men killed, and another sixty-eight wounded – more than any other British regiment. Aside from these simple facts, James Wolfe's own account of the battle and his part in it as told to his father may stand alone:[44]

The army was drawn out this day se'nnight between a wood and a river Maine, near a little village, called Dettingen, in five lines – two of foot and three of horse. The cannon on both sides began to play about nine o'clock in the morning, and we were exposed to the fire of theirs (said to be about fifty pieces) for near three hours, a great part of which flanked us terribly from the other side of the water. The French were all the while drawn up in sight of us on this side. About twelve o'clock we marched towards them; they advanced likewise, and, as near as I can guess, the fight began about one. The Gens d'Armes, or Mousquetaires Gris, attacked the first line, composed of nine regiments of English foot, and four or five of Austrians, and some Hanoverians. They broke through the Scotch Fusiliers, who they begun the attack upon; but before they got to the second line, out of two hundred there were not forty living, so they wheeled, and came between the first and second line (except an officer with a standard, and four or five men, who broke through the second line and were taken by some of Hawley's regiment of Dragoons), and about twenty of them escaped to their army, riding through an interval that was made for our horse to advance. These unhappy men were of the first families in France. Nothing, I believe, could be more rash than their undertaking.

The second attack was made on the left by their Horse against ours, which advanced for the first time. Neither side did much, for they both retreated; and our Horse had like to have broke our first line in the confusion. The Horse fired their pistols, which, if they had let alone, and attacked the French with their swords, being so much stronger and heavier, they would certainly have beat them. Their excuse for retreating – they could not make their horses stand the fire! The third and last attack was made by the foot on both sides. We advanced towards one another; our men in high spirits, and very impatient for fighting, being elated with beating the French Horse, part of which advanced towards us; while the rest attacked our Horse, but were soon driven back by the great fire we gave them. The Major and I (for we had neither Colonel nor Lieutenant Colonel),[45] before they came near, were employed in begging and ordering the men not to fire at too great a distance, but to keep it till the enemy should come near us; but to little purpose. The whole fired when they thought they could reach them, which had like to have ruined us. We did very great execution with it. As soon as the French saw we presented they all fell down, and when we had fired they all got up and marched close to us in tolerable good order, and gave us a brisk fire, which put us into some disorder and made us give way a little, particularly ours and two or three more regiments, that were in the hottest of it. However, we soon rallied again, and attacked them with great fury, which gained us a complete victory, and forced the enemy to retire in great haste. 'Twas luck that we did give way a little, for our men were loading all the while, and it gave room for an Austrian regiment to move into an interval, rather too little before, who charged the enemy with great bravery and resolution. So soon as the French retreated, the line halted, and we got the sad news of the death of as good and brave a man as any amongst us, General Clayton,[46] who was killed by a musket ball in the last attack. His death gave us all sorrow, so great was the opinion we had of him, and was the hindrance of anything further being done that day. He had, 'tis said, orders for pursuing the enemy, and if we had followed them, as was expected, it is the opinion of most people, that of the 27,000 men they brought over the Maine, they would not have repassed with half that number. When they retreated, several pieces of our artillery played upon them, and made terrible havoc; at last we followed them, but too late; they had almost all passed the river. One of the bridges broke, and in the hurry abundance were drowned. A great number of their officers and men were taken prisoners. Their loss is computed to be between six and seven thousand men, and ours three thousand.

His Majesty was in the midst of the fight; and the Duke behaved as bravely as a man could do. He had a musket-shot through the calf of his leg.[47] I had several times the honour of speaking with him just as the battle began, and was often afraid of his being dash'd to pieces by the cannon-balls. He gave his orders with a great deal of calmness, and seemed quite unconcerned. The soldiers were in high delight with him so near them. Captain Rainsford behaved with the greatest conduct and bravery in the world. I sometimes thought I had lost poor Ned, when I saw arms, legs, and heads beat off close by him. He is called "The Old Soldier", and very deservedly. A horse I rid of the Colonel's at the first attack was shot in one of his hinder legs, and threw me; so I was obliged to do the duty of an adjutant all that day and the next on foot, in a pair of heavy boots.

I lost with the horse, furniture and pistols which cost me ten ducats; but three days after the battle got the horse again, with the ball in him, – and he is now almost well again, – but without furniture and pistols.

A brigade of English and another of Hanoverians are in garrison in this town [Hochst], which we are fortifying daily. We are detached from the grand army, which is encamped between Frankfort and Hanau, about twelve miles off.

They talk of a second battle soon. Count Khevenhuller and Marshal Broglie are expected to join the two armies in a few days. We are very well situated at present, and in a plentiful country. Had we stayed a few days longer at Aschaffenburg we had been all starved, for the French would have cut off our communication with Frankfort. Poor Captain Merrydan is killed . . .

It was a famous victory but like all too many of them ultimately inconclusive. Having pushed the French aside, the Allies marched next day to Hanau – and stayed there. Worn out, Wolfe was "very much out of order, and I was obliged to keep my tent for two days. Bleeding was of great service to me . . ."[48] His health was never robust, but there may perhaps be a hint here that his weakness was at least partly psycho-somatic. The stresses of battle frequently if not invariably produce a lethargic reaction afterwards and while Wolfe was outwardly unmoved by the sight of those "arms, legs, and heads beat off", he may well have been rather more affected than he initially thought, and also depressed by his failure to exert his precarious authority in "begging and ordering the men not to fire . . . but to little purpose". This is perhaps hardly surprising, for an analysis of the ages of those men wounded at Culloden three years later shows that like their officers, the majority of the British infantry's rank and file at this period were comparatively mature men. Their mean age was about thirty-six, and a significant proportion were in their forties and early fifties. Such old sweats are unlikely to have responded well to the shrill cries of a skinny sixteen-year-old youth and it would be surprising if this did not in turn engender a certain insecurity in the acting adjutant – an insecurity which he was to display throughout his career. At any rate, an echo of it can still be heard in one of his more ascerbic outbursts to his father, penned in the aftermath of Braddock's disaster on the Monongahela in 1755:[49]

I have but a very mean opinion of the infantry in general. I know their discipline to be bad, & their valour precarious. They are easily put into disorder, & hard to recover out of it; they frequently kill their officers thro' fear, & murder one another in their confusion . . .

On the other hand, he had clearly made a favourable impression on the young Duke of Cumberland when he "had several times the honour of speaking with him . . ." On 13 July he was confirmed as adjutant and promoted to a vacant lieutenancy next day. The Duke of Cumberland's patronage was to be of considerable significance to Wolfe's career. Conventionally, most 18th-century European armies, and the British one is no exception, are seen as being the plaything of the aristocracy, with major appointments arbitrarily arranged through family and other connections at court and in the ministry. Superficially, this view, bolstered by many a dry analysis of the *Army List* and the apparent predominance of aristocratic titles in its upper reaches, might appear unassailable. Nevertheless, the reality was that in the 1740s at least, like many "old" armies it was still small enough for the officers to know each other and for the real power to lie with a tight-knit mafia of professional soldiers; men such as William Blakeney, Humphrey Bland, Henry Hawley, John "Daddy" Huske, John Ligonier, and of course, Colonel Edward Wolfe. Young as he was, James was very much a part of this mafia. It was where he came from and where he belonged, and ordinarily he might, ill-health or a musketball aside, have lived to grow gruff and grey in the service like the rest of them, remembered by history, if at all, only as a competent but undistinguished subordinate. Cumberland's royal patronage, however, dramatically accelerated his early promotion within the service and would ultimately bring him to the notice of those political gentlemen with the power to appoint commanders.

In the meantime, the army idly hung about in the region of Worms, feeling pleased with itself but studiously avoiding any offensive action. Eventually, after a frustrated Stair had been replaced by the decrepit Field Marshal George Wade, they marched back to winter quarters in Flanders. The 12th Foot and its new adjutant marched through Brussels on 22 November 1743 and then settled into winter quarters at Ostend. Traditionally, this was the signal for every officer with sufficient excuse to take himself off on leave, but although his younger brother Edward spent the next few months at home in pursuit of "the fair sex", James remained on duty with the battalion. As adjutant it was clearly much more difficult for him to obtain leave, but his youth and inexperience might also have counted against him. A quiet period in winter quarters also gave him an opportunity to consolidate his unpromising beginning – but in the event he was soon to leave the 12th Foot altogether.

In March 1744, James wrote to his brother, telling him that as it was shortly intended to encamp he had ordered a marquee for the two of them, which would cost in the region of £4, and intended to get a two-horse cart for another £10. Then, just before the campaign got underway everything changed in a flurry of exchanges and promotions. John Cossley became lieutenant colonel and stout old Captain Charles Rainsford succeeded to the majority, while Lieutenant John Stevens[50] went to the second troop of Horse Grenadier Guards. At first James hoped that this would provide Edward with the chance for a step, but he evidently missed it for in the end it was not until Lieutenant John Romer succeeded to a company in

Barrell's 4th Foot,[51] that the way was finally opened for Edward to purchase promotion – his father as usual providing the money. Finally, on 3 June 1744, at the still comparatively tender age of seventeen, James obtained a captaincy in William Barrell's 4th Foot. His new regiment was still in England at the time, but it was ordered to embark for Ostend on 9 June and so he and "Thickhead" Romer presumably joined it there. This was an important step in his career. As indicated in the previous chapter, a captaincy brought with it a number of privileges and perquisites, as well as a certain degree of independence. Wolfe was now the commander of a company, earning the princely sum of 10s per day and expected to earn it not only by leading them in battle, but also by knowing the names of all his men, inspecting their quarters regularly and keeping an "exact state" of their weapons, clothing, accoutrements and necessaries. Significantly, he was also now eligible to take up a staff appointment.

If Captain Wolfe and his fellow officers expected great things from their summer under canvas, they were to be disappointed, for if Stair had effectively blundered into a trap and then bludgeoned his way out of it again at Dettingen, old Grandmother Wade was determined to do neither. Unfortunately his anxiety to avoid making any mistakes meant that the army, although now 76,000-strong (made up of 22,000 British, 16,000 Hanoverians, 18,000 Austrians and 20,000 Dutch), remained inactive along the line of the Scheldt while the French overran Flanders, taking Courtai, Menin and Ypres in quick succession. Despite his promotion and the new responsibilities which it brought, it was consequently a dispiriting time for James – he always reacted badly to blatant incapacity – and it was made all the worse by Edward's death from tuberculosis in October. He and his brother had been very close and Edward's death affected James greatly:[52]

Poor Ned wanted nothing but the satisfaction of seeing his dearest friends to leave the world with the greatest tranquillity. He often called on us. It gives me many uneasy hours when I reflect on the possibility there was of my being with him some time before he died. God knows it was being too exact, and not apprehending the danger the poor fellow was in; and even that would not have hindered it had I received the physician's first letter. I know you won't be able to read this paragraph without shedding tears, as I do writing it; but there is a satisfaction even in giving way to grief now and then. 'Tis what we owe the memory of a dear friend.

Though it is the custom of the army to sell the deceased's effects, I could not suffer it. We none of us want, and I thought the best way would be to bestow them on the deserving whom he had an esteem for in his lifetime. To his servant – the most honest and faithful man I ever knew – I gave all his clothes . . . I gave his horse to his friend Parry, with the furniture. I know he loved Parry, and I know for that reason the horse will be taken care of. His other horse I keep myself. I have his watch, sash, gorget, books and maps, which I shall preserve to his memory. Everything else that I have not mentioned shall be taken care of, and given to proper persons.

He was an honest and a good lad, had lived very well, and always discharged his duty with the cheerfulness becoming a good officer. He lived and died as a son of you two should, which, I think, is saying all I can. I have the melancholy satisfaction to find him regretted by his friends and acquaintances. His Colonel is particularly concerned for him, and desired I would assure you of it. There was in him the prospect (when ripened with experience) of good understanding and judgement, and an excellent soldier. You'll excuse my dwelling so long on this cruel subject, but in relating this to you, vanity and partiality are banished. A strong desire to do justice to his memory occasions it.

There was no part of his life that makes him dearer to me than that which you have often mentioned – he pined after me. It often makes me angry that any hour of my life should pass without thinking of him; and when I do think of him, that though all the reasons I have to lament his loss are now as forcible as at the moment of his departure, I don't find my heart swell with the same sorrow as it did at that time. Nature is ever too good in blotting out the violence of affliction. For all tempers (as mine is) too much given to mirth, it is often necessary to revive grief in one's memory . . .

Mirth is not a characteristic often associated with Wolfe; indeed, if anything, there is a distinct perception of irascibility and constant impatience with the shortcomings of others. Yet the mirth was very real and it would be wrong to suggest that Edward's death may have soured him, for an amusement wholly absent from his father's rather stern pomposity looks out from Highmore's painting, and even from the hostile Townshend's watercolour sketched shortly before his death. His moods were certainly changeable. He was quick-tempered, sensitive, probably unduly so, and no doubt more than a little insecure, but he was certainly not humourless.

In the circumstances this was just as well, for the timid Wade had been recalled in October, leaving Sir John Ligonier in temporary charge until the Duke of Cumberland was officially appointed to command in February 1745. As the new campaigning season opened, the war took on a new urgency and the French pressed northwards to threaten the great Dutch barrier fortresses. Having been left behind in Ghent along with Rich's 4th Dragoons, Captain Wolfe and the 4th Foot missed the bloody battle at Fontenoy, but on 19 May they exchanged places with Huske's 23rd Fusiliers when various garrison regiments were called forward to replace those battalions which had suffered the severest losses in the battle. Then, a month later, the Duke of Cumberland signed Wolfe's commission as brigade major to Harry Pulteney's Brigade on 12 June 1745. The timing of this staff appointment was fortuitous, for a serious rebellion was about to break out in Scotland.

4
The Staff Officer

With the unlikely backing of a Franco-Irish consortium of slave-traders, the would-be Stuart heir, Prince Charles Edward, landed in Arisaig, on the west coast of Scotland on 25 July 1745. Initially his appearance, un-supported by French regulars, was received with rather more conster-nation than enthusiasm, but within a short time he gathered a small army and began marching on Edinburgh. Alarmed by the inexplicable failure of Sir John Cope to stop the Jacobite advance, the Government immediately set about recalling regiments from Flanders. Needless to say, this came at an extremely awkward time for Cumberland. Fontenoy had been fought and lost in a vain attempt to raise the siege of Tournai. With its fall on 20 June the French were pressing northwards once more, threatening Ostend, which also fell on 26 August, and Ghent which followed soon afterwards. Nevertheless, the defence of the United Kingdom took precedence.

On 4 September positive orders were sent to Cumberland, requiring him to send ten battalions home immediately. Wolfe may have crossed with the first lift under Sir John Ligonier, which got into the London river on the 23rd, for although most of the regiments were cantoned at Dartford to cover the capital from a possible French landing, two battalions, including Pulteney's 13th Foot were immediately sent on up to Newcastle upon Tyne. The evidence, however, firmly points to his having been in the second lift, brought over by the Earl of Albemarle. In response to the unexpected news of Cope's total defeat at Prestonpans, outside Edinburgh on 21 September, eight more of Cumberland's battalions were ordered to embark for Newcastle upon Tyne at once, and the rest of the army warned to hold itself in readiness to follow.

Predictably, finding sufficient shipping for all these troops at short notice proved well-nigh impossible and the Earl of Albemarle only sailed from Helvoetensluys on 13 October with just seven of the designated battalions: Thomas Howard's 3rd (Buffs), Barrell's 4th, the 8th (whose new colonel was a certain Major General Edward Wolfe), Price's 14th, Fleming's 36th, Monro's 37th, and Francis Ligonier's 59th/48th.[53] It was a bad crossing. Five days out the convoy was scattered by a heavy south-westerly gale. Some of the transports got into the Tyne two days later carrying half of the Buffs, while the other half of the regiment together with the 37th and five companies apiece of the 4th and the 8th, had straggled in as well by 2 November. The rest of the convoy, reported Albemarle rather hopefully, was believed to be at Berwick.

James himself must have arrived at Newcastle about the beginning of November, for on the 14th of the month he wrote to his mother, replying to a letter in which she had offered financial assistance in respect of a recent "accident". The nature of this catastrophe is not explained, but the obvious inference is that he had been complaining of the loss of his horses, and probably his tent and that cart as well, which had presumably been abandoned when his brigade sailed from Helvoetensluys. It was quite common for all regimental officers to be forced to abandon their baggage animals when moving by sea, and only those whose military duties positively required them to be mounted could expect to have their riding horses shipped. Ordinarily, as a major of brigade Wolfe would have been so privileged, but in the circumstances of this particular move it was probably impossible to accommodate his chargers. Even Rich's 4th Dragoons, for example, had to be left behind for want of sufficient horse-transports. At any rate, according to Beckles Willson, a surviving order signed by Wade, who was then in command at Newcastle, directed "Major Wolfe to be paid £930 for allowance for 93 baggage horses to the seven battalions lately come from Flanders."[54]

Thus compensated at least in part for his losses, Wolfe gratefully declined his mother's offer of help, but did mention his having met his father, who was also serving under Wade. Promoted to major general on 27 May, he was commanding his troops from the comfort of a post-chaise, rather than from the more traditional saddle of a spirited charger.[55] Otherwise, there was little to celebrate. The Jacobites, having destroyed Sir John Cope's army at Prestonpans, chose to march into England by way of Carlisle, thus avoiding a direct confrontation with Wade. He for his part displayed all the fumbling ineptitude which had characterised his command in Flanders the year before. An attempt to relieve the beleaguered garrison of Carlisle foundered miserably in the ice and snow before the army had gotten the length of Hexham, and he moved equally slowly in his reluctant attempt to keep pace with the rebels as they marched south. To the undisguised relief of all concerned he was replaced, after the rebels had turned back from Derby, by Lieutenant General Henry Hawley and at the end of December the army marched into Scotland.

Hawley has tended to be dealt with less than sympathetically and all-too-frequently characterised as a vicious martinet of very limited ability. Yet outward appearances can be deceptive. Hawley was unpopular in certain quarters it is true, and an undoubted black sense of humour has been interpreted all too literally by his enemies, but like Wolfe he took his soldiering seriously and had little time for those officers who failed to live up to his professional standards.

By 10 January Hawley had completed his concentration at Edinburgh and three days later began a cautious advance towards Stirling. The town itself fell to the rebels on the 8th but Major General Blakeney was still holding out in the castle. On 16 January Hawley encamped at Falkirk, some ten miles short of the town. A major battle with the rebels was imminent, but his cavalry's failure to patrol aggressively enough meant that he was almost taken by surprise when they suddenly came looking for him next day. The importance of the high ground of Falkirk Muir was obvious to both sides and on the news of the rebel approach Hawley galloped to the top and sent one of his ADCs, James MacKenzie, "to order the Cavalry to move that way immediately and the Infantry and Artillery to follow them as fast as possible."[56] They won the race, but only just, and in a breathless, confused, scrambling affair which began at about 4 p.m. and ended amidst a wild thunderstorm, a substantial part of both armies fled in all directions. The battle opened with an over-hasty cavalry charge on the left by Hawley's three regiments of dragoons. A tightly controlled rebel volley broke it up in disorder, and some of the supporting infantry were then swept away in the Highland charge that followed. Nevertheless, Hawley's right wing held firm while a substantial part of the rebel left wing and most of their second line ran away in turn. The whole debacle was remarkably similar in many respects to the battle of Sheriffmuir in 1715, where, as the old song famously recorded, "we ran and they ran and a'body ran away man". While, as on that occasion, the British regulars initially held the field and rallied first, Hawley judged it expedient to retire under cover of darkness first to Linlithgow and then all the way back to Edinburgh.

As usual Wolfe was sadly reticent about his own role in the battle. The army's brigade structure had been altered when it was so hastily brought back from Flanders (and was to be altered at least once more before Culloden) so that although James still held the temporary rank of major, we really do not know how he was employed. He may well have been back with his own 4th Foot who, as it happens, stood fast and acquitted themselves very creditably indeed. On the other hand, he may already have been serving as an ADC to General Hawley himself. All that we know with any certainty is that in a letter he expressed the widespread belief that, while the army had retreated, it had not been beaten.[57]

> If you have not seen the *Gazette*, you will have heard of our late encounter (for 'twas not a battle, as neither side would fight): and possibly it will be told you in a much worse light than it really is. Though we can't have been said to have totally routed the enemy, yet we remained a long time masters of the field of battle, and of our cannon, not one of which would have been lost if the drivers had not

left their carriages and run off with the horses. We left Falkirk and part of our camp because the ammunition of the army – on which we only depend – was all wet and spoiled; but our retreat was not molested by the enemy, as affecting our superiority. The loss of either side is inconsiderable, and we are now making all necessary preparations to try once more to put an end to this rebellion, which the weather has hitherto prevented, and in my opinion can at any time be the only objection.

Most of the other officers who wrote of the battle did so in pretty much the same vein and, unlike the rebels, they were ready and willing enough to try again. On 30 January the Duke of Cumberland arrived in Edinburgh to take command. Wasting no time, he marched for Stirling the next day but to the disappointment of all concerned the rebels declined to wait for him and instead retreated northwards in considerable confusion. Despite their bombastic claims of victory, they too were in no doubt as to the true outcome of the battle. Having crossed the Forth, they split into two divisions, one of which retired into the hills while the other retired up the east coast. With the worst of the winter still to come, Cumberland declined to force matters, hoping perhaps that the combination of defeat and bitter weather would see the rebellion die of its own accord. Instead, he slowly moved up the east coast, entering Aberdeen on 27 February and putting his army into winter quarters until the beginning of April.

For Wolfe, meanwhile, the campaign was providing another opportunity for advancement. At some point either before or after Falkirk, General Hawley, who knew talent when he saw it, had taken him on as one of his ADCs.[58] According to the satirical *Advice to the Officers of the British Army:*

> An aid-de-camp is to his general what Mercury was to Jupiter, and what the jackal is to the lion. It is a post that few can fill with credit, and requires parts and education to execute its duties with propriety. Mistake me not; I do not mean that you are to puzzle your brain with Mathematics, or spoil your eyes with poring over Greek and Latin. Nor is it necessary you should understand military manoeuvres, or even the manual exercise. It is the graces you must court, by means of their high priest, a dancing master. Learn to make a good bow; that is the first grand essential; the next is to carve and hold the toast; and if you aspire to great eminence, get a few French and German phrases by rote: these, besides giving you an air of learning, may induce people to suppose you have served abroad. Next to these accomplishments, the art of listening with a seeming attention to a long story, will be of great use to you; particularly if your general is old, and has served in former wars, or has accidentally been present at any remarkable siege or battle . . .[59]

James was, of course, a young man of genuine parts and some education and he really had served abroad to boot, but his first recorded appearance as Hawley's ADC certainly had something of the air of the jackal. On arriving in Aberdeen, Cumberland had been offered an apartment in Marischal College, one of the burgh's two universities, but, as it was not "convenient" for some reason, he instead took up his quarters in a Mrs Thompson's house in the nearby Guestrow, while General Hawley and his staff moved in next door to Mrs Gordon's. Before moving out to make way for her unwelcome guests, however, Mrs Gordon took great care to lock up all her moveables, leaving Hawley with only the use of her roof and the furniture. Unsurprisingly, the General was unimpressed and soon sent for the keys, thus affording us the first impressions of Wolfe by an outsider:[60]

> General Hawley sent two messengers to command me to send him every key I had. And so I did, still thinking when he had satisfied his curiosity he would send them to me again. But about six o'clock in the afternoon he sent one of his aid-de-camps to me (whose name is Wolf), who, after telling me rudely enough that he had a great deal of trouble to find me out, said that he was come to let me know that I was deprived of everything I had but the cloths on my back . . .
>
> I then desired to have my tea, but the Major told me it was very good, and that tea was scarce in the army, so he did not believe I could have it. The same answer was made me when I asked for my chocolate. I mentioned several other things, particularly my china. That, he told me, was, a great deal of it very pretty, and that they were very fond of china themselves, but as they had no ladies travelled with them I might perhaps have some of it. I then desired to have my pictures. He said he supposed I would not wish to have them all. I replied that I did not pretend to name any except my son's. He asked me if I had a son, where he was? I said I had sent him into the country to make room for them. To what place? said he. I answered, To Sir Arthur Forbes's. He asked, How old my son was. I said about fourteen. Fourteen, said he, then he is not a child[61] and you will be made to produce him. And thus we parted. This Major Wolfe was aid de camp to General Hawley.

High-handed and a touch facetious young James might have been, but what the indignant (and partisan) Mrs Gordon neglected to mention was that her absent husband, George Gordon of Hallhead, was at that very moment riding with the cavalry troop raised in Aberdeenshire by the rebel Lord Pitsligo. Mr Gordon had in fact been one of the first in Aberdeen to join in the rebellion so it is hardly surprising that Hawley and Wolfe should now consider his tea and chocolate fair game. Soon they would be marching north in search of the man himself.

On 17 March Major General Humphrey Bland pushed forward to Strathbogie with a small brigade, and a more general advance commenced on 8 April. The army crossed the Spey on the 12th and then steadily closed up on the rebel headquarters at Inverness. The rebels were initially too dispersed to offer much resistance, but once they had assembled sufficient men they essayed a counter-attack on Cumberland's camp outside Nairn on the night of 15 April. Poorly planned and worse executed, the attack was aborted in shambolic circumstances and the rebel army had barely returned to its concentration area on Culloden Moor when word was received that the British Army was in full march towards it.

This time Wolfe would write at least two letters, both of them providing extremely useful details of crucial aspects of the battle, but once again saying next to nothing of his own part in it. Nevertheless, the fact of his serving as an ADC to Hawley means that it is possible to trace his movements and to find two possible glimpses of him.

Initially, the greater part of Cumberland's cavalry, commanded by Major General Humphrey Bland, was posted on the left wing, not (according to Wolfe) with any particular purpose in mind but simply because the ground was drier and firmer there than anywhere else on the waterlogged moor. Bland quickly realised that it would be possible to outflank the rebels by moving through some stone-walled enclosures, and so sent to acquaint his immediate superior, Hawley, of this happy possibility. By the time Hawley (and presumably Wolfe as well) got down to have a look, a start had already been made on pulling down the walls and, preceded by a half battalion of infantry drawn from the 64th Highlanders and the Argyle Militia, the cavalry trotted forward. Unfortunately, having cleared the enclosures and swung northwards to regain the moor in the rear of the Jacobite army, Hawley found his path blocked by a feature variously described as a "hollow way" or a "ditch". This was not a sunken road around the steading at Culchunaig, as is stated in many secondary sources, but the re-entrant and stream stretching back for about 500 metres along the hillside from Culchunaig to Balvraid.

Alerted to Hawley's approach, four Jacobite battalions were hastily deployed on the far side of the re-entrant together with some cavalry. As it happened they were also lining the crest of the moor and Hawley halted, quite unable to see from his own position what if anything was behind them. In fact, at this point he and Wolfe were quite blind and could see nothing of the battlefield at all. Significantly, in a letter written next day to his friend, Major Henry Delabene,[62] James noted that once in position Hawley halted the cavalry and made no attempt to cross the re-entrant until the sound of firing began to slacken on the moor.

At this point we may catch a telling glimpse of Wolfe, for there was considerable disagreement amongst the surviving participants as to when that firing began, but three of them concurred that it began "about one in the afternoon". They were James Wolfe, Captain Alexander Stewart of Kerr's 11th Dragoons, and a volunteer named James Ray, who was riding with Cobham's 10th Dragoons. Significantly all three men may have been within earshot of each other at the beginning of the battle and it is very tempting, therefore, to picture Wolfe, who was prone to making dramatic gestures, loudly calling out the time when ordered by his general to make a note of that important event.

Unseen by the cavalrymen, the battle on the moor was short and vicious. Despite repeated claims in subsequent histories that the bombardment lasted as much as an hour or more, those who were actually there and troubled to record it by their watches reckoned that less than ten minutes passed before the rebels charged forward. In the past the feared Highland charge had inspired panic in the opposing troops, but this time they held firm and although Wolfe's own regiment, Barrell's 4th, was overwhelmed,[63] "Daddy" Huske quickly counter-attacked with four battalions from the second line. Hemmed in on three sides the Jacobites were mown down in a terrible cross-fire at point blank range. By the time the cavalry had finally scrambled over the re-entrant and gained the moor the battle was all but over. The four Jacobite battalions which held the crest retreated in good order and were allowed to get off pretty well unscathed, but the dragoons succeeded in cutting off and capturing a part of the *Eccossois Royal* – a Scots regiment in the French service – and then set off along the Inverness road, after the fugitives.

Wolfe too may well have joined in the chase, although a well-established popular legend associates him with an ugly incident on the battlefield itself. One of the many "atrocity" stories eagerly recounted in *The Lyon in Mourning* by Robert Forbes concerned the fate of an Aberdeenshire man, Charles Fraser of Inverallochie, who was badly wounded while commanding Lord Lovat's Frasers:

> The gentleman lying on the ground wounded was young Inverallachy. It was told by the sogars that one officer of distinction and then another were ordered by C———d to shoot that man, which they refusing to do, C———d inquird a common sogar if his gun was chargd. He replying it was, C———d ordered to shoot that man, which he did.[64]

Whether this incident ever happened is open to question. Forbes, himself a fervent Jacobite, constantly led and coached his witnesses outrageously and this particular one, James Hay, made a habit of producing detailed if far from consistent stories upon demand. In outline it sounds convincing, but while this original version of the tale clearly refers to a number of officers "of distinction", by the end of the century it was just Wolfe alone who figured in it. Indeed he was firmly stated by no less a personage than

Sir Walter Scott to have been the officer in question, "on the authority of Mr Steuart of Allantoun", though just what that gentleman's authority might have been remains somewhat unclear. Some modern versions of the story even substitute Hawley's name for that of Cumberland, on the grounds that Wolfe was serving on his rather than on the Duke's staff. None, however, seem to have troubled themselves to enquire as to whether the young major really was an actor in the drama in the first place. On the contrary, if, as seems probable, he was wearing his usual plain red frock that day, he is unlikely to have had the appearance of an officer "of distinction." Consequently his later association with the alleged incident is almost certainly founded on nothing more than wishful thinking, and a desire that the hero of Quebec's involvement in the battle should be presented in as favourable a light as possible. Perhaps also the fact that one of the battalions which later stood with him on the Plains of Abraham was a Highland one led by Inverallochie's one-time commanding officer, Simon Fraser, the *soi-disant* Master of Lovat, might also have suggested a pleasing coincidence.

There is no doubt, however, about what happened afterwards. Having beaten the rebels and occupied Inverness, Cumberland waited there for over a month, hoping for a formal surrender. Unfortunately on 30 April two French frigates landed £35,000 in gold and with this unseasonable supply of money in their pockets the surviving Jacobite leaders momentarily took leave of their senses and decided to fight on, despite having been abandoned by the Young Pretender himself. Their crack-brained defiance lasted only a few days but it was enough to provoke Cumberland into establishing a new base of operations at Fort Augustus and embarking upon a series of punitive raids into hostile territory. Although these raids were initially aimed at searching out and destroying any rebel troop concentrations, the last remnants of the Jacobite army had disintegrated after an abortive rendezvous on 18 May, and priority shifted to the seizure of the rebels' livestock and other moveable goods.

As a busy staff officer, it is unlikely that Wolfe personally took part in any of the raids, but some surviving correspondence shows that he was actively involved in co-ordinating them and settling disputes as to the division of the spoils. On 19 May, for example, shortly before leaving Inverness he wrote to Captain Charles Hamilton of Cobham's 10th Dragoons:[65]

> I am ordered by General Hawley to acquaint you that he has shown your letter to his Royal Highness, who approves of everything you have done, and desires you will continue that assiduity in apprehending such as have been in open rebellion or are known abettors, and that you will be carefull to collect all proffs and accusations against them, and deliver them to Major Chaban,[68] and

let the Major know from General Hawley that he is to receive and keep together all such accusations as shall be sent him from you, or any other officer under his command, that they may more conveniently be had when called for. You know the manner of treating the houses and possessions of rebels in this part of the country. The same freedom is to be used where you are as has been hitherto practised, that is seeking for them and their arms, cattle, and other things that are usually found . . .

Imperial historians understandably endeavour to portray Wolfe's part in this particular campaign in something of a heroic light, preferring the fanciful legend of his chivalrous refusal to execute Inverallochie to the more robust reality revealed here, and in his treatment of Mrs Gordon. However, in Scotland and later again in Canada he consistently behaved as the ruthless professional soldier he was, impatient of any obstruction, restraint or interference by the indigenous civilian population. Yet this should not surprise us, for although he was unquestionably accounted a gentleman by his contemporaries he came from a rather more robust background than the respectable military squirearchy of Victorian times. As he later observed to William Rickson, "You know I am but a very indifferent scholar. When a man leaves his studies at fifteen, he will never be justly called a man of letters."[67] Nor, for that matter, when he was bred up to be a soldier by similarly dedicated professionals such as Cossley, Duroure, Pulteney and Hawley, could he be expected to have much knowledge of or sympathy for "civil society". This is not to say that his character was defective as a result, but rather that it should not be judged by modern standards, which would be quite alien to him.

Be that as it may, Wolfe's staff appointment came to an end with Cumberland and Hawley's return southwards in July that year. It would appear that he had all along been an "extra" ADC rather than a regular one, and now, returned to regimental duty, he was sent with his company to reconstruct the little barracks at Inversnaid, which had been burned by the rebels early in the rising. There he remained until late in November when he was finally summoned back to Flanders.

Granted six weeks' grace, Wolfe spent Christmas at home in London. It was evidently not an entirely happy visit, for as usual he was short of money and while his surviving correspondence is silent upon the matter, it appears that he was hoping for a loan from his father with which to purchase promotion. In fact the relevant Commission and Notification Books record "Capt. James Wolfe of Barrels Regt., to be Major to Majr. Genl. Johnsons Regt., in the room of Majr. Lacy, who retires, & Capt. Of a Company in the said Regt." and his commission was dated 5 February 1747.[68] Then on 9 May the Duke of Cumberland also wrote to the Earl of Chesterfield, recommending that Major James Wolfe should be permitted to purchase the vacant lieutenant-colonelcy of the 8th Foot, and adding that Wolfe had served constantly and well during the past two years as a major of brigade and proved himself capable and desirous to do his duty.[69] As James would obviously not have been eligible to purchase a lieutenant colonel's commission without already holding a substantive major's one, Cumberland was presumably anticipating his purchase of Lacy's majority in the 33rd. Unfortunately, both that particular promotion, and consequently Wolfe's further elevation to the lieutenant colonelcy of the 8th fell through. Either Thomas Lacy changed his mind about retiring, for he soldiered on with the 33rd until 1753, or else Wolfe's father was unable to advance him the necessary loan. The latter is certainly the likelier explanation for Edward Wolfe's own pay as Inspector General of Marines was then considerably in arrears, and the accounts of his old 1st Marines would not be cleared for some years to come. The fact that the business evidently dragged on for over three months suggests that James may have tried very hard to raise the money, but it was to no avail. Consequently, although Wolfe would obviously have been very pleased to join his father's regiment, he returned instead to the Continent still as a Captain of Barrell's 4th Foot, but this time as Major of Brigade under Sir John Mordaunt.[70]

While he was serving in Scotland the military situation in Flanders had deteriorated. Antwerp and Namur were now in French hands and Ligonier had been defeated at Rocoux; but Cumberland, once more in the saddle as Allied Commander-in-Chief, was planning a counter-offensive. Unfortunately, French control of the mouth of the Scheldt hampered the movement of supplies and the Dutch and Austrians failed to provide promised reinforcements. Unwilling to launch a frontal assault on the French positions near Antwerp, Cumberland instead turned on a detached corps quartered near Tongres. Perhaps predictably, the various Allied contingents moved too slowly and by the time the Duke was in position *Marechal* Saxe had lunged forward to within striking distance of Maastricht. Instead of attacking, on 21 June an outnumbered Cumberland was forced into a defensive battle variously known as Maastricht, Val or Lauffeldt.

The battle was long, bloody and badly handled from the outset. Cumberland and Sir John Ligonier disagreed over the importance of holding the villages of Lauffeldt and Vlytingen which lay in front of the Allied position. Cumberland wanted them abandoned and set on fire, while Ligonier advocated holding them as forward redoubts to break up the anticipated French attacks, just as the farms of Hougoumont and La Haye Sainte were later to do at Waterloo. In the end Sir John won the argument, but by then it was too late to fortify the villages properly and not all the troops allocated to the defence of Lauffeldt were in position when the battle began.

Nevertheless, the fighting for both villages was fierce and sustained. Four times the French stormed in and four times they were thrown out again. At length, a fifth assault spearheaded by the infamous Irish Brigade took Lauffeldt and drove the defenders out and up on to the long slope behind the villages. Undaunted, Cumberland then counter-attacked and initially regained some of the lost ground, but now that they were clear of the villages the French cavalry were able to intervene with decisive effect. For a time the battle still hung in the balance, but it ended in a tactical defeat for the Allies.[71]

Wolfe apparently wrote nothing at all about this particular battle, although he did allude some years later to the bravery of his servant Roland, who was wounded after bringing up a spare horse. He did at least have some excuse for his reticence this time, for like many another staff officer he had once again discovered the hard way that sitting on top of a horse in the middle of an infantry formation can be very dangerous. At Dettingen it was only his borrowed horse that had been wounded, but this time he was not so lucky. Although the exact nature of his wound does not appear, he was evidently shot through the body and injured seriously enough to merit being carried off first to a field hospital, and then to England.

He remained at home, slowly recuperating, until the following March. Yet he did not miss much. With the Allies' attention firmly focused on Maastricht, the French suddenly stormed Bergen-op-Zoom, but otherwise both sides were becoming increasingly weary of the war and its awful cost. Formal peace negotiations did not begin until March of 1748, but military operations were already winding down. On 10 November 1747 five battalions were ordered home, which looks very much like a thinning out of one battalion from each brigade, and although four of them and two fresh ones besides were sent out again in February, this was no more than a showing of teeth for the benefit of the French peace commissioners.[72]

One of those teeth was James Wolfe, who having been ordered back to duty was now serving under Major General Thomas Fowke. Shortly after his arrival, he wrote an extremely interesting letter to his father concerning the military situation and his own prospects for promotion:[73]

General Fowke is left here with four regiments of Foot, and eight pieces of cannon,[74] to assist in defending this part of Holland. The troops are cantoned in the village, two leagues from Breda and one from Gertruidenberg, and wait the orders of him who is appointed to lead the army here; 'tis at present the Prince of Wolfenbuttel, but we are apprehensive of losing him.

As a Major of Brigade, and the first of that rank, I am here, though I took some pains to avoid it. The corps that I hear is intended to assemble in this quarter will be of thirty-five or forty battalions and some squadrons, unless the enemy's present undertaking should require them upon the Maese. I hear Maestricht is invested. Marshal Lowendahl passed the Maese with some troops at Namur, was joined by those that wintered in Louvain, marched through a country that is almost impassible in the finest seasons, seized Limbourg, and is, we are told, on the other side of the river, where our army lay the greatest part of last campaign; while M. de Saxe moves with the larger part of the French army, and invests Maestricht on this side. If so, the body of Austrians there will be inferior to either of these corps, and will certainly retire, or rather has retired, and leave the unhappy fortress to its garrison and a Dutch commander. I am at a loss to know whether that place is thought of such worth as to risk a battle with disadvantage, especially in numbers; though the situation is such that a fortunate stroke might be the total ruin of the besieging army, from the extreme breadth of the Maese, and difficulty of retiring with a beaten army over a bridge or two. But if in two or three days these regiments should move, I shall think the attempt a thing determined, and be out of doubt as to our destination.

The Prince of Orange is expected here soon. Marshal Bathiany is laid up with the gout (and in an evil hour) at Bois-le-Duc. H.R.H. has been ill again at Venlo, but is something better, and perhaps gone to Roremonde; the greatest part of the army is in full march to that place. Neither the English regiments to the north, nor that expected from the river, are yet arrived, though never so much wanted as at this unlucky time.

I am writing to tell you the purport of a conversation with Colonel Yorke, the then Adjutant General, to whom I addressed myself on being ordered to remain here. He said some civil things in relation to having a person with these people that was acquainted with the country, and the customs of the army; and proceeded to tell me that the Duke, in discourse with him, had expressed great concern at not having it in his power to serve me, but that his intention was just, and he would take an opportunity soon of making it appear. And Yorke, as a secret, told me H.R.H. intended that Field should succeed Cossley, and that he would give me the Major's commission of Bragg's regiment for nothing, and (as he was pleased to say) in order to my being Lieutenant-Colonel to it, for Jocelyn is dying. Cossley, you know, is to go out with a government, and the sale of his company only. If this be true, you will make the proper reflections on it, and think me not much hurt. I am sure the thing is yet far off, possibly may fail as heretofore; but with sincerity I assure you, I am out of the reach of disappointment . . .

Once again a fairly complicated scheme was afoot. Cumberland had, of course, been trying to do something for Wolfe for some time. Bragg's 28th Foot was a notoriously rough and ready outfit that verged upon being a laughing stock. Cumberland not unnaturally wanted to appoint an efficient new commander capable of turning the regiment around, and by giving Wolfe the job he would kill two birds with one stone. Major Field of the 28th was to be transferred into the 12th in succession to Wolfe's old friend Lieutenant Colonel John Cossley. As the latter was to be provided for by being made governor of some minor fortress, Field was to have his lieutenant colonel's commission for nothing. Consequently, Wolfe would get Field's majority in the 28th without purchase, and with it the exciting expectation of succeeding the dying Jocelyn.

Had this scheme come to fruition it might have been interesting to observe the results of Wolfe's arrival in this shabby corps, but once again as he feared it fell through. Peace was signed less than three weeks later and with it came the usual round of reductions and disbandments. Seeing his opportunity, Cumberland tried to have Bragg's 28th disbanded in place of Conway's 59th/48th. The move made considerable sense but it would have flagrantly flouted the "custom of the service" which dictated that in such circumstances the "young" regiments were invariably broken first. Had Cumberland succeeded in his aim, no matter how justified, he would have set a dangerous precedent and the design was frustrated by a widespread storm of protest. Little wonder then, that his original notion of placing Wolfe in command was also dropped.

James soon decided that he was not "out of the reach of disappointment" after all. The ending of hostilities meant an end to his staff appointment and a return to ordinary regimental duty. This, as he afterwards confessed to William Rickson, was a "mortifying circum-stance."[75]

> Disappointed of my sanguine hopes, humbled to an excess, I could not remain in the Army and refuse to do the duty of my office while I staid in Britain. Many things, I thought, were and still are wanting to my education. Certain never to reap any advantages that way with the regiment; on the contrary, your barren battalion conversation rather blunts the faculties than improves my youth and vigour bestowed idly in Scotland; my temper daily charged with discontent; and from a man become a martinet or a monster . . .

NOTES

1. WO4/35, p91. The regiments in question were Guise's 6th, Onslow's 8th, Charles Howard's 19th, Campbell's 21st (Royal Scots Fusiliers), Wentworth's 24th, Blakeney's 27th, William Handasyd's 31st, Descury's 32nd Fusiliers, Cavendish's 34th and Bland's 36th Foot.

2. WO4/35. Although invariably designated and officially referred to as the 1st to 6th Marines (and joined a year later by the 7th to 10th Marines) they actually took precedence as the 44th to 49th Foot. Spottiswood's (later Gooch's) American Regiment briefly ranked as the 61st Foot until it was disbanded in 1742.

3. Willson, Beckles, *The Life and Letters of James Wolfe* (1909), pp2-3. Firth and Davies *Regimental History of Cromwell's Army*, pp107, 320, 325, 647. The claim by Ferrar that the Edward Wolfe who died at Youghal was actually an elder brother of the Limerick George Woulfe is certainly stretching things rather too far, and more enterprising than credible.

4. There is no foundation whatever for the often repeated story that the Colonel was road-building in Scotland at the time. The Footguards were never employed on such operations.

5. "His naive representations did not fall on deaf ears, for, indeed the veteran knew the stuff the boy was made of, and secretly indulged his military precocity. Far otherwise it was with Mrs Wolfe. What she had long dreaded was come to pass. She knew she could not prevent her eldest-born from finally embracing the profession of arms, but was it not madness that a child of his years and constitution should be exposed to the dangers and hardships of foreign service?" (Beckles Willson, op.cit. p12.)

6. Newport, Isle of Wight, 6 August 1740. (Beckles Willson, ibid. pp13-4.)

7. The expeditionary force had already been augmented by Cavendish's 34th and Bland's 36th Foot, two of the regiments earlier brought from Ireland, and more would follow.

8. Atkinson, C.T. "Jenkins' Ear, the Austrian Succession War and the Forty-five" *JSAHR*, XXII (1943-44), pp288-9.

9. Guy, A.J., *Oeconomy and Discipline* (1985), treats the complicated subject of pay and allowances in considerable detail.

10. Simes, (Captain) Thomas, *The Military Medley* (1768), pp197-8.

11. Ibid. pp195-6.

12. A "fuzee" or rather fusil was a lightweight firelock carried by the officers of grenadiers and fusiliers. An "espontoon" was a form of half-pike supposedly carried by all other officers when serving on foot. In reality most either carried a fusil or relied upon their swords when on active service, and in 1786 the espontoon was officially ordered to be laid aside. Sergeants, for their part, carried a halberd, which was very similar in appearance, except in having an ornamental axe-blade below the spear-point. In 1792 it was replaced by the lighter espontoon, but rather confusingly continued to be referred to as a halberd.

13. Although white spatterdashes (gaiters) were supposed to be worn by all dismounted officers on parade, surviving orderly books from the period invariably direct officers (including those serving in Highland units, who invariably wore breeches in the 18th century) to wear boots on active service.

14. Infantry officers' waistcoats in Wolfe's day were supposed to be red, although many wore pale buff-coloured ones by way of affectation. White waistcoats were officially introduced in the Clothing Regulations of 1768.

15. Quoted in Guy, A.J. op.cit. p98.

16. Unpublished Kinlochmoidart papers. The complete bill for his kit, including boots, shoes, bedding, toiletries and a deal box in which to pack it all, came to £59 1s 8d.

17. The 20th Foot's orderly book 1 June 1748 (in *Wolfe's Instructions to Young Officers*, pp12-13) intriguingly states that "No officers to do duty with arms, but in their regimentals, or in red or blue; the officers that go on the roads are

to march in red clothes." There appears to be a clear implication that some officers were wont to appear on parade not only in a variety of regimentals, red frocks and blue greatcoats, but sometimes in so-called "coloured" or civilian clothes rather than in their proper uniforms.

18. WO31/40. 16 December 1795. Both sons were commissioned into the 4/60th.
19. Undated. (Beckles Willson op.cit. pp297-8.) Lord Charles Hay was appointed Colonel of the 33rd Foot in November 1753.
20. Ghent, 12 September 1742. (Beckles Willson op.cit. p23.)
21. The most notable and certainly the most useful diary is the one kept by John Peebles of the 42nd Highlanders while serving in North America from 1776-1782. This records his social as well as his military activities in considerable detail and provides an unparalleled picture of daily life in an 18th-century infantry battalion. (Gruber, I. (Ed) *John Peebles' American War 1776-1782*.)
22. Ghent, 27 August 1742. (Beckles Willson, op.cit. pp21-22.)
23. Madras Mayoral Court Register, Vol.61: 7 July 1759.
24. Devizes, 18 July 1756. (Beckles Willson, op.cit. pp295-297.)
25. Turpin de Crisse, Comte de, *Essai sur l'Art de la Guerre*, 2 vols., (1754).
26. It is unclear which book Wolfe is recommending here. The Prussian *Regulation for Foot* appeared in translation in 1754, but the cavalry did not appear in English until 1757. He may have been referring to an earlier French edition of both.
27. Santa Cruz, Marquis de, *Reflexions militaires et politiques*, 12 vols., (1735-40).
28. Feuquieres, Lt. Gen. Antoine de Pas, Marquis de, *Memoirs Historical and Military . . .Trans. from French with preliminary remarks by the Translator.* 2 vols., (1735-6).
29. Montecucculi, R. de, *Memoires, ou principes de l'art militaire*, (1712).
30. Folard, le Chevalier de, *Commentaire sur Polybe*, (1754).
31. Saint-Remy, Sieur de, *Memorial de l'Artillerie*, 2 vols., (1693)
32. This may be a confused reference to Turpin de Crisse's work (q.v.).
33. Grandmaison, M., *La Petite Guerre, ou Traite de Services des troupes Legeres en Campagna*, (1756).
34. Puysegur, Marechal J.F. de, *L'Art de la Guerre*, 2 vols., (1748).
35. John Muller produced four extremely popular books between 1746 and 1757: *A Treatise Containing the Elementary Part of Fortification, Regular and Irregular* (1746, reprinted in 1756, 1774, 1782 and 1799); *The Attack and Defence of Fortified Places* (1747, revised edition 1756, and reprinted in 1770 and 1791); *A Treatise Containing the Practical Part of Fortification* (1757, reprinted in 1764 and 1774); and, *A Treatise of Artillery* (1757, revised edition 1768 and reprinted 1780). It was presumably the first of these which Sime recommended should form a part of every subaltern's kit.
36. Kane, Brig. Gen. Richard, *Campaigns of King William and Queen Anne; From 1689, to 1712. Also, A New System of Military Discipline, for a Battalion of Foot in Action; with the Most Essential Exercise of the Cavalry . . .* (1745).
37. *General Wolfe's Instructions to Young Officers*, (1780) ppv-vi.
38. Ligonier (1680-1770) was a talented Huguenot officer, and despite his French origin was pretty universally referred to as "Ligoneer". For a good biography see Whitworth, R., *Field Marshal Lord Ligonier*, (1958).
39. St. Trond, Liege, 12 February 1743. (Beckles Willson, op.cit. pp25-6.)
40. Camp near Aschaffenburg, 21 June 1743. (Ibid. pp30-2.)
41. Charles Rainsford, Captain, 12th Foot, 2 October 1731. Evidently an old acquaintance of Colonel Wolfe, his first commission dated back to 24 May 1705.
42. The term "ammunition" was widely used to cover anything, from bread to

boots, issued by the Army to a standard specification rather than purchased individually

43. Captain Robert Blakeney, 31st Foot. As he had been a Captain since 23 April 1720, he was certainly possessed of some experience.

44. Hochst, 4 July 1743. (Beckles Willson, op.cit. pp36-8.)

45. Colonel Scipio Duroure was still serving as adjutant general. The lieutenant colonel's absence is unexplained, but he too may have been serving on the staff, leaving Major John Cossley in command. The latter's first commission dated back to 11 June 1706.

46. Lieutenant General Jaspar Clayton. Another old professional first commissioned in 1695 and colonel of the 14th Foot since 15 June 1713.

47. An unfortunate side effect of this wound, which never properly healed, was to be his infamous girth. He appears to be of normal size, perhaps even a little thin, in the official portrait of King George at Dettingen, yet within a few years he had become extremely fat.

48. Beckles Willson, ibid.

49. Southampton, 4 September 1755. (Beckles Willson, op.cit. p274.)

50. Wolfe (21 March) calls him Stephens, but his name is spelled thus in the *Army List*. He was also the surgeon of the 12th Foot and went to the Horse Grenadier Guards in that capacity. (Beckles Willson, op.cit. pp42-3.)

51. Wolfe (Beckles Willson, ibid.) appears to suggest that "Thickhead" Romer's father, Captain John Romer, was serving in the 12th Foot at the time, but this was not the case.

52. Wolfe to his mother. Ghent, 20 October 1744. (Beckles Willson, op.cit. pp46-7.)

53. Atkinson, op.cit. pp292-3. A composite battalion of Footguards was left behind.

54. Beckles Willson, op.cit. p52.

55. Newcastle, 14 November 1745. (Beckles Willson, op.cit. p53.)

56. HMC Trevor MSS p139.

57. Edinburgh, 20 January 1746. (Beckles Willson, op.cit. pp56-7.)

58. As a lieutenant general, Hawley was allowed two ADCs at the government's expense, and at Falkirk he certainly had the services of James Stuart Mackenzie and James Masterton. At Aberdeen, and presumably at Culloden as well, he was also attended by a Colonel George Watson, Major James Wolfe, of course, and probably another officer named Edward Mason.

59. *Advice to the Officers of the British Army* (1782) – 2nd ed.(1946) p22.

60. Forbes, R. (Ed) *The Lyon in Mourning*, Vol.III, (1895) pp169, 174-5.

61. As Wolfe was only just short of fifteen years old himself when he received his first commission, his attitude here is understandable enough. Young master Gordon was quite old enough to go for a rebel.

62. Inverness, 17 April 1746. (Beckles Willson, op.cit. p63.)

63. Barrell's 4th Foot lost a total of 17 killed and 108 wounded out of 325 of all ranks present. One officer, Lord Robert Kerr, was killed and five others were wounded, including "Thickhead" Romer. Wolfe was well out of it. For fuller accounts of this action see the author's *Like Hungry Wolves* (1994) and *1745: A Military History of the last Jacobite Rising* (1996).

64. Forbes, op.cit. p56.

65. Inverness, 19 May 1746. (Beckles Willson, op.cit. p68.)

66. Major Peter Chaban, first commissioned a cornet, 22 July 1715.

67. Glasgow, 2 April 1749. (Beckles Willson, op.cit. pp92-4.)

68. WO25/90, f154 (Commission Book) and WO25/136, p66 (Notification Book). The same phantom promotion is noted in *Wolfe's Instructions to Young Officers*

p3. I am extremely grateful to Dr. John Houlding for providing the relevant references at short notice.

69. Quoted thus in Fortescue's *History of the British Army*, Vol.II, p157. Cumberland's warm recommendation once again clearly demonstrates that Wolfe did not "decline in his favour" after that apocryphal incident on Culloden Moor.

70. The exact composition of the brigade is uncertain, but it appears to have included Pulteney's 13th, and Crawford's 25th. The third battalion *might* have been Wolfe's 8th.

71. The British contingent comprised five regiments of dragoons: Craufurd's 2nd (Royal North British), Rich's 4th, Rothes' 6th (Inniskilling), Cope's 7th and Cumberland's 15th; two battalions of Footguards (in Vlytingen) – the 1st and 3rd – and twelve battalions of the line formed in four brigades: Thomas Howard's 3rd (Buffs), Barrell's 4th, Wolfe's 8th, Pulteney's 13th, Charles Howard's 19th, Campbell's 21st (Royal Scots Fusiliers), Huske's 23rd (Royal Welch Fusiliers), Crawford's 25th, Douglas's 32nd Fusiliers, Johnson's 33rd, Dejean's 37th and Conway's 59th/48th. The last two regiments seemingly had no casualties. Fortescue errs in omitting Wolfe's 8th.

72. Atkinson, op.cit. p298. The regiments ordered home were Thomas Howard's 3rd (Buffs), Pulteney's 13th, Sackville's 20th, Douglas's 32nd Fusiliers and Fleming's 36th. Those which were sent back out in February were Skelton's 12th, Pulteney's 13th, Sackville's 20th, Beauclerk's 31st, Leighton's 32nd Fusiliers and Fleming's 36th. It will be noted that Francis Leighton had succeeded William Douglas to command of the 32nd in the intervening period.

73. Osterhout, 12 April 1748. (Beckles Willson, op.cit. pp78-80.)

74. In October Cumberland had requested two short 6 lbrs for every battalion in Flanders. (WO4/44).

75. Glasgow, 2 April 1749. (Beckles Willson, op.cit. pp92-3.)

CHAPTER III
A Battalion of Infantry
James Wolfe and the 20th Foot

James Wolfe returned to Scotland not as a captain in the 4th but as the major of Lord George Sackville's 20th Foot. His substantive regimental appointment had at last been effected on 5 January 1749, but like so many long-anticipated events the reality at first failed to live up to his fond expectations. The 20th's lieutenant colonel, Edward Cornwallis, was shortly to go out as Lieutenant Governor of Nova Scotia and although this would leave Wolfe in day-to-day charge of the battalion, the prospect was far from appealing, as he grumbled to his old friend William Rickson:[1]

> Cornwallis is preparing all things for Nova Scotia; his absence will over-bother me; my stay must be everlasting; and thou know'st, Hal, how I hate compulsion. I'd rather be Major upon half pay, by my soul! These are all new men to me, and many of them but of low mettle. Besides, I am by no means ambitious of command when that command obliges me to reside far from my own, surrounded either with flatterers or spies and in a country not at all to my taste. Would to God you had a company in this Regiment,[2] that I might at last find some comfort in your conversation. Cornwallis asks to have Loftus[3] with him. The Duke laughed at the request and refused him . . .

Notwithstanding these doubts, Wolfe soon buckled down to the job in hand and was destined to do it well for the next eight years. At this point, therefore, it is necessary to digress from his story and look at the men he was to command; where they came from, and how they were recruited, trained and employed.

1
Thomas Lobster

It would probably be fair to say that considerably more nonsense has been written and said about the ordinary British soldier in the 18th century than about almost any other aspect of Anglo-American military history.

"Bloody-backs" and "scum of the earth" are only amongst the most widely reported of the many epithets bestowed upon the friendless redcoats, first by hostile politicians and pamphleteers at home and revolting colonists abroad, and then blithely repeated and embellished by generations of careless and uncaring historians. Some of the more damning terms of endearment were even expressed by the officers who led them – including Wolfe at his most irascible. In 1761, for example, Jack Calcraft wrote to Sir Jeffrey Amherst memorably describing the 97th and 98th Foot as "a corps and sort of man you never saw in Europe and if you had, you'd never wish to see elsewhere . . ."[4]

Equally colourful variations upon this theme abound throughout the 18th century, but however honestly or justifiably uttered, the complaints are all too frequently plucked out of time and context. Criticisms applied to the Army in 1794, were not necessarily applicable fifty years before. While politicians and rebels alike generously extended their near-routine denunciation of rude and licentious soldiery to any man in a red coat, those who attracted the genuine opprobrium of military men quite literally belonged in a class of their own. Ordinarily, as we shall see, the Army was relatively particular about its recruits, but in wartime all restraint was frequently lost. Standing regiments were driven to frantically beat up for substantial numbers of new recruits in order to complete their enlarged wartime establishments – and make good any drafts taken to build up other units – while at the same time Letters of Service were freely granted to a whole host of unsuitable individuals for the raising of entirely new regiments. Considerable profits could be made at almost every level in the raising of these mushroom units, but only if the required number of men or something very near it could be paraded before an inspecting general within the prescribed time. Not surprisingly, this produced an air of cut-throat competition and those involved grew increasingly unscrupulous about where and how they found the men to fill out the ranks. The result, at for example Belle Isle in 1761 and more strikingly still in Flanders in 1794, was that those battalions raised for rank, such as the 97th and 98th, were all-too frequently found to be padded out with old men and young boys.

Nor was the situation much improved when magistrates often conceived it to be their patriotic duty to turn petty criminals over to the Army rather than put the county to the expense of jailing or even hanging them. Although the worst offenders were normally assigned to units serving in the Caribbean, rather than to just any battalion which happened to be passing by, this dubious proceeding was afforded a certain official endorsement by occasional Acts (such as the two passed during the Jacobite emergency in 1745) encouraging magistrates to impress all "able-bodied men who do not follow or exercise any lawful calling or employment" and "all such able-bodied, idle and disorderly persons who cannot upon examination prove themselves to exercise and industriously follow some lawful trade or employment, or to have some substance sufficient for their support and maintenance." Unwanted by the Army and of dubious utility in any case, those "vestry men"[5] impressed in 1745 were generally employed after Culloden in battlefield clearance, burial details and prisoner handling before being discharged as swiftly as possible. They were thus responsible for some of the very few verifiable atrocities that can be laid at the British Army's door in the aftermath of the rebellion. Nevertheless, notwithstanding this unhappy experience similar Acts appeared during the later crises of 1755-57 and 1778-79.

From time to time prisoners of war were also enlisted. Some hundreds of captured Jacobites were turned over to serve in foreign garrisons in 1746: 250 men to Dalzell's 38th Foot on Antigua, 200 more to Jamaica for Trelawney's 49th and another 200 apiece to Shirley's 65th and Pepperell's 66th at Cape Breton.[6] In the following year, those not already combed out from the jails were given the opportunity to "volunteer" for service in the independent companies being raised for Boscawen's expedition to Pondicherry. Even foreign prisoners and deserters, such as men from the *Volontaires Etranger* who were taken into the 60th after the surrender of Louisburg, were sometimes acceptable, and on at least two occasions in the 1740s even the recruitment of Polish and Swiss prisoners into Richbell's 39th Foot was officially sanctioned.[7]

With these awful examples before us it would be easy to look upon the 18th-century British Army as some species of ambulant penal institution. Yet it is extremely important not to lose sight of the fact that the often sorry collection of individuals swept up in wartime were very different from the generality of the men serving in the Georgian army – and in particular from those serving under Wolfe in the 20th Foot during the early 1750s.

The majority of soldiers were traditionally found by "beating up" for volunteers and other than the prohibition on regiments carried on the Irish Establishment recruiting in that kingdom, all of King George's regiments were free to find their men anywhere within his British dominions and colonies. Ordinarily a recruiting party comprised no more than a subaltern, a couple of NCOs and a drummer – who obviously enough did the actual beating up. One or two of these parties had to suffice to maintain numbers in peacetime, but if larger numbers of men were required in a hurry then the process was naturally much more intensive and required a number of parties controlled by a senior officer based at a central rendezvous. However, this could not be done if a regiment was serving abroad and so in 1744 so-called "additional companies" were formed for those units serving Flanders. The sole purpose of these companies, staffed by officers drawn from the Half-pay, was envisaged to be the finding and processing of recruits for their parent battalions. In this they seem to have been quite successful and they were even temporarily brigaded into provisional battalions during the Jacobite emergency of 1745-46. Disbanded in 1748, they were authorised again in 1755 only to be re-assigned as cadres for the new regiments formed in the following year.

Howsoever constituted, recruiting parties required a "beating order" from the War Office which also helpfully required magistrates, justices and constables to provide all necessary assistance in the way of "Quarters, impressing Carriages and otherwise as there shall be occasion." From time to time the War Office also specified where the recruiting could take place. This was important for while the small individual recruiting parties could profitably beat up in competition, especially in built-up areas, it was obviously undesirable (and not a little impractical) for larger groups to work the same area when raising new units.

Certain regiments, particularly the Scottish ones, had traditional regional associations even at this early period. The 1st (or Royal) Regiment, for instance, seems to have drawn a significant number of both officers and men from the Scottish Highlands throughout the 18th-century, and even after the advent of designated Highland regiments. Curiously enough, although they had yet to be formally linked with the area, Guise's 6th Foot went recruiting in Warwickshire and in the adjacent counties when they returned from the West Indies in 1743. It was not until a year later, however, in April 1744 that regiments were explicitly linked with counties for the first time.[8] The criteria for assigning regiments to particular counties are unclear. While the 7th (Royal) Fusiliers were given a free hand in the City of London, Middlesex, Southwark and Westminster, no doubt because the regiment had always enjoyed a close association with London and its Liberties, other connections are less obvious and rarely correspond with the county titles formally granted in 1783. Occasionally, town corporations or county "associations" would sponsor the raising of entirely new regiments. John Parslow's 70th Foot, for example, raised in 1758 was initially known as the "Glasgow Greys" and for reasons which remain obscure, in the following year the burgh of Aberdeen provided a large number of recruits for John Craufurd's 85th Royal Volunteers.

With or without civic endeavours of this sort, towns and villages were the natural hunting ground of recruiters, especially on market days and during the periodic hiring fairs, for nowhere else were sufficient numbers of footloose men to be found gathered together. Although the instructions issued to recruiting parties for Samuel Bagshawe's 93rd Foot in 1760 rather optimistically enjoined that they were only to take such men "as were born in the Neighbourhood of the place where they are Inlisted in & of whom you can get and give a good account",[9] even at the best of times this was asking too much. It was inevitable that a great many of those putting themselves forward were *not* born in the neighbourhood. In an absolutely typical example only eleven out of eighty-nine men enlisted into Captain Hamilton Maxwell's company of the 71st Highlanders at Fochabers and Elgin in the north-east of Scotland late in 1775 actually came from those parishes in which they were attested. A further twenty did come from adjacent parishes, which might accord with Bagshawe's definition of "in the Neighbourhood", but thirty-two came from the next county and twenty-five from even further away – including two virtual foreigners from Lincolnshire![10]

As a rule, the enlistment of actual foreigners was officially discouraged, although there is ample evidence that it happened in wartime, and not just at a local level. For some reason there were at least five Dutchmen or Germans serving in Captain Lieutenant John Godwin's company of the Royal Artillery at Culloden[11] and, as we have seen, on at least two occasions in the 1740s Swiss and Polish prisoners were enlisted into Richbell's 39th. Why this particular corps should be considered a suitable repository for foreigners does not appear, but a certain uneasiness at the experiment is evidenced by the fact that when a large number of men were discharged from the regiment, on its being transferred to the Irish Establishment in 1748, only the English ones were allowed to re-enlist in other corps. The 62nd/60th (Royal American) Regiment, on the other hand, was planned from the outset to have been at least partially raised and officered by Swiss and Germans, though the fact that they were only to serve abroad made this prospect more acceptable than it might otherwise have been.[12]

Other supposedly forbidden categories of recruits included Roman Catholics, indentured servants and apprentices, and members of the militia, while the oath taken when attesting before a magistrate required the recruit to declare that he was neither ruptured nor lame, or troubled with fits and that he had the full use of his limbs. If the recruiters could afford to be choosy, no "Strollers, Vagabonds, Tinkers, Chimney Sweepers, Colliers, or Saylors to be Inlisted"[13] despite the fact that magistrates were generally as keen to wish such men upon the Army, as it was to avoid them.

While it is relatively easy to identify those men whom the Army didn't want, it can be rather more difficult to identify those who did in fact enlist. Some facts at least are easily established. In the first place, recruits were supposed to be at least five foot six inches high, although it was common (especially in wartime) to accept shorter men if "thought likely to grow." In February 1760, for instance, an inspection report on Staats Long Morris's newly raised 89th Highlanders noted that the men in the rear and centre ranks were "mostly young and unexceptional . . . according to the instructions for raising, which allow of low size, if well limbed."[14] For obvious reasons younger men were always preferred if they could be had and all but seven of those enlisted into the 71st by Captain Hamilton

Maxwell were under thirty years of age, and no fewer than fifty-nine out of the total fell into the comparatively narrow sixteen-to-twenty age band. This was not because younger men were supposedly fitter and healthier, (in fact, then as now, very young recruits tended to be weak and lacking in stamina), for as William Windham remarked in a preface to his *Plan of Discipline for the use of the Norfolk Militia* first published in 1759, officers "must expect to find many of the countrymen infinitely awkward and stiff, especially those who are turned thirty years of age, and have been used to hard labour. These, (though willing and attentive) cannot easily bring their limbs to execute what they are taught, although they perfectly comprehend it."[15]

While the physical requirements are therefore reasonably straight-forward, the real problem is that we know so very little about why men chose to join the Army at all. James Aytoun, for example, left a particularly interesting memoir of life in the ranks in the late 1780s, including a very detailed account of the enlistment procedure, yet at the same time he quite neglected to say anything at all about why he went for a soldier in the first place!

Even allowing for considerable popular prejudice, the Army might outwardly seem unappealing. The pay was relatively poor, living conditions were often bad and discipline could be harsh – and that was while regiments were still serving at home. On the other hand, a more reasoned assessment might concede that bad as some barracks and billets might be, labourers' cottages and lodgings were frequently worse; and while soldiers' pay might be bad, it was also constant and included the regular provision of good clothing. Day-labourers, by contrast, were paid only while they actually worked and a spell of bad weather could mean no work and no pay. Similarly, although the self-employed, such as weavers and small tradesmen, might ordinarily be better situated, they still had to find their own tools and materials and were extremely vulnerable to economic depressions which cut wages and often threw them out of work entirely. Significantly, both labourers and clothworkers were disproportionately represented in the ranks, to the exclusion of artisans and older, more settled farmworkers with families and tied cottages. Sticking with Hamilton Maxwell's would-be heroes we find that no fewer than sixty-two out of eighty-nine recruits were described as labourers and another eight might also have been accounted the same by a less sympathetic clerk – though conversely there is a strong suspicion that "labourer" was merely a catch-all term written down when a man declined to declare a trade.

While simple economics clearly played a considerable part in leading or driving men into the Army, it was by no means the only or even perhaps the primary factor. Like Aytoun, few if any of those who actually served in the ranks before the Napoleonic Wars troubled to give their reasons for doing so, although one of the verses in an old recruiting song for the 42nd Highlanders runs:

Oh it's in by the barn and out by the byre,
This auld farmer thinks you'll never tire,
It's a slavery job o' low degree,
So 'list my bonnie laddie and come wi' me.

Whatever its disadvantages the Army did at least offer something more than the endless and perhaps hopeless drudgery of labouring from dawn to dusk in the same parish for the rest of a man's life – especially if he was young and without family ties – or even running away from them, which provided the subject of the song's next verse. Alice was later to famously remark that "a soldier's life is terrible hard" but recruits, like the four young shoemakers who presented themselves together to Captain Grant of the 93rd in Leeds, often seem to have been attracted both by the perennial promise of adventure and by the very real prospect of a comparatively easy life. Surprisingly enough, in many respects it probably was an easy life. It is a frequently expressed truism that soldiering largely consists of boredom interspersed with brief moments of sheer bloody terror, but soldiering in King George's army must at times have seemed like a part-time occupation.

The actual process of becoming a soldier was a fairly lengthy one, for it was necessary on the one hand to give a potential recruit the chance to sober up in order to be able to demonstrate that he was indeed enlisting voluntarily – and if not, to ensure he paid for his round. On the other hand, the recruiting party also needed to fully satisfy themselves that he was indeed fit to die for his country. The first point of contact was normally with one of the NCOs in the recruiting party, who in addition to his repertoire of verbal blandishments would offer the would-be recruit an enlistment bounty of several pounds. The amount of money actually paid out could vary quite widely according to circumstances and was normally a matter for negotiation. Just as a man would haggle with a farmer or other master over his yearly fee or wages before accepting employment, so he expected to haggle for his bounty. If less than the budgeted sum was agreed on, then the sergeant and his officer went snacks on the difference; but if recruits were hard to come by it might be necessary to pay over the odds for a good one, which obviously bit into the anticipated profits. Once the bargain was struck it was traditionally sealed with a shilling, which was equally traditionally transmuted into alcohol at the earliest opportunity.

Notwithstanding popular legend, acceptance of the King's Shilling did not immediately turn a man into a soldier. He next had to be approved by the officer in charge of the party, and this was best done when the potential recruit was sober, after which he would be given a basic medical examination. A less than scrupulous officer could neglect to look over recruits and hurry them past a doctor with little more than a quick glance to ensure that they possessed the usual number of arms and legs, but this could be unwise, for if the man was subsequently rejected either on arrival at the regiment or by an Inspecting Field Officer, the recruiter would not only be held responsible for any monies already spent on him, by way of subsistence, accommodation and beer money, but he might also be required to bear the cost of sending the man home again as well! If, however, the officer was satisfied that the recruit would indeed be acceptable he was then taken before a magistrate or justice of the peace to be attested or sworn-in according to the usual form. The *Articles of War* specifically stated that this was to be done within four days, but not sooner than twenty-four hours, presumably in order to ensure that the recruit was sober and knew what he was doing. There were, in fact, two oaths. The first was a straightforward oath of allegiance to the King, whilst the other, as this typical example demonstrates, was a useful statement of particulars:

> I, John Sharp, do make Oath that I am a Protestant and by trade a Taylor, and to the best of my knowledge and belief, was born in the parish of Mortlich in the County of Banff; that I have no rupture, nor ever was troubled with fits; that I am in no ways disabled by lameness or otherwise, but have perfect use of my limbs; and that I have voluntarily enlisted myself to serve His Majesty King George the Third as a private soldier in General Fraser's new highland regiment and in Captain Maxwell's Company; and I have received all the enlisting money which I agreed for. As witness my hand, this 29th day of Dec., 1775. John Sharp.[16]

Although the recruit duly declared that he had received his bounty, it normally seems to have taken the form of a paper transaction in which the money was credited to his account. From this a number of deductions were in due course made for his "necessaries", including his knapsack and various items of clothing and cleaning materials. When James Aytoun enlisted into the 58th Foot he considered himself fortunate in this regard for "I received £1 11s 6d bounty and as I had plenty of shirts, Quartermaster Sergeant Elliott only bought for me out of my bounty two pairs of good shoes at five shillings a pair and two pairs of good, white stockings at two shillings per pair."[17]

Whether the money Aytoun received represented the whole of his bounty or merely the residue after his knapsack had been paid for does not appear, but if all of it was paid over in cash rather than written up as a credit there might be an obvious temptation for a recruit to squander the money, or worse still to run with it. Whether this solicitude was appreciated is questionable and in a number of instances the withholding of bounty money was one of the grievances advanced by mutineers – and occasionally advanced as a defence for deserting.

2
A Soldier's Life . . .

With or without some of his bounty money in his pocket, the recruit now required to be trained. This was something to which James Wolfe paid close attention. In May of 1750 he wrote that "The recruits are to be taught all parts of their duty with the utmost care; they are to be quartered with good and honest soldiers, and by no means suffered to associate with such as are of a different character, and known to be infamous." But his most detailed remarks on the subject date to the invasion scare of January 1755:

> The officers . . . take particular care that the recruits be regularly fed, and properly provided with necessaries, strictly observing former orders relating to the stoppages; and they are to look to their behaviour and manner of living, and to the company they keep, that a proper remedy may be applied in time when any thing is found amiss.
> One of the subaltern officers to be constantly with the recruits when they exercise, to see they are properly instructed; and he is to make his report to the commanding officer in town every day after it is over.
> Whatever the size of the recruit may be, he is to fire, kneeling and standing, to the front, to the rear, and obliquely, and from one rank to six deep; but this is not to be done till they are acquainted with the ordinary parts of the exercise, and either by an officer, the adjutant, or serjeant-major.

In the meantime, he had earlier ordered that no recruit was to be excused from mounting guard or to be allowed to work in his spare time "till he has been a twelvemonth in the regiment, and is thoroughly acquainted with the service."[18]

Ideally, as much of a soldier's time as possible should be spent in training, which to all intents and purposes in the 18th century meant variations upon what would now be called close-order drill. The precise nature of this training will be examined in due course but for the present it is sufficient to say that throughout most of the century the average British soldier spent astonishingly little of his time at it. In the most detailed study of the subject, Dr. John Houlding convincingly demonstrates that in peacetime most infantry battalions were not sufficiently concentrated to undertake anything much more complicated than the absolute basics for no more than 15-20% of the time.[19] All too often they were instead on the march, proceeding from one set of quarters to another, or widely dispersed in those quarters, and frequently carrying out a variety of jobs in aid of the civil power.

The army which Sir John Cope led to disaster at Prestonpans in 1745 provides a useful and, again, absolutely typical illustration of the problem. That summer the forces available to him as Commander-in-Chief Scotland comprised two regiments of cavalry, and three and a half battalions of infantry, while a fourth was still in process of being raised. One battalion, Guise's 6th Foot, was widely scattered between "Aberdeen and the Coast-Quarters", Lee's 55th/44th had five companies similarly spread between Dumfries, Stranraer, Glasgow and Stirling, and another five in Berwick (which lay outside Cope's jurisdiction), while Thomas Murray's 57th/46th was most widely dispersed of all in the Highland forts. Only the strategic reserve battalion, Lascelles' 58th/47th, was properly concentrated at Edinburgh and even then two companies of the regiment were doing duty as the Castle garrison.

These unpromising conditions were not improved by an absence of proper barracks. The first purpose-built barracks in England were erected at Berwick upon Tweed in 1721, and during the course of the century others were later built at Chatham, Hilsea (Portsmouth), Tynemouth, Plymouth and other locations requiring concentrations of troops. In Scotland and in Ireland a number of small forts and barracks were considered essential for policing purposes but otherwise recourse had to be made to mediaeval castles and other converted buildings, such as the notorious Savoy in London. All of them were overcrowded, usually in poor condition and generally considered to be insanitary, but the only other alternative was billeting, and most battalions serving in England (and to a lesser extent in Scotland) had to be dispersed in "quarters". Soldiers could be billeted upon private citizens in Scotland, but otherwise they had to be accommodated in pubs, or as the annual *Mutiny Act* defined them, "inns, livery stables, alehouses, victualling houses, and all houses selling brandy, strong waters, cyder or metheglin by retail to be drunk on the premises." A daily allowance for each man's accommodation, food and drink was paid to the landlord, but was generally reckoned inadequate by both parties. Needless to say, therefore, billeting was not only unpopular with landlords, but also resulted in an unsatisfactory dispersal of soldiers and consequent weakening of discipline. Regimental orderly books constantly required sergeants to go and find out where their men were billeted, to check up on what they were doing (and no doubt tell them to stop it) and also to make sure that they were eating properly and not spending all their subsistence money on the "brandy, strong waters, cyder or metheglin" being sold on the premises.

Lacking proper barrack facilities and parade grounds and generally denied the opportunity for any advanced training, soldiers were normally drilled for a few hours in the morning and then, if their other duties allowed it, dismissed to their quarters. At this point they were usually permitted to go about in search of casual employment if they so wished. Part-time working was not merely tolerated by senior officers but actively encouraged, as a 1750 entry in the 20th's orderly book makes clear:

> The Colonel thinks the soldiers cannot better employ themselves in the intervals of duty than in some sort of work, and would by all means encourage labour and industry, as the best way to preserve their healths, and enable them to undergo fatigue whenever they shall be called upon; but he will not allow the men to be engaged in any kind of dirty work, that may spoil or dirty their cloaths.[20]

The nature of this part-time work could vary enormously. At one end of the scale, those regiments, such as the 20th, quartered in Scotland were required to furnish parties to work on the roads each summer. This duty attracted extra pay and, despite the hard labour involved, was evidently a popular one. For the most part, however, soldiers seem to have worked at their old civilian trades, although large numbers also obtained leave to work during the harvest and a surprising number were employed about "gentlemen's houses", though it is not clear whether they were engaged in building them or working there as part-time servants. There were limits, though, and Wolfe himself disapprovingly noted in his orders to the regimentthat "It has been observed that the soldiers have of late been employed in all sorts of dirty work, such as carrying coals, filth, &c. in the streets, and have been busy in the holds of several ships; they likewise have condescended to clean the kennels: the colonel is ashamed and surprized to perceive that they are not below the meanest piece of drudgery for the meanest consideration."

Times must have been hard, for ordinarily soldiers did indeed draw the line at that sort of thing. In fact, the chain of events which led to the infamous "Boston Massacre" in 1770 began when an off-duty soldier of the 29th called at the ropewalk and was asked if he was looking for work. He answered in the affirmative, only to be invited to clean the "shithouse". This was correctly taken to be a deliberate provocation and a series of increasingly vicious brawls between soldiers and civilians followed.

The statement that soldiers were allowed to work in order to "preserve their healths, and enable them to undergo fatigue" was in a sense a polite fiction, for while it certainly kept them active and hopefully out of trouble, it was primarily undertaken in order to supplement their basic pay, which was small enough in all conscience.

If serving on the British Establishment an infantryman was supposed to receive the equivalent of just 8d per day, or only 7d if his regiment was carried on the Irish Establishment. As with officers' pay, only that part of it accounted as subsistence was actually issued to him by his captain in hard cash, usually on a weekly basis and subject to deductions or stoppages of up to 6d a week to cover the cost of "shoes, stockings, gayters, medicines, shaving, mending of arms, loss by exchange of remittance of their pay but nothing else except such things as may be lost or spoiled by the soldier's negligence and the captain is to accompt with them for the residue every two months." Whether any such residue from these stoppages actually manifested itself could be a doubtful matter. James Aytoun, by then serving in the badly run 30th Foot, observed that

> The men's account was never settled nor arrears paid off more than once in six months and frequently on a longer period. It was always observed that a careful soldier was severely watched by the adjutant and pay sergeants, more so than a prodigal, because the prodigal took from the pay sergeant shirts, shoes etc. at an extravagant price and sold the same for less than half their value. In doing so they were scarcely out of debt to the pay sergeant. Officers of companies seldom gave themselves any concern about their company's accounts. The pay sergeants were heirs at law and, as already observed, most men when dead were in debt in the company's books. It was very easy making a dead man 'debtor to balance' . . .[21]

It is hard to say how typical Aytoun's experience may have been or how much credence may be placed on his old soldier's grumbling, for he retold his story many years later and, like most such memoirs, it was undoubtedly improved in the telling. It is certainly the case that in some of the better-run units it was common to allow the men to purchase their own necessaries rather than stopping the cost out of their subsistence, although this was still a privilege rather than a right. On 20 April 1761, for instance, the 42nd Highlanders' orderly book directed that certain items, including black ribbons for new cockades, needed to be procured and it was to be "left to the Commanding Officer of Companys to allow such men as they can depend upon to provide these articles for themselves."[22]

The residue of the subsistence, and any additional money which might be earned off duty, had to cover the cost of all the soldier's food and drink when in quarters or on the march. In theory they were supposed to form messes of about six men (which, on campaign, was the usual number allocated to each wedge-shaped tent) and if not fed by their landlord to procure their food at weekly markets. The system was of course open to abuse and many officers, Wolfe amongst them, considered there was rather too much temptation to blow the subsistence on strong drink and then starve for the rest of the week. Again in May of 1750 Wolfe deplored the fact that "The shameful drunkenness observed among the men on pay-days in particular, is thought in a great measure to proceed from their not putting a proportion of their pay regularly into their messes."[23] Whether this was actually the case is by no means certain. At any rate, Aytoun recalled that when quartered in Ireland a butcher in his mess and some other men would periodically buy a sheep which, "when killed and all counted, cost us about 1d per lb", while others visited Downpatrick market to buy oatmeal for their porridge. If this informal system of purchasing their victuals in the High Street, so to speak, was impractical for any reason, then they could sometimes buy food at regulated prices from licensed sutlers accompanying the army. Only if neither was possible – usually because they were on board ship, stranded in a remote garrison, or swallowed up in the forests of North America – were rations issued to soldiers and to a more limited extent to their wives and children as well. Just how much was stopped out of the soldier's subsistence to pay for these rations obviously varied, but an effort was always made to ensure that at least some hard cash was paid over to the soldier, if only to avoid his selling his food in order to have some drink money.

Rations normally took the form of one pound of bread and either one pound of beef or nine ounces of pork each day, together with lesser quantities of "small rations" – oatmeal, butter or cheese, potatoes, pease or occasionally rice, all according to availability. In the summer of 1759 regiments serving in North America were even supplied with spruce beer "for the health and conveniency of the troops which will be served at prime cost".[24] Another North American speciality often issued to Rangers and Light Infantry was "parched corn" – now rather more familiarly served as popcorn. If local conditions allowed, the diet could in fact be varied and surprisingly healthy – providing once again that the food supplied was not sold or exchanged for drink. Like most soldiers James Aytoun spent a fair amount of his time thinking about food and although he complained of being half-starved on Dominica, he also described how:

> We sold all our butter, rice, pease and beef and part of our pork and brought green plantains, vegetables and roast coffee and treacle and made a shift to have a jug of coffee and a piece of bread for breakfast and an ounce or two of pork for dinner with a plate of tolerable good broth made from the salt pork . . . well heatened with Cayenne pepper. Any supper or third meal we had was a little pork brine, Cayenne pepper and the remainder of our bread and as much water as we could drink.

As for the off-reckonings which amounted to 2d per day irrespective of whether the soldier was serving on the British or Irish Establishments, these were rarely if ever issued as cash in hand for they were instead applied to the purchase of clothing. The individual soldier's entitlement to clothing was governed by a set of regulations laid down on 20 November 1729:[25]

> A good full-bodied Cloth Coat, well lined, which may serve for the Waistcoat the Second Year.
> A Waistcoat.
> A Pair of good Kersey Breeches.
> A Pair of good strong Stockings
> A Pair of good strong Shoes.
> Two good Shirts, and Two good Neckcloths.
> A good strong Hat, well laced.

> For the SECOND YEAR
> A good Cloth Coat well lined, as the First Year.
> A Waistcoat made of the former Year's Coat.
> A Pair of new Kersey Breeches.
> A Pair of good strong Stockings.
> A Pair of good strong Shoes.
> A good Shirt, and a Neckcloth.
> A good strong Hat, well laced.
> For the Fusilier Regiment, Caps once in Two Years.

> The new Waistcoat in the First Year, is only to be given to Regiments new-raised, and to additional Men; who are likewise to be furnished with Two Pair of Stockings, and Two Shirts.

The regimental colonel was able to buy this clothing in bulk and at a substantial discount, but the profit on it was accounted one of his perquisites and the only time when a soldier might be lucky enough to finger any of his off-reckonings was if it was necessary to refund him for any items of clothing which had either not been supplied or did not meet the customary specifications. Should any additional clothing be required, on the other hand, whether in the form of additional shoes and shirts, or the frocks and check shirts worn on board ships, or for working, these items were almost invariably accounted as necessaries, and paid for by additional stoppages from the soldier's subsistence, rather than from the off-reckonings.

The clothing itself, as depicted in contemporary paintings, such as the well-known series by David Morier, can often appear fussy, elaborate and altogether impractical to modern eyes, but all of it had a purpose. The characteristic gaiters or spatterdashes were intended to protect the soldier's stockings and breeches from mud and to prevent stones from getting into his shoes. His red coat was lined with a contrasting "facing" colour, which appeared on turned-back lapels, cuffs and skirts and served, together with the distinctive pattern woven into the worsted lace binding, to identify his regiment. Royal regiments traditionally had dark blue facings, while the others sported varying shades of yellow, buff and green, or less commonly red, black or white, or even unique shades such as the gosling green facings of the 5th Foot. On their heads most soldiers wore felt hats cocked up on three sides, while grenadiers had tall so-called "mitre" caps, whose actual origin as stocking caps was betrayed by the way in which they were jammed on to the soldiers' heads.

In fact, once they were removed from formal parade grounds, the rank and file of the Georgian army could often be just as casually dressed as their officers. Hair was normally brushed up under the hat or even cropped short rather than elaborately plaited or clubbed and powdered, and it was a very common practice to retain the previous year's clothing for ordinary duties long after the new year's suit had been issued, in order to preserve the new for formal parades and inspections. This was only sensible, but it hardly encouraged smartness at other times. A much less well-known but altogether more revealing and convincing series of water-colour sketches by an unknown artist from Penicuik depicts some extremely scruffy British regulars slouching around Edinburgh in 1746.[26] Unlike Morier's smartly-dressed heroes, their coat skirts are unhooked, their hat brims are unflapped, and even the grenadier contrives to look untidy. Almost as soon as he joined the 20th Foot James Wolfe had to issue an order that "The serjeants are always to wear their swords; they are not to put on great coats between troop-beating and tattoo, unless the weather should be remarkably bad: the corporals are never to be seen without their side-arms on."[27] A month later he was forbidding soldiers from appearing on the streets "with a leather apron on, or other mark of his profession, and his regimental coat on" and at the same time banning anybody at all, from sergeants on downwards, from wearing handkerchiefs about their necks. Initially neither order seems to have had much effect and in August he positively thundered that "No serjeant, corporal, drummer, or private man of any company, is to wear any other than his regimental coat, waistcoat and breeches, without the leave of his commanding officer". Apart from a later complaint about soldiers dirtying their clothes when working, this finally seems to have done the trick, but it has to be remembered that Wolfe was an unusually conscientious officer who deliberately set out to impose his will on what initially was a rather slack regiment. In some of the other corps, especially in Ireland and far away from parade grounds, reviewing generals and Swiss artists, sergeants no doubt continued to happily slouch around shrouded in heavy greatcoats, and sporting coloured handkerchiefs around their necks, while giving orders to equally scruffy gangs of vagabonds who just happened to be King George's soldiers.

At any rate, once paid for the clothing was the soldier's property and once it finally became surplus it was disposed of to second-hand clothes dealers – though just what they did with cast-off uniforms remains obscure. Inevitably, however, some of the old clothing also ended up on the backs of soldiers' wives.

Soldiers were routinely discouraged from marrying. While quartered at Banff in 1750, Wolfe felt it necessary to record in the 20th's orderly books that "The officers are desired to discourage matrimony among the men as much as possible; the service suffers by the multitude of women already in the regiment"[28] and shortly before the regiment returned to England he repeated the injunction in still stronger terms:

> The lieutenant colonel is informed that several soldiers have been married in this town in a clandestine and illegal manner, this practice is contrary to all order and discipline, and deserves an exemplary punishment, as well from the civil magistrates as from the military; the first soldier who shall disobey the repeated orders that have been given upon this subject, and shall presume to marry in this infamous manner, and without his officer's knowledge, must expect to be proceeded against with the utmost rigour. The lieutenant colonel further recommends to the soldiers not to marry at all; the long march, and embarkation that will soon follow, must convince them that many women in the regiment are very inconvenient, especially as some of them are not so industrious, nor so useful to their husbands, as a soldier's wife ought to be.[29]

The nature of that usefulness and industry varied but it would be fair to say that the presence of at least some wives (as distinct from unattached camp-followers) was indispensable to the regimental oeconomy. Officially they were supposed to be employed as washerwomen and during the later American Revolutionary War, at least one commentator suggested that the relatively healthier state of the British forces was at least in part down to the fact that the American forces did not employ washerwomen and so were noticeably dirtier as a result. Women were also drafted in from time to time to serve in the hospitals, and although they were regularly paid as well as fed for this work it was evidently undertaken unwillingly. On 20 August 1759 Wolfe was forced to direct that "If any woman refuses to serve as nurse in the hospital, or leaves it without being regularly dismissed by order of the director, she shall be struck off the provision roll, and if found afterwards in any of the camps she shall be turned out immediately."[30]

Occasionally, if the circumstances demanded it, the soldiers' wives could undertake a more active role and, on another occasion, Wolfe described how "several women turned out volunteers to drag artillery to the batteries" at the siege of Louisburg. Subsequently, some were employed in making up sandbags and wads for the Royal Artillery during Murray's defence of Quebec during the winter of 1759-60, whilst other women carried water and sometimes ammunition right up into the firing line. This must have happened with surprising frequency, for there is ample testimony to this hazardous, if largely unsung, role. Martha May, for example, the wife of an old soldier in Bouquet's 60th Foot, spoke of her willingness to carry water to her husband and officers "in ye Hottest Battle as I have done before."[31] She was far from alone in her conduct and by far the clearest and most unambiguous account of women's battlefield role comes from the diary of an officer serving in Flanders in 1794:

> It would be doing great injustice to the women of the army not to mention with what alacrity they contributed all the assistance in their power to the soldiers while engaged, some fetching their aprons full of cartridges from the ammunition waggons, and filling the pouches of the soldiers, at the hazard of their own lives, while others with a canteen filled with spirit and water, would hold it to the mouths of the soldiers, half choked with gunpowder and thirst, and when a man was wounded they would afford him all the assistance in their power to help him to the nearest house or waggon, in which friendly offices it was, as may be supposed, no uncommon thing for the females to get wounded as well as the men, many instances of the kind happening in the course of the campaign.[32]

While it is easy to imagine a woman defiantly insisting on bringing water or other comforts to her husband in spite of any orders to the contrary, resupplying ammunition is another matter entirely and can only have been undertaken with the active approval, if not indeed at the urgent behest, of the quartermaster and his assistants.

Less dramatically, it may also be safely inferred that the wives did much of the shopping and cooking for the messes to which their husbands belonged, but, notwithstanding this usefulness, industry and occasional bravery, the majority of officers, Wolfe included, still considered them to be an unmitigated nuisance. The principal causes of complaint centred around the sheer numbers of women who attached themselves to regiments. They took up valuable barrack space, when it was available, and their accompanying broods of children brought problems of their own. As far as possible, families were segregated, even to the extent of erecting rudimentary "married patches" outside forts and barracks,[33] or at least allowing married soldiers to take up lodgings of their own. This was not just for the sake of privacy, but also to ensure that other soldiers did not have their sleep disturbed by crying children. As we have seen, while Wolfe peevishly complained about the number of women attached to the

20th Foot in the 1750s he was unable or unwilling to go beyond urging his officers to discourage marriages.

On active service it was, or at least should have been, a different matter. Then strict limits could be and were applied to the numbers of women allowed to accompany each regiment. Only the fittest and least encumbered with children were supposed to be taken and the rest either left behind on the quayside, or in a base camp such as the one Major General Braddock established at Fort Cumberland. Needless to say, this policy occasioned both hardship and disappointment, not merely at the women's being parted from their husbands, but from their regiment as well. Ensign Keep of the 28th Foot – "The Old Braggs" in Wolfe's day – wrote to his brother how, as the regiment marched out of Berry Head Barracks bound for the Peninsula in 1812, it was watched by one of the older women "perching upon a rock and giving vent to her lamentations as we filed down the road before her on the way to Brixham, the tears rolling over her weather beaten features, and her fists clenched in a wild paroxysm of grief and heroism, crying out 'fight 28th – fight boys – fight 'em'."[34]

A limit of just six women per company is frequently quoted in secondary sources and although by no means as rigidly enforced as these sources assume, an attempt was certainly made to apply it in North America during the Seven Years War. It has to be stressed very strongly, however, that this entirely notional limit only applied and could certainly only be enforced in the allocation of space and victualling on board the transports carrying the troops overseas, and afterwards in the issue of pay and rations to women as well as to soldiers upon the march. Nevertheless, in 1755 General Braddock complained of "A Greater number of Women been brought over than those allowed by the Government", and after initially allowing six per company to march from Alexandria, tried to cut them back to only two.[35] Wolfe, for his part, imposed a limit of three women to a company of seventy and four to one of a hundred men when he sailed from Louisburg in 1759[36] – half the usual ratio – but once again it has to be stressed that in both instances the limits only extended to those wives actually borne on the rolls for rations and pay. Many other "unofficial" women continued to accompany the army, fending for themselves and causing endless problems for regimental adjutants. To quote but one example amongst many, on 25 June 1761 the "Supernumerary women" of the 42nd Highlanders were ordered to return to Ticonderoga next day. Unfortunately the order, like the earlier instructions for them to stay behind in the first place, was initially ignored. Consequently, two days later a plaintive note was entered to the effect that "The women who have absconded this morning and have not obeyed the order of yesterday must depart at Sun rising with their baggage, their husbands to be acquainted that if they again disobey that their names will be put in orders discharging them for ever from the regiment which they may say their accompts with."[37]

Those women who were officially authorised to follow Braddock's army in 1755 were allowed the same 6d per day issued as subsistence to the soldiers. When rations were issued a stoppage of 2d per day was made to pay for them, which Wolfe considered they could "very well afford, by their industry, to pay . . . the idle ones that cannot are better away."[38] This stoppage obviously still left them with 4d besides anything else they could earn, but as it was usual to allow only three-quarters of the usual rations for women and a half or less for children, it was quickly accounted for. Both the official women, and those unofficial or "Supernumerary" women who defied orders to determinedly follow their regiments, not only shared (or, worse still, bought) rations intended for soldiers, but they were also accused of selling excessive quantities of alcohol to pay their way, and repeatedly proved themselves to be the most formidable marauders. Worst of all, they were apparently little awed by the provost marshal.

3
Discipline

It was not only the sheer numbers of women and children which gave officers cause for concern, but also their widely perceived detrimental effect on good order and discipline. Since mediaeval times the provost marshal had traditionally been responsible for all matters touching upon military discipline in the camp and for so long as armies remained temporary organisations, assembled in time of war and disbanded immediately afterwards, the exercise of his authority was quite straightforward. However, the establishment of a standing army whose constituent units were widely dispersed throughout the country inevitably led to a diminution of his role. In large garrisons and on active service he remained responsible for the maintenance of "good order" in the camp, but by the middle of the 18th century his duties were very largely administrative[39] and his actual policing duties were pretty well confined to keeping sutlers, women and drunks in line – by flogging them if necessary. He also acted as a jailer both at home[40] and abroad when soldiers were brought before a general rather than a regimental court martial. After sentencing, he could also be called upon to act as a hangman, but for the most part the responsibility for the everyday maintenance of military discipline had, by Wolfe's day, very firmly passed to regimental officers and NCOs.

The Georgian army undoubtedly has a somewhat unenviable reputation for being harshly disciplined. It is unfortunate, therefore, that despite its importance, interest in the subject tends either to be superficial, or worse still more sensationalist and prurient than balanced and properly considered, for it is in this field that the greatest paradox is thrown up. A badly treated soldier is likely to simply run away and the poorly supervised dispersal of soldiers in what were essentially civilian billets made it extremely easy for 18th-century ones to do just that. Yet, while desertion was indeed real a problem, neither its scale nor the evidence regularly produced at deserters' court martials point to its being a response to harsh living conditions or a brutal disciplinary regime.

The legal foundation of the Army's disciplinary system was provided by the annual *Mutiny Act*, which in turn gave authority to the *Articles of War*, a quasi-legal code that operated independently of the civil one. When a man was enlisted as a soldier the second and sixth sections, dealing with mutiny and desertion, were to be read to him within four days and a man was not considered subject to its penalties unless this had been done. It was customary, therefore, for court martial proceedings to open with formal evidence to the effect that the accused had been properly enlisted and had the *Articles* read to him. Furthermore, since 1718 it had also been mandatory to have them read at the head of every regiment, company and troop at two-monthly intervals, otherwise in an age when illiteracy was common amongst the working population, ignorance could be a legally valid defence. Nevertheless, from a legal point of view the *Articles* were far from satisfactory, being poorly laid out, often vague, and unnecessarily cluttered up with administrative regulations, which had no direct bearing on the maintenance of military discipline.

Soldiers accused of ordinary criminal acts against civilians, such as murder, rape and robbery, were supposed to be turned over to civil magistrates, except on Gibraltar (which had none) or on active service in foreign parts. In practice, most officers were reluctant to do so unless a constable actually turned up on their doorstep with a warrant, and in October 1750 Wolfe entered a typically stern warning in the 20th's Orderly books that:

> The magistrates of Aberdeen made a complaint of a robbery, that is supposed to have been committed by two soldiers of this regiment; the colonel was in hopes that these practices were at an end, and that the number of villains he has been forced to whip out of the regiment, had given sufficient warning, and removed the evil; but since there are some still left, he desires they may be assured, that he will contribute all in his power to hang the first rascal that shall be found guilty of a crime of this sort; and such as are not delivered over to the civil power may expect the severest and most exemplary punishment that the martial law can possibly inflict.[41]

In other words, it was all to be kept in the family unless there was no alternative but to surrender the offender to the magistrates.

Ordinary "military" crime, on the other hand, fell into three very broad and sometimes overlapping categories. There were minor disciplinary offences such as losing (or selling) kit, embezzling official funds, being late and/or drunk on parade (or absent from it altogether), transgressing a variety of regimental standing orders and so on. Generally speaking, these crimes are poorly documented, no doubt because they were usually dealt with by company or troop commanders and merited only relatively light punishments such as small fines or stoppages, extra guard duties, fatigues, confinement to quarters, or most effective of all, a withdrawal of permission to seek outside work. For instance, the Articles of War stated anyone making "reproachful or provoking Speeches or Gestures" was required to ask "Pardon of the Party offended, in the Presence of his Commanding Officer."

Petty stuff like that undoubtedly accounted for most crime, but more serious offences were in the first instance dealt with by regimental courts martial, normally comprising five commissioned officers headed by a captain, although just three were allowed if this number could not be readily assembled. The frequency with which regimental courts sat could vary enormously. The first entry in Captain Stewart's orderly book is for 18 February 1759 and he records no fewer than twelve regimental courts-martial taking place between 3 March and 6 April, including five in the eight days between 9 and 17 March. Since the regiment was still in its winter quarters in New York State at the time, the apparent high incidence of crime may well be explained by boredom and slack control. At any rate, once they moved into the field it was a completely different story and no more regimental courts are recorded until 20 July 1760. Once again, these courts are poorly documented, but an idea of the sort of crime normally dealt with may be had from other surviving orderly books. A surprisingly frequent complaint turning up in more than one regiment's books is the wanton destruction or damage of farm boundaries, fishing, shooting or any form of poaching with nets and snares, and in 1759 several complaints are even recorded in the 42nd's orderly book about soldiers using fences for informal target practice! Rather more conventional offences appear to have included sentries accepting money or drink to turn a blind eye to whatever was being smuggled in or out of the barrack gate, "the unsoldier-like practice of not coming to the places of parade and exercise", and absconding from guard. Chiefly, however, the courts appear to have dealt with those perennial favourites, gambling and drunkenness.

The proceedings could evidently be surprisingly informal, especially if they sat as a court of inquiry rather than a court of military law, and in 1750 Wolfe had to issue a reminder that "When court-martials assemble all sort of order and decency is to be observed. No officer to appear as a member in a regimental court of judicature, but in red cloaths and his sash on; and the president and gentlemen who compose such courts cannot be too exact and circumstantial in their enquiries, that the sentence may be given upon sure ground, and with the strictest regard to justice."[42] There was good reason for this since regimental courts had the power to award corporal punishment, subject to confirmation by the commanding officer – who could not be a member of the court. The extent of this power, when exercised,[43] is a touch uncertain since the *Articles* invariably left the actual sentencing to the court's discretion. Inevitably, therefore, there could be a wide variation in the punishments ordered according to the views of individual commanding officers. Lieutenant Colonel Robert Rich, the actual commander of Barrell's 4th Foot during Wolfe's time with the regiment, was a notorious flogger and lampooned as such in at least one contemporary caricature; but at the other end of the scale Lieutenant Colonel Matthews Sewell of Richbell's 39th could write to Sam Bagshawe in 1750 that "I have ordered a Cat of nine Tails to be bought, in terrorem, but I hope we shall have no Occasion to use them."[44]

Whether the cat was kept *in terrorem* or not, it is unlikely that regimental courts awarded more than about 300 lashes,[45] although on at least one occasion a grenadier of the 20th named Rigby was awarded 600 for accepting a bribe from a civilian.[46] Any offence meriting a greater punishment properly fell within the competence of a general court martial, comprising no fewer than thirteen members and normally presided over by a colonel. Naturally enough, assembling sufficient officers to constitute such a court was not always easy, particularly since it inevitably required the presence of more than one regiment upon the spot. However, it was the only court competent to try offences by officers, and to award death sentences – subject to confirmation by the local commander-in-chief. Consequently, not only did general courts deal with the most serious offences (such as murder, rape, robbery or mutiny), but they also seem to have considered themselves morally obliged to convict and award exemplary punishments.

Mutiny naturally demanded the most exemplary retribution, though the term literally covered a multitude of sins. Bloody uprisings attended by the horrible murder of unpopular officers were seldom if ever enacted in King George's army. Nevertheless, mutiny was essentially distinguished from insubordination by the actual striking of superior officers, or at least threatening to do so, and the *Articles* also very prudently enacted that any failure on the part of an offender's comrades to disclose foreknowledge of the same, or to hesitate in assisting to restrain and apprehend him, was equally culpable.

In his study of the contemporary Georgian navy N.A.M. Rodger postulates that, with some few exceptions, nautical mutinies were conducted according to certain unwritten rules, well understood by both officers and men, which ensured that they seldom moved beyond what would now be termed industrial disputes. Perhaps not without tongue in cheek, he summarised this informal code as ruling that mutiny should not take place on the high seas or in the presence of the enemy; that no personal violence should be employed, although tumult and shouting was permissible; and thirdly, that mutiny could only be resorted to in the pursuit of objectives sanctioned by the immemorial custom of the service[47] – surprisingly enough, the same may have been true of military mutinies!

Much depended upon individual circumstances, but a rational re-assessment of the detailed case evidence contained in John Prebble's useful (if polemic) account of mutiny in the 18th-century Highland regiments reveals that while they were not conducted according to precisely the same rules as naval ones, some very close parallels did exist.[48] In the first place, with the exception of an obscure incident at Gibraltar in 1760,[49] nearly all the known mutinies occurred at home rather than abroad, and like naval ones they certainly never took place when actually engaged in operations against an enemy. On the contrary, for the most part they involved newly raised units, and most frequently occurred on the point of embarkation for service overseas. While various contributory factors emerged from time to time, the principal cause of discontent, just as in the navy, appears to have centred around arrears of pay and bounty money.

In some cases the actual protest took the form of little more than a polite refusal to embark on the transports, while in others it was attended by noisy outbreaks of mobbing and rioting in the very best 18th-century radical tradition. Unpopular officers could sometimes be beaten up if imprudent or unfortunate enough to be caught alone, but it was very rare indeed for anything more serious to happen. Moreover, although ringleaders were occasionally identified and later punished, it was much more common for the incident to end with senior officers giving in to the mutineers' demands. Extraordinary as this apparent lenience or weakness might appear to modern eyes, it was simply a recognition of the fact that, far from being bloody revolts against established authority, the majority of mutinies were nothing more than relatively routine industrial disputes, conducted according to familiar, if rowdy, 18th-century grievance procedures. In May 1750, for example, Wolfe simply warned that "If any man of the party for the roads presumes on any occasion, or for any cause whatever, to shew the same sort of disposition to mutiny and disobedience, as was observed in some soldiers of the last year's detachment, particularly in the castle of Stirling, Captain Trapaud, and the officers ordered to command them, are to make an immediate and severe example of the offenders". Since he then went on to say that anyone committing crimes of a "high nature" or who was "remarkably idle" was to be immediately sent back to the regiment, it may safely be inferred that the "mutiny and disobedience" in question was indeed no more than a disposition to complain about pay and working conditions.[50]

As far as can be ascertained, other than the Gibraltar incident there were in fact no serious mutinies during the Seven Years War proper, although, according to Stewart of Garth, when Campbell's 88th Highlanders were disbanded at Linlithgow in July 1763

> . . . one of those unfortunate collisions of opinion occurred . . . In the hurry of the campaign, new clothing had not been served out to the soldiers for the year 1763, and when they were disbanded, it was thought they had no occasion for military uniforms. The soldiers thought otherwise, and said they were fully entitled to pay, clothing, and all that had been promised, and therefore due to them. The thing was at first resisted, but the men persevering, it was at length acquiesced in, and an allowance in money given them in lieu of the clothing. In this resistance to authority, for the support of what they considered their rights, some indications of violence . . . were manifested.[51]

During the American Revolutionary War, on the other hand, there were at least five major incidents between September 1778 and January 1783 which probably illustrate the whole spectrum of military protest. The most violent of them occurred in Leith when an attempt to forcibly draft sixty-four recruits originally intended for the 42nd and 71st Highlanders into the 83rd Royal Glasgow Volunteers ended in a pitched battle on the dockside in which fourteen men were killed. Although it approximates to the popular Hollywood image of mutiny, this affair was altogether untypical both as to its cause and bloody ending, and was regarded even at the time as wholly exceptional. The others, however, were much more typical as to cause, course and outcome. An equally short-lived mutiny in the Argyllshire Fencibles, for example, had its roots in discontent over arrears of pay and bounty money, exacerbated in this case by excessive stoppages for necessaries. At first the men's protests took the form of a refusal to accept new-style accoutrements, but then a mismanaged and rather too heavy-handed attempt to deal with what was still at that stage little more than insubordination sparked a brief revolt and a noisy occupation of Edinburgh Castle. The whole affair was all over within an hour, with one ringleader being sentenced to death and the other to 1,000 lashes – which seems to have been the customary tariff. Equally typically, both men afterwards had their sentences commuted to five years' service in the West Indies.

Like the Argylls, both Seaforth's 78th/74th Highlanders and Lord MacDonald's 76th Highlanders were entirely new regiments raised for rank by officers who were for the most part as inexperienced as their men, and once again their discontent primarily stemmed from unpaid arrears of pay and bounty money. In both cases the protest was manifested in a point-blank refusal to embark on transports until the money owing was paid, and complaints of alleged ill treatment by the officers redressed. Only the first "mutiny" involved a certain amount of mobbing and scuffling in the High Street of Edinburgh, in the course of which the commanding officer was knocked to the ground; the other was a peaceful, well-conducted affair. While deploring the affront to good order and discipline, Lieutenant General Oughton, the Commander-in-Chief Scotland, ordered the men paid, promised to look into their other grievances – and took no disciplinary action.

The fifth and last incident initially involved Murray's 77th Highlanders, yet another new unit raised for rank and only for the duration of the American War. Despite this limitation on its service, orders were given to embark for India *after* the war had ended. Not surprisingly the men declined to go and underlined the point with some rather noisy mobbing and rioting in the streets of Portsmouth, and an equally traditional beating-up of the unpopular commanding officer. An immediate attempt by the 41st (Invalid) Regiment to quell the disturbance was then seen off with one dead and two wounded. Characteristically, the mutineers publicly regretted the old veteran's death, but encouraged by this apparent success their mutinous example was followed not only by Gordon's 81st Highlanders, but also by Lambton's 68th (Durham) Regiment as well. With the Portsmouth defences occupied by the mutineers and the unrest spreading to the fleet, a humiliating climbdown followed a week later and although the 68th were successfully re-embarked for the West Indies, both Highland regiments secured their disbandment – and the customary full remission for their sins.

Even the most famous of all the 18th-century revolts, the Black Watch mutiny of 1743, was in reality pretty tame stuff by Hollywood standards. It certainly resulted in three of the ringleaders being put up against a wall and shot, and about a hundred others being condemned to serve in the West Indies, but when all the accumulated mythology surrounding the incident is stripped away, an entirely familiar pattern of grievance and protest emerges in which the fact of their being a Highland regiment was merely incidental. Instead, the significant features were that the then 43rd Regiment was a recent and still unstable creation, which had largely been cobbled together from a number of paramilitary police units, and had not yet been on active service. Both money and clothing were owing to the soldiers and they were ordered to embark for Germany with only the promise of it. There were other aggravating factors, it is true, including a widely-believed rumour that they were destined for the West Indies rather than Germany, but at the end of the day the so-called mutiny amounted to no more than some noisy but harmless tumults and a collective attempt at desertion on the part of little more than a hundred or so of the men – who subsequently surrendered without a fight. Dramatic though it appeared, both at the time and in retrospect, the most unusual feature of the Black Watch mutiny was probably the fact that it ended up in a general court martial at all, and even then that can be put down to the attempted mass desertion rather than to the "revolt" itself.

Desertion was in fact by far the most common offence dealt with by general courts martial, and all too often it was casual and half-hearted enough to be more justly accounted absence without leave, rather than a desperate attempt to escape supposedly intolerable living conditions. Sometimes it could even happen by accident. One of Wolfe's men, Richard Rothwell of the 20th Foot, in an entirely typical example deserted in Glasgow on 24 December 1752 and when asked what he had to say in his defence, claimed;

> . . . that after he got his pay he met with some soldiers and townsmen with whom he play'd at cards and lost his money, and not knowing what to do he sold one of his shirts in order to regain it, but having lost that he sold another and lost that money also, and being very drunk he returned to his quarters late but was shut out and wandered four miles away from Glasgow, where finding himself upon sober and considering that it was the day he should have been upon guard, he durst not return to the regiment for fear of punishment . . .[52]

Judging by extant court martial records, this sort of thing was probably a lot commoner than might be supposed, and even when a man deliberately absented himself there were different degrees of culpability. It was not always easy or even wise to assume that it was his fixed intention to desert. In one particularly fascinating case recorded in Sam Bagshawe's correspondence, Lieutenant Archibald Grant of the 39th Foot wrote on 10 December 1747 to inform the then Major that: ". . . three of your Men viz. Josh. Beains, Joseph Harrison and William Ward had Deserted that morning." Ominously he added, "they went off armed with a case of pistolls and cutlash each". Bagshawe, however, reassuringly replied that he was sceptical about them intending to desert as they had "particular Obligations to me" and rather oddly expressed a hope that they were only off on "some drinking scheme". As it happened, they had indeed returned before his reply reached the unfortunate Lieutenant and mysteriously explained to him that ". . . they were only on an Intriguing scheme":[53] The fact that all three of them went off armed to the teeth rather suggests that the intrigue was a of a criminal nature, but nevertheless none of them appear to have been punished in any way.

Despite the outward severity of the Army's penal code, offenders escaped punishment with some considerable frequency. Recruits were hard enough to come by without hanging, flogging or shooting them at the slightest excuse. Much obviously depended upon the circumstances and the gravity of the particular case. Eight of the twenty-six deserters brought before general courts martial in Scotland between 1751 and 1753 were second offenders who had previously been pardoned, or in just one instance, had already been flogged by their own commanding officers. It is not surprising therefore to find that they were then dealt with harshly by the higher court. Five of the condemned were sentenced to death and the others to floggings; seven got 500, one 600, two 800 and the rest 1,000 or occasionally 1,500 lashes apiece. Only three were pardoned, including Isaac Walton of Bocland's 11th Foot, who was recommended to mercy by the court on account of his "youth, ignorance and natural stupidity."

Conversely, of twenty-four men recorded in Captain Stewart's orderly book as having been convicted of desertion in a similar time period between 1759 and 1761, eight – a third – were sentenced to death and a further six to what was obviously a standard tariff of 1,000 lashes. At first sight this suggests that in wartime offenders were more harshly dealt with, but in fact only eleven sentences were carried out and the other three offenders, together with ten others whose original sentence is unspecified (or who may still have been awaiting trial), were pardoned and returned to their units without punishment.

One of those whose sentence was carried out, Jonathan Barns (or Burns), was doubly condemned for having been found serving in the enemy's ranks. Despite its own readiness to enlist German and other foreign prisoners of war,[54] the army generally took a dim view of deserters who ran *to* the enemy rather than away from him. In the immediate aftermath of the battle of Culloden in 1746 no fewer than eighty-one British soldiers were discovered amongst the "French" prisoners, and having been taken in arms, as the saying was, they were promptly condemned to death by a drumhead court martial. Few of them had actually deserted. Most only joined the Irish Picquets under duress and in order to escape the exceptionally harsh treatment to which they had been subjected while prisoners of war. Consequently it appears that while up to thirty were actually hanged, the rest were returned to their units. Wolfe himself had a brush with would-be deserters to the French Army's Irish Brigade while he was stationed at Dover Castle in 1753 and his response was nothing if not robust:

> Hazle, of Capt. Maxwell's[55] is not hereafter to be suffered to go without the castle gates; the lieut. colonel does not mean by this to prevent his deserting, but to punish him for his insolence: but he desires that Hazle, and Findas the grenadier, who has already been condemned for treason, may know, as well as those who have been in the service of France, or desire to be there, that he sets no sort of value or estimation upon them, and that he had much rather they were in the Irish brigades than in the army of Great Britain; but if ever he hears that any deserter shall dare hereafter to threaten to desert, he'll

be immediately whipped out of the regiment, with every mark of infamy, contempt and disgrace, as unworthy to continue in it, and as a fit recruit for the rebel battalions, hired by the French to serve against their country.[56]

This declaration, and indeed his manner of dealing with what could have been a serious disciplinary matter, was typical of Wolfe. There is no doubting the outward harshness of the Army's disciplinary code and the sentences routinely handed down by general courts martial, but just as in the wider administration of 18th-century justice apparent severity was in very large measure leavened by an unregulated exercise of humanity. So long as a suitable example could be made from time to time, the Army was generally content at every level to turn a blind eye to what might seem like an alarming range of misdemeanours and petty crime and to almost routinely pardon more serious offences. There was a resigned acceptance of the fact that, in an Army largely made up of spirited young men, a certain amount of casual misbehaviour was inevitable. Excessive drinking and gambling were certainly (if sometimes rather primly) discouraged as likely to lead to more serious offences, but on the whole it was widely recognised that a needlessly oppressive disciplinary regime was incompatible with a soldierly spirit.

Recruiters usually made a point in their speeches about only looking for men of spirit, who were, in the immortal Sergeant Kite's words, "fit for a cap" (i.e. to be grenadiers) and generally speaking they got them too. In the very nature of things, misdemeanours, crimes and punishments tend to be much better recorded than the good behaviour that is actually the norm. The British Army undoubtedly had its bad days and its villains and failures like any other, but on the whole it performed well and often exceptionally well. It would be tedious to reel off a bombastic recital of stirring deeds that won the empire, but glimpses of that spirit can nevertheless be seen at an individual level. When our old friend Sam Bagshawe had the misfortune to have a leg shot off at L'Orient in 1746 he providentially happened to be talking at the time to a Royal Artillery surgeon named James Butler, who saved his life by promptly administering first aid. However, Bagshawe still lay critically injured within range of the French guns until a party of grenadiers crawled some distance with him behind a stone wall and then afterwards, under cover of darkness, carried him another eleven miles to safety. That was hardly the behaviour of a drink-sodden rabble kept in line only by fear of the lash; and nor was the gallant way in which a number of wounded men ("who to their honour were many") fell in behind Henry Clinton for one last assault on the American redoubt at Bunker Hill in 1775. In both these cases it might be argued that the men were simply sticking by their officers, but no officers were present when Sergeant Terry Molloy defiantly retorted that he "would take my Chance" when Jacobite rebels threatened to hang him if he did not surrender Ruthven Barracks in 1745. Take his chance he did, and with just twelve men he beat off an attack by several hundred rebels.

Good order, discipline and a soldier's motivation are inextricably linked. To be effective an army needs to be well disciplined. It is overwhelmingly evident that British soldiers were led, not driven, into battle and that once arrived there they were generally successful because they were part of a well-disciplined and well-motivated organisation. Unlike the Duke of Wellington, who once bluntly stated that his soldiers only enlisted for drink or to escape paternal responsibilities, James Wolfe, born and bred a soldier, recognised their innate spirit and was rather given to encouraging his men in an almost Napoleonic style, as when he addressed his beloved 20th Foot in December 1755:

> The men should consider that they are on the point of entering into a war for the defence of their country against an enemy who has long meditated the destruction of it: that a drunken, vicious, irregular army is but a poor defence to a state; but that virtue, courage and obedience in the troops are a sure guard against all assaults: that the troops that are posted in this country (*i.e.;* Kent) are designed to repel the enemy's first attempt; and that they should be in readiness to execute their part with honour and spirit, and not give themselves up to every excess, and to every irregularity in times like these; both officers and soldiers should exert themselves in every part of duty, and shew their countrymen that they deserve their esteem and consideration; and they should endeavour in a particular manner to recommend themselves to his majesty, and to the captain-general, by their zeal, fidelity and valour. [57]

4
Fighting Tactics

No matter what a man's zeal, fidelity and valour, there is rather more to soldiering and fighting tactics than simply giving him a firelock and bayonet and then pointing him in the general direction of the enemy.

When Wolfe first joined the Army, British infantry tactics centred almost exclusively around the lethal application of firepower. Just how much actual firing could be done in training varied according to whether a battalion was maintained on the British or the Irish Establishment, for up until 1755 all infantry battalions were allowed sufficient powder for 45,000 rounds per anum, which roughly equated to 60 or 120 rounds per man depending on whether the battalion was at full or cadre strength. This was just about sufficient to practise platooning (of either variety) with blanks, but astonishingly only two to four rounds of ball were issued each year which barely sufficed to accustom soldiers to the very different kick from a live round, let alone master the rudiments of marksmanship. As in the naval service, however, conscientious officers would sometimes eke out this niggardly allowance by purchasing additional ammunition out of their own pockets, or at least acquiring it by methods best not enquired into – which no doubt explains why, in March 1755, Wolfe referred to his friend Captain Trapaud at Fort Augustus having "a parcel of musket balls that belonged to us". On the other hand, with war then plainly approaching, live ammunition could more or less be had for the asking and in that same letter he told Rickson:

> We fire bullets continually . . . firing balls at objects teaches soldiers to level incomparably, makes the recruits steady, and removes the foolish apprehension that seizes young soldiers when they first load their arms with bullets. We fire, first singly, then by files, 1, 2, 3, or more, then by ranks, and lastly by platoons; and the soldiers see the effects of their shot especially at a mark or upon water. We shoot obliquely, and in different situations of ground from heights downwards and contrarywise.[58]

Platoon firing or platooning had originally evolved at the end of the 17th century as a means of optimising the limited effectiveness of muzzle-loading firearms and covering that vulnerable thirty seconds or so which it took for the average soldier to reload his firelock. The earliest and simplest drills that preceded it had involved deep bodies of musketeers firing by one rank at a time in the pious hope that by the time each had fired in sequence the first rank would be reloaded and ready to begin the cycle afresh. The French were still employing a variant of this technique at Dettingen in 1743, but the British Army was by then firmly wedded to the intricacies of platooning.

Although it allowed a much shallower deployment in three (and later in just two) ranks, rather than the four then being favoured by the French, the basic principle of platooning was still that only a certain proportion of the men standing in the firing line were actually expected to be shooting at any one time. Just before the commencement of the action, the regiment's major and his faithful assistant the adjutant rode down the line telling the men off into *ad hoc* platoons, each more or less the same size – twenty to thirty men being reckoned to be the optimum number. The grenadier company was left alone, but otherwise these platoons were formed and officered without any regard to the ordinary company organisation. At the same time the platoons were grouped into four grand divisions, both for fire control and manoeuvring purposes and each individual platoon assigned to one of three "firings". There were a number of minor variations on the system, but essentially when the word was given to open fire, the platoons of each "firing" did so in sequence. It was assumed that if the firefight was carefully controlled, the soldiers making up the platoons in the first firing would have been able to reload in time to pick up the sequence after the third or fourth firing, and in theory, a series of small volleys would ripple up and down the line until either a specified number of rounds had been expended, or until one side or the other gave way.

This technique, as refined by good old Humphrey Bland and enshrined in the 1728 and 1748 *Regulations,* no doubt looked very impressive at a stage-managed review in Hyde Park or in Phoenix Park. Sometimes it could be taken to extreme lengths and after the 13th and 20th Foot were reviewed by the Duke of Cumberland at Reading in 1753, Wolfe noted in the latter regiment's orderly book that:

> His Royal Highness thought that general Pulteney's Regiment fired their platoons and subdivisions quicker than we did, wherefore Lord Bury (the 20th's colonel) has commanded that we practise the same platoon exercise that they do; for to the difference between their platoon exercise and ours, his lordship ascribes their superiority in this point; and as his lordship is very desirous that no regiment should exceed his own in the performance of every part of their duty, and in matters of discipline, he desires we may begin to practise this platoon exercise as early as possible.[59]

The precise form of the platoon exercise then being practised by Pulteney's 13th is uncertain, for ordinarily Cumberland was firmly opposed to innovations in this line, or at least to deviations from the uniform practices laid down in successive official regulations. This was unfortunate, for despite a certain amount of tinkering in the 1749 *Regulations,* platooning had not worked at all well under the stress of actual combat. The Jacobite adjutant general, Colonel John Sullivan, was to remark after the 1745 rebellion that "the English . . . are the troops in the world yt fires best"[60] but even at Dettingen, with a peacetime-trained army, the platooning had broken down almost at once and it was certainly asking too much of wartime levies to master it.

Consequently, the early 1750s saw the quite unofficial emergence of the much simpler and altogether superior Prussian-style "alternate firing". Contemporaries were in no doubt that James Wolfe was the man responsible for introducing the alternate fire into the British service, as we shall see in the next chapter, but his own first enthusiastic mention of it occurs in the 20th's Orderly Book on 31 January 1755:

> As the alternate fire by platoons or divisions, or by companies, is the most simple, plain and easy, and used by the best disciplined troops

111

in Europe, we are at all times to imitate them in that respect, making every platoon receive the word of command, and to make ready and fire from the officer who commands it; because in battle the fire of our artillery and infantry may render it difficult to use any general signals by beat of drum.[61]

Rather than carving up the battalion into *ad hoc* platoons without regard to the existing company organisation, the alternate system was indeed simple and effective. The eight battalion companies were each designated as a platoon or subdivision under their own officers and then paired off to form the four grand divisions. During the 1740s the grenadier company had also been divided into two little platoons, one of which was posted on each flank of the battalion, but now they were to remain in one body on the right flank, while the protection of the left was to be undertaken by a French style "Picquet". This was effectively a second, *ad hoc* grenadier company formed of men temporarily drafted from the ordinary battalion companies, and became forerunner of the later Light Company.

For fire-control purposes, the platoons or subdivisions could still fire in a predetermined sequence either from one flank to the other, from the two flanks in to the centre, or from the centre out to the flanks; but it was also recognised that in action, after the first few rounds, the captains commanding each grand division would be left to their own judgement as to when to fire and could direct each subdivision to fire alternately without regard to what the rest of the battalion might be doing. It was not as pretty as Bland's system, or the equally complicated "improvement" devised by Colonel Robert Napier, but it was much more likely to stand up to the stresses of actual combat. At the outset of the new war with France, Wolfe's "alternate fire" would gain widespread adoption in spite of Cumberland's opposition.

A study of drill books alone can give a very skewed picture of how a battalion was supposed to behave in action, for while it can present a very good picture of how a particular manoeuvre (or system of platooning) is supposed to work, it rarely explains when and under what tactical circumstances it ought to be employed. However, in anticipation of a French invasion, Wolfe issued a set of *Instructions for the 20th Regiment* at Canterbury on 15 December 1755.[62] Unfortunately, although he had very definite and very sensible ideas about how a battalion should fight, Wolfe never learned how to set them out in a clear and logical fashion. Tactical instructions are interspersed with exhortations about honour and duty, and generally speaking the running order in which the different paragraphs (or rather, instructions) appear in the original follows no discernible logic. In preparing the summary below a considerable amount of editing and rearrangement has therefore been necessary.

Before a battle begins, and while a battalion is marching towards the enemy, the officer commanding a platoon is to be at the head of his men, looking frequently back upon them to see that they are in order, the serjeant in the mean while taking his place in the interval, and the officers are not to go to the flanks of their platoons till they have orders, or a signal so to do from the officer commanding the battalion, and this should only be given a little while before the action begins.

If the battalion should be crowded at any time, or confined in their ground, the captain or officer commanding a grand division may order his center platoon to fall back till the battalion can extend itself again, so as to take up its usual ground.

All the officers upon the left of the colours are to be upon the left of their platoons; the captain of the piquet is to be on the left of his piquet, and the ensign in the centre.

Every grand division consisting of two companies as they now are, is to be told off in three platoons, to be commanded by a captain, a lieutenant, and an ensign, with a serjeant to each; the rest of the officers and non-commissioned officers are to be distributed in the rear to compleat the files, to keep the men in their duty, and to supply the places of the officers or serjeants that may be killed or dangerously wounded.

If the firing is ordered to begin by platoons, either from the wings or from the center, it is to proceed in a regular manner, till the enemy is defeated, or till the signal is given for attacking them with the bayonets.

If we attack a body less in extent than the battalion, the platoons upon the wings must be careful to direct their fire obliquely so as to strike upon the enemy. The officers to inform the soldiers of his platoon, before the action begins, where they are to direct their fire; and they are to take good aim to destroy their adversaries.

There is no necessity for firing very fast; a cool well levelled fire, with the pieces carefully loaded, is much more destructive and formidable than the quickest fire in confusion.

If the battalion attacks another of nearly equal extent, whose flanks are not covered, the grenadiers and piquet may be ordered to detach themselves, and surround the enemy by attacking their flank and rear, while the eight companies charge them in front. The grenadiers and piquet should therefore be accustomed to these sort of movements, that they may execute their orders with a great deal of expedition.

If the battalion is to attack another battalion of equal force, and of like number of ranks, and the country quite open, it is highly probable, that, after firing a few rounds, they will be commanded to charge them with their bayonets, for which the officers and men should be prepared.

The battalion is not to halloo or cry out upon any account whatsoever, although the rest of the troops should do it, until they are ordered to charge with their bayonets; in that case, and when they are upon the point of rushing upon the enemy, the battalion may give a war-like shout and run on.

The eight companies of the battalion are never to pursue the enemy, without particular orders to do so; the piquet and grenadiers will be detached for that purpose, and the battalion is to march on in good order to support them.

Wolfe was not alone in increasingly stressing the aggressive use of the bayonet in place of platoon firing, for the Jacobite campaign had provided a salutary shock to the advocates of controlled firepower. The problem remained a simple arithmetical one. The normal movement rate of infantrymen drawn up in line was around seventy-five paces a minute. For all practical purposes, this was also reckoned to be the optimum effective range of the common firelock. Ordinarily, once a unit began taking casualties there was (and still is) a natural tendency to halt and return fire. If, on the other hand, a unit was willing to absorb those casualties and press forward, there might only be time for one volley before both sides came into physical contact, and it was more than likely the defenders would be so intimidated by the attackers' resolution as to decline such a meeting.

This was exactly what happened at Prestonpans and may also have happened at Falkirk. Platoon firing, in whatever form, simply could not inflict enough casualties quickly enough to stop a really determined attacker. At Culloden, on the other hand, it is clear from the surprising number of eyewitness accounts written by British soldiers that platoon firing was *not* employed there and the otherwise dangerous tactic of firing by whole ranks – and perhaps even by whole battalions – was used instead. The result was a famous victory and Cumberland's junior officers, Wolfe among them,[63] appeared to have learned two important lessons. First, there was the rather obvious point that firepower was much more effective when delivered by massed volleys rather than by relatively small platoons; and secondly, that the obvious dangers of then being left with unloaded weapons could be obviated by the prompt and effective use of the bayonet.

The problem that remained was that the method of bayonet-fighting then in use had been borrowed from the pike-fighting drills of a hundred years before, and the requirement for the soldier to stand at right angles to his front, with the firelock and bayonet levelled shoulder-high, meant that any advance would be slow and far from intimidating. Once again, the

1. Major James Wolfe by Joseph Highmore c 1749
The best of Wolfe's portraits, depicting him in the silver laced regimentals of the 20th
Foot and capturing his confident good humour. (National Archives of Canada/C-003916)

2. The old vicarage, Westerham, Kent – James Wolfe's birthplace.

3. *The George and Dragon*, Westerham. A plaque records Wolfe's stay there in December 1758, but it may also have been one of the inns "ruined" when Wolfe marched the 20th Foot into the West Country in March 1754.

4. British infantrymen as depicted in 1746 by an unknown artist in the Penicuick area and looking very different from the stiffly pipeclayed figure in more conventional paintings.

5. A British grenadier after the same artist.

6. Corporal Jones of the 13th Foot after
Lieutenant Baillie, 1753 . . .

7. . . . and as recreated by a member of the
re-enactment group *Lace Wars*

9. British infantryman
after Paul Sanby c 1760

8. British infantryman
after Paul Sanby c 1760

10. Gunner, Royal Artillery, 1742

11. Grenadier's mitre cap

12. Grenadier "pushing" his bayonet, after William Baillie of the 13th Foot, 1753

13. Wolfe's much improved Prussian-style "Charge your Bayonet", as depicted in Windham's *Norfolk Discipline*, 1759.

14. An unflattering but instantly recognisable caricature of Wolfe at Quebec, after Brigadier Townshend.

15. An important portrait of Wolfe in mock-heroic pose at Quebec by Captain Smyth. The plain red "frock" coat depicted here was probably worn throughout his service since the large cuffs suggest it was made for him in the early 1740s.

16. The unashamedly heroic statue of Wolfe, based on Smyth's sketch, which now stands in the marketplace at Westerham. As befits a hero he is waving a sword, although Smyth's drawing shows that he did not bother with one.

solution came from the Prussian Army, where the soldier faced his front, levelled his bayonet waist high and could indeed rush in upon the enemy.[64] The earliest known illustrations of this being done by British soldiers appear in William Windham's admirable *Plan of Discipline composed for the use of the Militia of Norfolk,* first published in 1759. Windham rather grudgingly admitted the technique's Prussian origins and rather more significantly paid tribute to the assistance of regular officers, belonging to the 67th and 72nd Foot, in writing the book. The 67th was, of course, James Wolfe's own regiment trained up exactly as he wanted, while the 72nd was commanded by his protégé, the Duke of Richmond. It would not, therefore, be going too far to attribute the introduction of this improved bayonet drill (as well as the alternate fire) to Wolfe.[65]

Increasingly during Wolfe's time, British infantry tactics shifted away from platooning to a much more aggressive firing of just one or two big volleys, before charging with the bayonet. This is not to say that they abandoned platoon-firing altogether, but rather that British officers became tactically more sophisticated, and this is illustrated by Wolfe's willingness to even contemplate mounting column attacks as advocated by the French theorist, the Chevalier de Folard:

> If the order of battle be such (and the country admit of it) that it is necessary to make breaches in the enemy's line for the cavalry to fall in upon them, the grand divisions of the regiment are each to form a firing column of three platoons in depth, which are to march forward and pierce the enemy's battalion in four places, that the cavalry behind us may get in amongst them and destroy them. In such an attack, only the first of the three platoons should fire, immediately present their bayonets, and charge. These four bodies are to be careful not to run into one another in their attack, but to preserve the intervals at a proper distance.

Even more interestingly, Wolfe was also in favour of mixing columns and skirmishers in the attack, should the circumstances justify it:

> If an intrenchment is to be attacked, the troops should move as quickly as possible towards the place, not in a line, but in small firing columns of three or four platoons in depth, with small parties between each column, who are to fire at the top of the parapet when the columns approach to divert the enemy's fire, and facilitate their passing the ditch, and getting over the parapet, which they must endeavour to do without loss of time.
>
> It is of little purpose to fire at men who are covered with an intrenchment; but by attacking in the manner above-mentioned one may succeed.

As to acting on the defensive, on the other hand – as he was to do at Quebec in 1759 – Wolfe evidently fully anticipated meeting and breaking column attacks. His instructions on this point are therefore of particular interest, for the regiments *Bearn* and *Languedoc* were to do just that:[66]

> If the center of the battalion is attacked by a column, the wings must be extremely careful to fire obliquely. That part of the battalion against which the column marches, must reserve their fire, and if they have time to put two or three bullets in their pieces, it must be done. When the column is within about twenty yards they must fire with a good aim, which will necessarily stop them a little. This body may then open from the center, and retire by files towards the wings of the regiment, while the neighbouring platoons wheel to the right and left, and either fire, if they are loaded, or close up and charge with their bayonets.

Unfortunately, as Wolfe was about to learn, his superiors did not appreciate this tactical virtuosity . . .

NOTES

1. Wolfe to William Rickson, Glasgow, 2 April 1749. Willson, Beckles *The Life and Letters of James Wolfe*, (1909) p93.
2. William Rickson was originally commissioned an ensign in the 8th Foot on 4 February 1740, and had become acquainted with Wolfe in Flanders. At the time this letter was written he was serving in Colonel Peregrine Lascelles' 47th Foot – having replaced one of that regiment's Prestonpans casualties.
3. Captain Arthur Loftus was another officer in the 8th Foot, at this time stationed in Gibraltar. Edward Cornwallis had also served in the regiment, which explains his request and the fact that Rickson would later exchange into the 40th Foot when Cornwallis had it.
4. WO34/99.
5. So called because £3.00 per man was paid into his parish's vestry account for the maintenance of any dependants that he might leave behind as a burden upon it.
6. Atkinson, C.T., "Jenkins' Ear, the Austrian Succession War and the Forty-five", *JSAHR* XXII (1943-44), p296.
7. Ibid. pp290, 297.
8. Ibid. p290.
9. Guy, A.J. *Colonel Samuel Bagshawe and the Army of George II*, (1985) p210.
10. Bulloch, J.M., *Territorial Soldiering in North-East Scotland*, (1914) pp34-5.
11. WO10/28-34.
12. In the event it was very largely recruited in North America although about half of the original recruits were Pennsylvania and New York "Dutch", i.e. of German origin.
13. Guy, op.cit. p210
14. WO1/164. It may at this stage be worth mentioning that, contrary to popular belief, the tallest men were not automatically posted to the regiment's

grenadier company. Although, in default of any other criteria this was sometimes the case in newly raised corps such as the 89th, in longer established ones the grenadiers were quite literally picked men, selected from amongst the steadier and most experienced soldiers, irrespective of their height. Article CXVII of Cumberland's *Standing Orders,* collected together in 1755 from orders issued during the last war, stated that the grenadier companies were "to be compleated out of the best Men of their respective Regiments, and to be constantly kept so." The fact that they were generally older men also led to their irreverent nickname, the "Grannies".

15. Windham, William, *Plan of Discipline for the use of the Norfolk Militia* (1759) Part II pp1-2.
16. Bulloch, op.cit. p32.
17. Aytoun, James, *Redcoats in the Caribbean* (1984), p1.
18. Anon: *General Wolfe's Instructions to Young Officers,* (1780) pp34-35.
19. Houlding, John, *Fit for Service: The Training of the British Army 1715-1795* (1981).
20. *Wolfe's Instructions,* p26.
21. Aytoun, op.cit. p24.
22. Unpublished typescript orderly book of Captain James Stewart's Coy. 1759-1761.
23. *Wolfe's Instructions,* p20.
24. Fort Edward Camp, 11 June 1759, (Stewart orderly book).
25. WO26/17 f307.
26. Brown, I.G. & Cheape, H., *Witness to Rebellion* (1996), figs. 27, 28 & 42. Although labelled by the editors as loyalist volunteers, no doubt on account of their extreme scruffiness, the men depicted in these particular sketches can in fact be identified as British regulars by their swords, knapsacks and canteens – items conspicuously lacking in sketches of genuine loyalists.
27. *Wolfe's Instructions,* p7.
28. Ibid., pp27-28.
29. Ibid., pp29-30. Despite official disapproval, by both military and ecclesiastical authorities, so-called clandestine marriages were in fact quite legal in Scotland. All that was required was that the principals should formally declare their purpose of marriage in a public place and in front of two witnesses.
30. *Wolfe's Instructions,* p97.
31. Quoted in Dr. Paul Kopperman, "The British High Command and Soldiers' Wives in America, 1755-1783" *JSAHR* LX no.241, p30 – Wolfe's reference to women dragging cannon can be found in Beckles Willson, p390.
32. Quoted in Lawson, C.C.P., *A History of the Uniforms of the British Army,* Vol.III (1961), p107.
33. An example of just such a married patch appears in a contemporary sketch map of Bernera Barracks and its environs, labelled as "Hutts for the Soldiers' Wives and Families". Significantly there are at least fourteen "Hutts" attached to a fort which never held more than seventy men and usually far fewer. (Tabraham & Grove, *Fortress Scotland and the Jacobites*).
34. Fletcher, I. (ed), *In the Service of the King; The Letters of William Thornton Keep at Home, Walcheren, and in the Peninsula, 1808-1814,* (1997), p102.
35. Kopperman, op.cit., pp26-8.
36. 17 May 1759, *Wolfe's Instructions,* p68.
37. Stewart orderly book.
38. Kopperman, op.cit., p22.
39. The tasks still allotted to the provost and his deputies were many and varied,

ranging from the mundane (such as ensuring that sutlers were not overcharging their customers) to the downright unpleasant (such as ensuring that latrines were regularly shifted and the carcasses of horses and other animals buried). However, there was obviously considerable scope for delegating some of the dirtier work to petty offenders.

40. Chiefly at the notoriously unhealthy Savoy Barracks in London, which simultaneously served as a military prison, a hospital for soldiers suffering from venereal diseases and a depot for recruits destined for regiments in the West Indies or the Mediterranean. All of its occupants were considered (with some reason) equally likely to run away if not closely confined.

41. *Wolfe's Instructions,* pp25-6.

42. Ibid., p27.

43. Conviction by a regimental court martial did not invariably lead to a flogging. Depending on the severity or otherwise of the offence, a man might simply be sentenced to a period of imprisonment in the "Black Hole" – a semi-underground prison cell – although this obviously depended on the regiment having access to one. Sometimes flogging was the only practical punishment.

44. Guy, op.cit., p97. "The Expence 7^d – a Company, which I apprehend must be stopt out of the Drum Maj^{rs} allowances."

45. The whole question of corporal punishment is a difficult one to tackle objectively. There is no doubt that the Army tended to award what were on the face of it much heavier sentences than the navy. On the other hand, for some unknown reason, soldiers regarded naval cats as being heavier and more brutal. In theory a ship's captain, possessed of the equivalent authority of a regimental court martial, could only award up to a dozen lashes in contrast to the 300 which looks like having been the upper limit on land. At any rate writing from Gibraltar in 1757 Lord Tyrawley opined "that 300 lashes are as much as the strongest man can bear at one time by the opinion of the surgeons that attend these Punishments . . . and that such criminal will be two months at least before he will be in a condition to be further punished."

46. *Wolfe's Instructions,* p28 – as it happened Wolfe pardoned him on account of his "youth and former good behaviour".

47. Rodger, N.A.M. *The Wooden World* (1986), p238.

48. Prebble, John, *Mutiny: Highland Regiments in Revolt 1743-1804,* (1975). Unfortunately Prebble's work is badly flawed by his wilful insistence on treating mutiny and its causes as a phenomenon unique to the Highland regiments, rather than setting the various incidents in their wider context – or acknowledging the important fact that most of the incidents described involved new recruits who still retained an essentially civilian perspective on protest.

49. All that is now known with any certainty is that it occurred at 10 o'clock on the evening of 29 September 1760. Exactly what happened is unknown, but when a general court martial was convened less than 48 hours later, the whole garrison was confined to barracks and arms taken off all soldiers not actually on duty. Private Robert Reid of the 6th Foot was subsequently found guilty of mutiny and sentenced to death, while two privates of the 13th, John Adkinson and Thomas Jones, received 1,000 lashes apiece and a fourth man, Samuel Peal, got 500. The circumstances suggest that boredom and alcohol were contributory if not the principal factors in this particular case, although the temporary disarming of the garrison is an indicator of its potential seriousness. (WO284/4)

50. *Wolfe's Instructions*, p21.
51. Stewart, David, *Sketches of the Highlanders of Scotland*, Vol.2 (1822), pp34-5. The money given in lieu of clothing was of course no more than a refund of their off-reckonings.
52. McCorry, Helen, "Besides he was very drunk at the time . . ." *JSAHR* LXXII no.291 p145. He was evidently believed for the court martial let him off with only 500 lashes.
53. Guy, op.cit., pp64-5, 285.
54. To be fair, the British Army generally confined itself to enlisting prisoners from mercenary units such as the *Volontaires Etrangers* captured at Louisburg in 1758, rather than from French national regiments.
55. Captain John Maxwell – he subsequently distinguished himself in command of a composite grenadier battalion in Germany.
56. *Wolfe's Instructions*, p31. Rather more prosaically he also went on to say that "As there is reason to believe that recruits are embarked at Dover Castle for the French army, and that deserters from our troops escape in the same vessels, any soldier of the regiment who can make discovery of such recruits, or apprehend any of these deserters, shall be rewarded over and above the allowance granted by act of parliament; the soldiers that lie in town have the finest opportunity for these sort of discoveries; and the lieutenant colonel desires they may be informed, that diligence and prudence in this matter will be very agreeable to him, and advantageous to themselves."
57. *Wolfe's Instructions*, pp54-55.
58. Exeter, 7 March 1755 (Beckles Willson, op.cit., pp354-5).
59. *Wolfe's Instructions*, pp31-2.
60. Taylor, A.H. (ed.), *1745 and After* (1938), p153.
61. *Wolfe's Instructions*, p35.
62. Ibid., pp46-53.
63. It is remarkable just how many of the officers who fought at Culloden went on to achieve great things: besides Wolfe, both Stringer Lawrence and Eyre Coote were present, to name but two.
64. Knox of the 43rd was, however, distinctly unimpressed when he saw it demonstrated at a review on 15 July 1759: "The left hand under the swell below the lowermost rammer-pipe, and the right hand a-cross the brass at the extremity of the butt – Thus was the firelock secured, which he poked out before him, in like-manner as an indolent hay-maker turns hay with a forked pole . . . I thought it ludicrous." *An Historical Journal of the Campaigns in North America*, (1914-16), Vol.I. p422.
65. It is in fact tempting to speculate, given the acknowledged assistance of the officers of the 67th, just how much of the immensely influential "Norfolk" discipline sprang from Windham's fertile genius, and how much of it actually represents James Wolfe's unwritten teaching.
66. *Wolfe's Instructions*, p52.

CHAPTER IV
The Road to Command
Colonel of Foot and Brigadier General

By 1755, when Wolfe was openly advocating the Prussian alternate firing and a few other radical ideas besides, he had obviously settled down well to the business of commanding a battalion. In the early months of 1749, however, it was still a very different matter. In the first place he was chronically short of cash and as heavily dependent as ever upon regular parental subsidies. In about 1750 the similarly impecunious Sam Bagshawe itemised both his annual income and his expenditure for his uncle's benefit and concluded that, frugal as his lifestyle was, the latter exceeded the former by £104 5s 7½d – and that was on a lieutenant colonel's pay![1] Wolfe will naturally have found it considerably cheaper to live in Glasgow than in Dublin, and unlike Bagshawe he did not require to buy a new wooden leg each year, but otherwise his expenses will have been very similar and he only had a major's pay on which to support them. Moreover, far from celebrating his substantive promotion to field rank at the third attempt, he bemoaned the fact that the appointment of Edward Cornwallis as Lieutenant Governor of Nova Scotia would prevent him from taking himself off on an extended leave. Instead, he complained, he was to be condemned to the drudgery of regimental soldiering amidst remote and uncongenial surroundings. Suddenly, however, he was off on another tack entirely and writing an odd letter to his father which opened with what amounted to a short essay on military philosophy:

> That variety incident to a military life gives our profession some advantages over those of a more even and consistent nature. We have all our passions and affections roused and exercised, many of which must have wanted their proper employment, had not suitable occasions obliged us to exert them. Few men are acquainted with the degrees of their own courage till danger prove them and are seldom justly informed how far the love of honour or dread of shame are superior to the love of life. This is a knowledge to be best acquired in an army; our actions are there in presence of the world, to be freely censured or approved. Constancy of temper, patience and all the

virtues necessary to make us suffer with a good grace are likewise parts of our character, and, as you know, frequently called in to carry us through unusual difficulties. What moderation and humility must he be possessed of that bears the good fortune of a successful war with tolerable modesty and humility, and he is excellent in his nature who triumphs without insolence. A battle gained is, I believe, the highest joy mankind is capable of receiving, to him who commands; and his merit must be equal to his success if it works no change to his disadvantage. Lastly a defeat is a trial of human resolution, and to labour under the mortification of being surpassed, and live to see the fatal consequences that may follow to one's country, is a situation next to damnable.[2]

1
Promotion, Preferment and Problems

Having delivered himself of these somewhat romanticised sentiments, James then rather abruptly turned to the real purpose of his letter, which was to anxiously speculate on the likelihood that Edward Cornwallis's anticipated promotion in far off Nova Scotia would now result in a new lieutenant colonel being brought in to the 20th Foot over his head:

> Your letter and several others mention Cornwallis's new officers. He will certainly get the regiment in America,[3] and I shall as certainly have a Lieutenant Colonel put in. In this great demand for employment, Lord George's interest, or even the Duke's own, will hardly be sufficient to keep out a new man. The Ministry must manage their people, and secure them by obligations. Let it be as it will, the sooner 'tis determined the greater share I shall have of freedom, and be more at liberty to visit you in the south.

On the face of it this letter represents a remarkable turnabout from Wolfe's complaint to Rickson, just five days earlier, that Cornwallis's prolonged absence would result in his being stuck in Scotland for the foreseeable future, far away from his friends and relations. The arrival of a second field officer with the battalion should have been welcome, for it would have allowed him to take that long leave which he wanted. In those five days, however, something had changed. Wolfe had been told something which might be to his advantage and one would give a good deal to know more about the intervening correspondence. Far from being temporary, Cornwallis's absence from the 20th was now confidently expected to be permanent and James seems to have been encouraged by his father, and perhaps by Sackville as well, to believe that he could be in line for the resulting vacancy.

All of this hearkened back, of course, to the earlier scheme proposed in January or February of 1748, whereby he was to have been put in as major of the 28th Foot solely in order to be on hand to succeed to the lieutenant colonelcy of that sorry corps when the unfortunate Jocelyn shuffled off his mortal coil. This time the Duke of Cumberland was preparing the ground much more thoroughly. It is obvious that Cornwallis's departure for Nova Scotia just as Wolfe joined the 20th was no coincidence. Sackville was one of the Duke's trusted circle and there had accordingly been no difficulty in putting Wolfe in over the heads of the 20th's captains when the then Major Cornwallis received his step up to lieutenant colonel. At the same time Cornwallis was promptly shuffled off out of the way (albeit to Nova Scotia rather than to the grave) and was obviously destined to succeed to the command of the 40th once Phillips gave up the ghost. Nevertheless, as James revealed to his father, although he was almost certainly aware of the real purpose of these manoeuvres, he was also sceptical as to the outcome – or perhaps even fearful that once again Cumberland's influence might not be sufficient to carry the day in the face of other competing interests.

In the event, and quite worryingly, Cornwallis did not immediately succeed to the command of the 40th Foot. Richard Phillips, whose first recorded commission – as a captain – dated back to 1702 and who had commanded the 40th from its first formation in 1717, was an unconscionable long time a-dying. Consequently, Cornwallis was to remain as the absentee lieutenant colonel of the 20th for another eleven long months. Had he been so minded, Sackville could no doubt have exerted both his influence and his prerogatives to have him replaced sooner, but that might have meant Cornwallis selling out to the highest bidder. As it eventually turned out both Sackville and Cumberland were determined that come what may Wolfe should have the job.

In the meantime the unexpected delay brought a further complication. Edward Cornwallis was still on the 20th's books when Sackville himself was promoted to the command of the 12th Dragoons and George Keppel, Viscount Bury, succeeded him as Colonel of the 20th Foot on 1 November 1749. This came as a considerable blow to Wolfe. He and Sackville got on well, but Bury was altogether a different kettle of fish. Significantly, as he explained to his father on 23 March 1750, James's first intimation that Cornwallis had at last been promoted a week earlier, and that consequently the lieutenant colonelcy of the 20th Foot was now vacant, came not (as might have been expected) from his new colonel, but from his old friend Sackville:

> The words of Lord Bury's two last letters seem calculated to make me imagine his lordship wishes me success, at the same time that they

express his difference of it. I am not able to extract enough of his real opinion, to determine whether I am, or am not, to be his Lieutenant Colonel. He says indeed, that the Duke is our friend, but does not affirm that he won't be prevailed upon, to give up this point. Lord George Sackville sent me the first information of the vacancy with the strongest assurances of his aid and service. As I know he is very sincere, I rely chiefly upon him. Whichever way the business turns, I shall be glad to know from you who the persons are that seem the most to concern themselves in it; that I may thank them for their endeavours whether they succeed or not.[4]

Bury's reticence at this critical juncture is curious and hints that there was indeed real competition for the lieutenant colonelcy – and that the low-born Wolfe may not have been the man he personally had in mind. At any rate, Wolfe wrote that letter to his father unaware that his friends had already triumphed. His commission as lieutenant colonel of the 20th Foot had been signed three days earlier, at the determined instigation of his old patron, the Duke of Cumberland, and as he delightedly wrote:

The Duke has employed his power and influence upon this occasion where, at least, it is sure to be remembered. There are not many opportunities in life, and the prospect, as things stand at present, very distant; but if ever he commands an army of this nation in its defence, I shall wish to be with him, and glad to contribute something to his success. This is the only return that can justly be made from me to him, and all, I believe, he would expect. I think myself much obliged to Lord George Sackville, and have writ to him the strongest assurances of it. What he said some time ago to his Royal Highness left, no doubt, a favourable impression, and forwarded this succession. I did not forget to tell Colonel Napier that some thanks are certainly due to him. The last three years of the war I was immediately about his person, and without his friendship and approbation, things could not have gone on so smoothly.

A clearer illustration of the crucial importance of patronage and influence, rather than the application of hard cash, in arranging promotions could not be asked for. By preferring Cornwallis to the colonelcy of the 40th, Cumberland had engineered a non-purchase vacancy in the 20th and then insisted that Wolfe should get it.

Once again, however, though Wolfe seems not to have realised it at first, Cumberland was killing two birds with one stone. Unlike Wolfe, Bury, who was only three years older, owed his present happy situation and his future prospects to his weighty aristocratic and political connections, rather than to any conspicuous display of soldierly skill. His predecessor,

Sackville, was also an aristocrat, of course, being the third son of the Duke of Dorset, but notwithstanding his unfortunate facial resemblance to a sheep (and rumoured homosexuality) it was widely admitted that he was also an able soldier. After he had commanded the 20th Foot at Culloden, Cumberland wrote approvingly to his father "he has shown not only his courage, but a disposition to his trade which I do not always find in those of a higher [social] rank."[5] Bury, on the other hand, had held a commission in the Coldstream Guards since 1738, served on the Duke's staff at Culloden and would later, as Earl of Albemarle, command at Havanna in 1762,[6] but at this stage in his career he was better known as a rake and a dandy.[7] It is more than probable that although he was a member of the Duke's military household, Cumberland considered him professionally unqualified to be left in sole charge of an infantry battalion. As part of the Duke's master plan, therefore, the inexperienced Bury was surely intended all along to be seconded by the talented Wolfe in his command of the 20th.

To be fair to Bury, he did in fact take a close interest in the welfare and efficiency of his new regiment, but only in so far as its behaviour might reflect well upon its noble commander. For the most part he also exercised his command of it at a comfortable distance and through the medium of a weekly exchange of letters. In January of 1750, for example, Wolfe commented that

> My Colonel and I have a very exact correspondence. He is extremely bent upon procuring all the knowledge of regimental affairs that the distance between us will allow of; in order, I suppose, to make such alterations and amendments as seem requisite, and to be the better prepared against he comes amongst us. I answer his letters very punctually, and endeavour all in my power to satisfy him in such particulars as are properly within my sphere; confining, however my judgement of men and things to what is purely military, and belonging to my office.[8]

Bury may indeed have been well aware why Wolfe was forced upon him as his lieutenant colonel and it is sometimes hard to escape the impression that his subsequent instructions to Wolfe on regimental matters, such as changing the platoon exercise, have more of the character of a nobleman corresponding with the steward of his estate, rather than with his second-in-command. Conversely, while Wolfe did his best to get on with his new commanding officer, it is clear that he sometimes considered him to be an amiable buffoon and reposed neither confidence nor respect in him. "Lord Bury," he wrote, "professes fairly, and means nothing; in that he resembles his father, and a million other showy men that are seen in palaces and in the courts of Kings. He desires never to see his regiment, and wishes that no officer would ever leave it."[9]

Bury's penchant for spending as little time as possible with the regiment was particularly galling to Wolfe as he himself appeared unable to get away from it. He had, of course, complained of this ever since he was first appointed to the 20th, but initially at least there was nothing to be done about it since he was the sole field officer actually present and was therefore forbidden by regulation from absenting himself for more than a few days. Now there were two field officers with the regiment, but neither Bury nor the Duke would consent to his taking an extended leave of absence, even for the laudable purpose of completing his military education. Consequently, as James wrote to his father in April:

> If it were possible while I am capable of improvement, and young enough to apply, I could wish to be allowed an interval to be bestowed upon myself; a year and a half or two years, would wear off the rough, unpolished coat, and give a gloss to all my future actions. It may be reasonably said that I have not for seven years past been at liberty to acquire the common accomplishments, much less to embellish or refine. I'm persuaded you would have thought it necessary, had not the war prevented your intentions, to have sent me from England to some place proper for the purpose. I hope you still think it not too late, and this the fairest opportunity. Turin seems the best calculated to answer my ends. I shall be glad to have your opinion, and to know whether you approve my choice and inclination, and what steps should be taken for effecting it.[10]

Whether the Lieutenant General did approve of his son's desire to go abroad in search of an education at this time does not appear, but it was certainly discussed in the family. Lord Bury, however, was flatly against the idea and said so, insisting that his lieutenant colonel should remain with the regiment at least until November. This, Wolfe grumbled, was "by no means correspondent with my way of thinking", but there was nothing he could do about it, especially as he was initially unwilling to go over Bury's head to the Duke.

By July he had given up on Turin and was talking instead of taking ten months off and going to the famous artillery school at Metz, even though well aware by now that Cumberland too was far from keen on the idea of his absenting himself for any length of time: "If the Duke consents, it will be with regret; for the perfection of military knowledge, in his Royal Highness's eye, is the command of a regiment to men of our rank, and his notion of care and diligence centres entirely in sticking eternally at the same point, viz. the battalion."[11] There was more to it than that, of course, for Bury rarely showed his face in Scotland except for a few months in the summer and Cumberland clearly believed – perhaps with some reason –

that if Wolfe was absent as well the regiment was likely to go to the dogs. Nevertheless, James remained hopeful and in a long letter written in October to his old friend William Rickson he reckoned on spending the winter at Metz and then enjoying the summer rambling up the Rhine to Switzerland and then back through France and the Netherlands – but to his intense disappointment, his long looked-for leave of absence was finally granted only on the condition of his not going abroad. This was again down to the Duke of Cumberland, and as James complained in a subsequent letter to Rickson:

> I got powerful people to ask the Duke no less than three times, for leave to go abroad, and he absolutely refused me that necessary indulgence: this I consider a very unlucky incident, and very discouraging; moreover he accompanied his denial with a speech that leaves no hope – that a Lieutenant Colonel was an officer of too high a rank to be allowed to leave his regiment for any considerable time. This is a dreadful mistake, and if obstinately pursued, will disgust a number of good intentions, and preserve that prevailing ignorance of military affairs that has been so fatal to us in all our undertakings . . .[12]

Thus disappointed, he took himself off to London in November and proceeded to get into trouble. Despite his continual protestations that he needed the time off to study the theoretical aspects of his chosen profession, Wolfe's preoccupations were far from confined to the military sphere. There was also the thorny matter of Miss Elizabeth Lawson. A niece of his old brigade commander, Sir John Mordaunt, Wolfe had first met her in London while recovering from his Lauffeldt wound late in 1747:

> The winter we were in London together I sometimes saw Miss Lawson, the maid of honour, G. Mordaunt's niece. She pleased me then; but the campaign in view, battledore and dangerous, left little thought for love. The last time I was in town, only three weeks, I was several times at her, – sometimes in public, sometimes at her uncle's, and two or three times at her own house. She made a surprising progress in that short time, and won all my affections. Some people reckon her handsome; but I, that am her lover, don't think her a beauty. She has much sweetness of temper, sense enough, and is very civil and engaging in her behaviour. She refused a clergyman with £1300 a year, and is at present addressed by a very rich knight; but to your antagonist's advantage, he has that of being mad added, so that I hold him cheap. In point of fortune, she has no more than I have a right to expect, viz. £12,000. The maid is tall and thin, about my own age, and that's the only objection! I endeavoured, with the assistance of all the art I was master of, to find out how any serious proposal

would be received by Mordaunt and her mother. It did not appear that they would be very averse to such a scheme; but as I am but twenty-two and three months it is rather early for that sort of project; and if I don't attempt her, somebody else will. The General and Mrs Wolfe are rather against it, from other more interested views, as they imagine. They have their eye upon one of £30,000. If a company in the Guards is bought for me, or I should be happy enough to purchase any lieutenant-colonel's commission within this twelvemonth, I shall certainly ask the question; but if I'm kept long here, the fire will be extinguished. Young flames must be constantly fed, or they'll evaporate.[13]

And that was the trouble. Wolfe may well have made an impression on Elizabeth before he went to Scotland, but three factors conspired against him. First, as he admitted to Rickson, he considered himself too young and impecunious to "attempt her" at that time. Secondly, his parents, who might otherwise have been persuaded to bail him out financially, favoured a Miss Hoskins instead. Thirdly, there was the simple fact of his prolonged absence on duty. Wolfe undoubtedly sustained himself in his Caledonian exile with thoughts of her, but that passion may not have been reciprocated. At any rate, something went badly wrong that winter which is only hinted at in the surviving correspondence.

Naturally enough, James initially took up residence with his parents, but very quickly had a serious falling out with them over the charming Miss Lawson, and in a letter of apology, which he subsequently wrote to his father, he admitted that:

> You justly ridicule the situation I was in: it was truly ridiculous, I am as sensible of it as any man can be; but, however, it must be allowed that it is not the first of that kind, and the effects are often very extraordinary. I am concerned that you had any share of the uneasiness. I wish it had all been mine own since I brought it upon myself. Most of my thoughts and inconsistency of action, receive their bias from hence. I do not say all; for I never heard it accused of producing either pride or vanity. Impatience of temper, restlessness of disposition and an indifference about all, even the most important affairs of life, are the constant attendants of that pernicious distemper.[14]

There speaks a disappointed lover if ever there was one.[15] With a certain lack of originality, he then proceeded to drown his sorrows, and as he explained to Rickson: "In that short time I committed more imprudent acts than in all my life before. I lived in the idlest, dissolute, abandoned manner that could be conceived, and that not out of vice, which is the most extraordinary part of it."[16]

Sober again, recovered from anything nasty he might have picked up, and for the moment at least contrite, Wolfe for a time reconciled himself to peacetime soldiering in Scotland. He even developed a taste for deer stalking and fishing, but the question of leave still rankled:

> Lord Bury comes down in April; he'll stay six weeks and then swear there's no enduring it any longer and beg leave to return. 'Wolfe, you'll stay in the Highlands; you can't with any face ask to quit the regiment so dispersed; and when you have clothed and sent them to their different quarters, towards the end of November you shall come to London, my dear friend, for three months.' This will be his discourse, and I must say 'My Lord, you are very kind!'[17]

Bury did indeed object to the notion of his going off on leave, but afterwards he changed his mind. Once again, however, he only allowed it on condition that Wolfe did not leave the kingdom – a qualification which this time James interpreted as broadly as he dared by taking himself off to Ireland, in order to visit his uncle, Major Walter Wolfe, in Dublin. The visit evidently turned out to be more congenial than expected, for a year or two later Wolfe had to explain to his mother that a woman who had recently written to him care of the Blackheath address was the widow of an officer killed at Fontenoy, whom he had met "by accident on my journey through Ireland, so you see I did not go there for nothing."[18] Despite this transparent attempt to throw his mother off the scent, the unidentified widow can have been no casual acquaintance, for Wolfe's *bête noire*, Colonel Townshend, subsequently drew a number of irreverent sketches of an "Irish Venus" lamenting his death at Quebec.

At any rate, not content with this holiday, Wolfe afterwards went straight from Ireland to his parents' new house at Blackheath and at last obtained the long-desired permission to go abroad for the winter – to Paris, where Bury's father, the Earl of Albemarle, was British ambassador.

Again he evidently enjoyed himself, but after nearly five months of genteel dissipation he fixed on the notion of visiting the French, Austrian and Prussian armies during their annual summer manoeuvres. At first he was actively encouraged in this design by Albemarle himself,[19] only to receive a peremptory letter of recall at the beginning of March 1753. At first Wolfe was inclined to blame the unreasonableness of the Duke but in a second letter Bury explained that Wolfe's presence was indispensably necessary since he himself would be unable to visit Scotland that year and mentioned "a fit of apoplexy that seized the Major some time ago and has impaired his health considerably".[20] There was no alternative then but to return, although there can be little doubt that his tongue was very firmly pressed into his cheek as he related the terrible scene of woe which greeted him on his arrival in Glasgow:[21]

Officers ruined, impoverished, desperate, and without hopes of preferment; the widow of our late Major and her daughter in tears; his situation before his death and the effects it had upon the corps, with the tragical end of the unhappy man in everybody's mouth; an ensign struck speechless with the palsy, and another that falls down in the most violent convulsions. He was seized with one the first night I came to the regiment (after supper) that so astonished and affected all that were present, that it is not to be described. I should have fallen upon the floor and fainted, had not one of the officers supported me, and called for immediate relief; and this as well as I can remember, for the first time in my life. Some of our people spit blood, and others are begging to sell before they are quite undone; and my friend Ben[22] will probably be in jail in a fortnight.

At least an end was in sight to his Scottish exile, for in August came orders to march south, into England to take up temporary quarters in Dover. The castle was then in a dilapidated state and apparently haunted to boot, but after so long in Scotland it must have seemed to the rank and file like the Promised Land. Complaints abound in the 20th's orderly book at this time of drunkenness, consorting with loose women, and even of agents seeking recruits for the French service. Despite his own personal inclinations in at least two of those directions,[23] Wolfe was clearly unimpressed both with the place and its temptations. However, in March the 20th Foot was ordered into the West Country, and a year later Bury succeeded his father as Earl of Albemarle. Social elevation was immediately accompanied in the military sphere by translation from the 20th Foot to the rather more prestigious (and lucrative) colonelcy of the 3rd Dragoons. By now rumours of war were abroad and although Wolfe discounted his mother's suggestion of trying for the command of some newly raised marines,[24] his own all-too brief hopes of taking over the 20th Foot were dashed when Philip Honeywood was preferred to the command on 8 April 1755.

2
The Prussian Drillmaster

Wolfe and Bury (or rather Albemarle, as he was now) had in time established a certain *modus vivendi* and after his departure remained on good terms, but James does not appear to have got on so well with Honeywood, or with William Kingsley who succeeded him on 22 May 1756. At any rate, he makes little real mention of either of them in his surviving correspondence. The disappointment at being passed over for the command brought his deep-seated discontent to a head for, despite his now being much closer to the centre of things in England, advancement appeared as far away as ever. "All my hope of success must be grounded upon right and just pretensions," he wrote. "I must serve and serve well or I cannot get forward; for who will be at the trouble to solicit for me out of pure friendship?"[25] The problem quite simply was that his present rank had been attained primarily through the patronage and accommodation of the "old army" mafia, and the Duke of Cumberland. Now, as a lieutenant colonel, he was no longer a client but a competitor for higher rank or office. Moreover, not only was he coming to an acute awareness of this, but he was also becoming increasingly disillusioned with other aspects of the old firm's hold on the Army, something all too apparent on his hearing the news of General Braddock's defeat on the Monongahela River.

The origins and shape of the conflict in which Wolfe would ultimately meet his destiny will be discussed in their proper place, but his first solid intimation of the impending war came in January 1755, when he was ordered to turn over a draft of one hundred men from the 20th to reinforce Dunbar's 48th Foot – one of two regiments ordered to North America under Major General Edward Braddock. Then in early September came the astonishing news that Braddock had been ambushed and killed.

> The accounts of Mr. Braddock's defeat are not yet clear enough to form a right judgement of the cause of it; but I do myself believe that the cowardice and ill-behaviour of the men far exceeded the ignorance of the chief, who though not a master of the difficult art of war, was yet a man of sense and courage. I have but a very mean opinion of the Infantry in general. I know their discipline to be bad, and their valour precarious. They are easily put into disorder, and hard to recover out of it. They frequently kill their officers through fear, and murder one another in their confusion. Their shameful behaviour in Scotland, at Port L'Orient, at Melle, and upon many less important occasions, clearly denoted the extreme ignorance of the officers, and the disobedient and dastardly spirit of the men.
>
> Was there ever such a slaughter of officers as upon this expedition? and did ever the Geneva and piss of this country operate more shamefully and violently upon the dirty inhabitants of it under the denomination of soldiers? I am sorry to say that our method of training and instructing the troops is extremely defective, and tends to no good end. We are lazy in time of peace, and of course want vigilance and activity in war. Our military education is by far the worst in Europe, and all our concerns are treated with contempt or totally neglected. It will cost us very dear some time hence. I hope the day is at a distance, but I am afraid it will come. [26]

Notwithstanding his scathing juxtaposition of soldiers, "Geneva and piss," it is abundantly clear that Wolfe recognised that the real problem lay not with the rank and file – for after all, a hundred of them were his own men from the 20th[27] – but rather with their training and with their officers. As his angry letter reveals, he had come to find himself increasingly at odds with the attitudes and teaching of those who had once been his closest colleagues and mentors. This was particularly true of Henry Hawley. In 1746 Wolfe had happily served under him as one of his ADCs – as his jackal – without complaint, adverse comment or the slightest hint that either man was dissatisfied with the other. However, by 1751 James was writing to his father from Inverness that:

> I have surveyed the field of battle of Culloden with great exactness, and find room for a military criticism as well as a place for a little ridicule upon some of the famous transactions of that memorable day. The actors shine in the world too high and bright to be eclipsed; but it is plain they don't borrow much of their glory from their performance on that occasion . . . You would not have left those ruffians the only possible means of conquest, nor suffer multitudes to go off unhurt with the power to destroy.[28]

Since he went on to specifically deny that he was referring to Cumberland, it is plain that his criticism was directed at Hawley and his failure to force the re-entrant south of Culchunaig. Four years later, waiting for a possible French invasion, James was even more direct.

> General Hawley is expected in a few days to keep us all in order; if there is an invasion they could not make use of a more unfit person. The troops dread his severity, hate the man, and hold his military knowledge in contempt.[29]

That Hawley, an experienced and intelligent officer who had taken the young Wolfe under his wing, and produced a few military theories of his own in his time, should now be regarded as an incompetent martinet is revealing enough; but even more so is an earlier throwaway reference to Bland, perhaps the most influential British military writer of the previous generation as, "Old Doting Humphrey"![30] Wolfe may just conceivably have been alluding to the old fellow's newly married state but in the circumstances there is no reason to doubt that he actually considered him to be in his dotage – and therein lay the problem, for the Duke of Cumberland was himself the most faithful disciple of that particular generation of professionals. Although a more than ordinarily effective administrator and an adequate if undistinguished military commander, Cumberland was neither an intellectual soldier nor an innovator. It is axiomatic that armies will usually go into a new war using the tactics of the previous one, and indeed it would be very strange if they did not, but by relying on Bland's teaching the Duke was in effect content to draw not upon recent experience in Flanders, but on Marlborough's campaigns of forty years before! Admittedly Robert Napier, the Adjutant General, had made some effort to tidy up the platoon-firing a little in the 1749 *Regulations*, and he and Alexander Drury of the 1st Footguards would produce the 1757 *Regulations* to Cumberland's order, but to all intents and purposes Bland's clumsy and ineffectual "chequer" lay at the heart of the British infantry's tactical doctrine for so long as the Duke was Commander in Chief.

Wolfe too had cut his teeth on Bland's *Treatise of Military Discipline* but while he considered it indispensable to the military education of young officers, he was only prepared to recommend it in so far as it covered matters of routine and procedure such as parades and the mounting and dismounting of guards. When it came to the tactical handling of a battalion, it was a very different matter. Privately he might also be prepared to admit the virtues of those two other Marlburian veterans, Kane and Molesworth, but none of the three made it on to his essential reading list. There can be little doubt that, notwithstanding their many good points, this was because he considered it on balance positively unhelpful to puzzle and confuse aspiring young officers with what Francis Grose would pithily describe as "some old exploded system". Instead he enthusiastically recommended the Prussian regulations.

In 1783 Grose (or whoever else wrote *Advice to Officers*) satirically suggested that colonels and lieutenant colonels promoted to the command of a regiment from some other corps should "show them that they were all in the dark before, and, overturning their whole routine of discipline, introduce another as different as possible."[31] By January of 1755 Wolfe had taken advantage of Bury's fundamental lack of interest to do just that and had trained the 20th Foot in the Prussian-style "alternate firing" as well as in ordinary platooning. Two years later he had the further courage of his convictions to go on to teach it to a much wider and positively enthusiastic audience in the teeth of the express disapproval of his old patron, the Duke of Cumberland.

Ironically enough, the introduction of a Prussian-based drill during the 1750s is often confused with the near simultaneous appearance of Napier and Drury's 1757 *Regulations*, but as Dr. Houlding points out, these official regulations were merely yet another variation upon Bland's outdated platooning, and Wolfe found them sadly wanting:

> The side-step has been introduced by mistake, I imagine, instead of the oblique step; one is as absurd as the other is useful. Wheeling by division to the right or left may be called a principle of motion; this excellent evolution is abolished, and the ridiculous wheel upon the centre introduced in its place. The ranks are opened to a very

inconvenient distance for no reason that I can conceive, unless to double the ranks by the side-step with more ease. Here one absurdity has produced another. Practising the platoon firing with the ranks open, as front ranks, as centre ranks, &c., is all nonsense; every soldier should be trained to fire in each rank and obliquely. A company or battalion should as readily fire to the rear as to the front, and this they acquire in learning the platoon exercise, – that is, they should be so taught. When soldiers are the masters of the use of their firearms and of their bayonets, the next great object is their marching in battalion, as your Lordship [Sackville] knows full well. For this no good instructions have ever been given in my time, nor any principles laid down by which we might be guided. Hence the variety of steps in our infantry, and the feebleness and disorderly floating of our lines. General Drury, I think, has the merit of the late inventions; 'tis unlucky, however, that our great master in the art of war, Frederick of Prussia, was not preferred upon this occasion. He has made the exercise simple and useful; we cannot choose so good a model.[32]

Past acquaintanceship and an appointment to the Irish staff secured Wolfe a place on Sir John Mordaunt's staff for the Rochefort expedition in 1757, and with it came a free hand. The Duke of Richmond, briefly a company commander in the 20th under Wolfe and now lieutenant colonel of the 33rd, wrote on 9 September that Mordaunt

> . . . has broke through all the absurd regulations that General Napier has been puzzling the army with since he has been Adjutant-General. He has abolished the manual exercise both old and new, and draws up all the regiments as Kingsley's [20th] used to do . . . and practises no other firing but by companies from right and left; and they practice the same kind of evolutions as Kingsley's used to do and no such absurdities as squares, etc.[33]

As commander of the expeditionary force Mordaunt bore ultimate responsibility for this policy, and he certainly got it in the neck when Cumberland discovered what was going on. In August the Duke wrote from Germany to Barrington, the Secretary at War, ordering him to

> . . . acquaint all General officers commanding Corps, Sir John Mordaunt not excepted, that I am Surprised to hear that my orders. . . [the new 1757 *Regulations*] approved & confirmed by His Majesty, are changed according to the Whim & Supposed Improvements of every fertile Genius; and that therefore it is my positive order, that in the Forming & Telling off of Battalions, they conform exactly to those Standing orders, which they have all received; and that no-one

presume to introduce new Schemes, without their having been approved of by His Majesty or by my orders.[34]

Notwithstanding his thus being singled out, the sixty-year-old Mordaunt was long past such independent behaviour, as his dismal performance at Rochefort was to prove. There can be no doubt, therefore, that his one-time brigade major, James Wolfe, was the real begetter of the changes – or that Cumberland's jibe about a "fertile Genius" shows that the Duke too was well aware of the fact. The reprimand, however, was quite literally a dead letter, for Cumberland had been badly defeated in the battle of Hastenbeck, outside Hameln, on 26 July[35] and was in full retreat when he wrote it. Pressed hard by the French, he capitulated a week or two later and signed an armistice – the infamous convention of Kloster Zeven. The King (and Elector) was furious and in the middle of October the Duke was dismissed, leaving no impediment thereafter to the spread of Wolfe's Prussian drill.

In the meantime, in September James had embarked on his first amphibious expedition and learned yet again how not to conduct military operations.

3
Step Aboard of the Transport

Britain's deepening involvement in what would afterwards be termed the Seven Years War saw a revival of old arguments between colonialists and continentals – between those who advocated concentration of the available military and naval resources on the security and expansion of Britain's overseas possessions, and those advocating direct intervention in Europe. Predictably enough, what initially emerged was an unsatisfactory compromise, primarily aimed at avoiding any commitment of British troops to Germany. While the Duke of Cumberland was despatched to Germany to take command of the Hanoverian army, he was given no British troops to assist him in defending the Electorate. Instead, direct British intervention was to take the form of a series of raids, launched on the French coast with the twin objects of diverting French troops from Germany and at the same time inflicting as much damage as possible on shipping and harbour facilities. To that end, Lieutenant General Sir John Mordaunt was ordered to assemble a force of ten battalions on the Solent by the end of July 1757[36] – one of them being the $1/20^{th}$ Foot led by its lieutenant colonel, James Wolfe.

That he was still only a lieutenant colonel at this time was hardly for the want of trying, for in December of 1755 he had sounded out his mother on another scheme to take over the 8th Foot from his father:

I have no prospect of preferment; nor no right to expect it in the common course; but if I knew how to secure £500 a year to my father in case he should give me his regiment and I miscarry, I believe I could manage to get it done. If the Duke should say that he should have his regiment again, in case I fell at the head of it, or £500 a year from my successor – would the General in that case consent to part with it, taking the sale of the Lieutenant Colonel's commission for his use?[37]

The General did not consent. Wolfe, so far as can be ascertained, had not purchased the lieutenant-colonelcy of the 20th from Edward Cornwallis, and consequently he had no assured right to sell or assign it to his father. Whether from this or some other cause, the scheme foundered without trace, as did his scarcely less sanguine hope that an appointment as Quartermaster General in Ireland would bring with it the brevet rank of full colonel. The Duke of Bedford, apparently another old acquaintance of Wolfe's father, was good enough to offer the post to James when it fell vacant on the death of Lord Forbes. However, while expressing a very proper appreciation of the favour, Wolfe readily admitted from the start that the appointment was "quite out of the course of my practice" and muttered darkly that if it did not come with the customary rank of colonel he would give it up immediately and go back to his battalion. As he wrote to Rickson, who was now himself acting as Deputy Quartermaster General in Scotland:

. . . this new office does neither please nor flatter me, as you may believe when I tell you that it was offered with the rank of Colonel, which the King, guided by the Duke, afterwards refused. His Royal Highness's reasons were plausible; he told the Duke of Bedford (who applied with warmth) that I was too young a lieutenant-colonel that it could not be done immediately.[38]

Viewed objectively, it is hard to disagree with Cumberland's opinion that Wolfe needed to serve his time, though no doubt Wolfe's constant importunities to go off on extended leave had been an irritation. It may seem odd too that James should have been so hungry to obtain the empty honour of a brevet colonelcy, but he no doubt reasoned that, once elevated, he should have a better claim to the command of a regiment should one fall vacant. As it happened, there was then every prospect that such an opportunity would transpire. On 25 August 1756 second battalions were authorised for a number of regiments including the 20th Foot, and while the 2/20th was presently under the command of Major John Beckwith,[39] Wolfe had hopes of being appointed to the colonelcy should it eventually be taken into the line as a regiment in its own right.

Consequently, he kissed hands for the Quartermaster General's appointment on 29 March, but when the expected brevet promotion to colonel failed to materialise, James had no hesitation in advising Bedford that he felt himself obliged to embark with his battalion.[40]

The choice of Rochefort as the primary objective of Sir John Mordaunt's expedition was made in a frighteningly casual fashion. Three years earlier a young Scots engineer officer, Robert Clerk, had passed through the town on his way home from Gibraltar. Paying a courtesy call on the governor "in his Regimentals", he politely asked to be shown around the fortifications and the dockyard. With equal courtesy the governor obliged and Clerk noted with considerable interest that, "There were parts of a rampart in existence round the town but it was incomplete and about 25' high at most." In July of 1757 this important intelligence was passed on to the Secret Committee by Sir John Ligonier, and when questioned, Clerk positively asserted that the town could be taken out of hand by escalade, without any time-consuming artillery preparation. Suitably impressed, the Committee agreed on 24 July to commit ten battalions to the purpose and to appoint Sir John Mordaunt to command the expedition.

Wolfe was at the time overseeing the training of both battalions of the 20th Foot at Bradford Heath, near Blandford, but Mordaunt evidently took him along to the conference on the 24th, because three days before he had rather gloomily written to Rickson from London:

> We are about to undertake something or other at a distance, and I am one of the party. I can't flatter you with a lively picture of my hopes as to the success of it; the reasons are so strong against us in whatever we take in hand, that I never expect any great matter; the chiefs, the engineers, and our wretched discipline, are the great and insurmountable obstructions. I doubt yet if there be any fixed plan; we wait for American intelligence, from whence the best is not expected, and shall probably be put into motion by that intelligence. I myself take the chance of a profession little understood and less liked in this country. I may come off as we have done before; but I never expect to see either the poor woman my mother, or the General again – she is at present dangerously ill, he is infirm with age. Whether my going may hurry their departure, you are as good a judge as I am. Besides their loss, I have not a soul to take charge of my little affairs, and expect to find everything in the utmost confusion, robbed and plundered by all that catch hold of them.[41]

The "wretched discipline" or training, at least, he was able to tackle while they waited to embark, for Mordaunt gave him a free hand. In fact, Wolfe got rather more time for it than he or anyone else might have anticipated since the Navy dragged its heels over providing both transports and escort. It had been agreed at the conference that the Channel Squadron under Admiral Hawke should be committed to the purpose, but the Navy was primarily concerned with intercepting two French squadrons expected to return shortly from Louisburg and the West Indies. News of their probable sailing was evidently the "American intelligence" referred to by Wolfe and so final approval for the expedition was not given until 4 August. Even then it took a further month for the transports to be assembled, brought round to Cowes and the troops embarked.

The expedition eventually sailed on 6 September and then took twelve days to cross the Channel and pass into the Bay of Biscay. Not only did this delay give the French time to learn that something nasty was afoot and prepare themselves accordingly, but the window of opportunity before Hawke would have to look out for the American squadrons was closing fast. Despite the frequent calms that dogged their progress, Wolfe, aboard HMS *Ramillies* was wretchedly seasick: "I have not myself been one hour well since we embarked, and have the mortification to find I am the worst mariner in the whole ship. General, secretary, and aides-de-camp are all stouter, all better seamen than myself. If I make the same figure ashore, I shall acquire no great reputation by the voyage."[42]

As it turned out, no one was to make much of a reputation from the voyage, although Wolfe at least emerged with more credit than most. Everything had depended from the beginning upon surprise and speed. From the outset the general idea had been to arrive, land the troops and storm Rochefort out of hand, but instead delay mounted upon delay and it soon became apparent that, beyond these general intentions, no proper planning had been carried out. Landfall was finally made during the afternoon of 20 September and Vice Admiral Knowles was ordered to lead the fleet through the Pertuis d'Antioche, past the Isle d'Oleron and so into the broad anchorage called the Rade de Basque or Basque Roads. Unfortunately, just at that point a large French man-of-war blundered unsuspectingly into the midst of the fleet. Three ships were directed to give chase and eventually drove her ashore near the mouth of the Bordeaux River, but by the time the excitement was all over Knowles judged that it was too dark to attempt the passage. Then, next morning, "just as the whole fleet was getting within the Pertuis the wind took them short, and they were obliged to stand out again; and here we are now, beating on and off, waiting for a better day and a more favourable gale."

Not until midday on the 23rd was it possible to effect a landing on the Isle d'Aix, which guarded the lower end of the Basque Roads. As soon as the French fort on the island surrendered at about half past one, Wolfe went ashore to interrogate the prisoners. While he was doing so, Major General Harry Conway, Mordaunt's second-in-command, proceeded to reconnoitre another fort situated on the sandy promontory of Fouras. It was thought that possession of this second fort would provide the expedition with a secure beachhead on the mainland within easy striking distance of Rochefort itself, but that evening's entry in a serial letter which Wolfe was writing his father reveals that the expedition was already starting to go wrong:[43]

> Isle d'Aix, 23rd, in the evening, – The fort of the Ile d'Aix taken by Captain Howe,[44] in the 'Magnanime', with a few distant shot from the 'Barfleur'. There were five great ships upon this business; but as Captain Howe led, he saved the rest the trouble of battering, and confounded the defendants to that degree with the vivacity of his fire that they deserted thirty pieces of cannon and eight mortars, and struck after thirty-five minutes of resistance. There were 500 men in the fort of which very few were killed; and the 'Magnanime' lost but three killed, and eight or ten wounded. Mr Howe's manner of going down upon the enemy, and his whole proceeding, have raised the opinion people had of his courage and abilities to a very high pitch . . .
>
> We are preparing to land somewhere between Rochelle and Rochefort, for the sake of mischief more than any success we can propose to ourselves after such long preparations and notice to the enemy. I believe the expedition will end in our landing and fighting, and then returning to our ships; and we may bombard Rochelle, put the isles of Rhe and Oleron under contribution, blow up the fortress of the Isle d'Aix, and spread terror all along the coast. If we had set out upon this business in time, I believe we should have been thought very troublesome . . . I have been told that General Conway, with three battalions, went down with Mr. Knowles' division to assist in the attack; but they were not wanted, only to take possession and guard the prisoners.

A number of interesting points stand out from this letter. First, Wolfe makes no mention of his having reconnoitred the fort at Fouras, as is sometimes claimed, and in fact he makes no mention at all of a proposed assault on it. Instead he appears to have believed that the next landing was to be made in one of the two sandy bays flanking the village of Chatelaillon to the north-east. Most worryingly, he had formed the clear impression that the expedition's primary objective of storming Rochefort had already been abandoned – and that it now had no clear objective beyond shooting up any French troops who might casually be encountered. This point in particular is noteworthy. The evidence produced at the subsequent inquiry suggested that the decision to try for a landing by Chatelaillon was only taken the next day, after it proved impossible to bring either warships or bomb-ketches in close enough to bombard Fouras. However, Wolfe's contemporary letter clearly reveals that the beach landing was under active consideration on the day *before*[45] and certainly implies that there was already a great deal more dithering going on than was admitted at the subsequent inquiry. In fact, in a later letter to his uncle, Major Walter Wolfe, James summarised the unfolding fiasco in scathing terms:[46]

> The season of the year and the nature of the enterprise called for the quickest and most vigorous execution, whereas our proceedings were quite otherwise. We were in sight of the Isle of Rhe, the 20th September . . . and it was the 23rd before we fired a gun. That afternoon and night slipped through our hands – that lucky moment of confusion and consternation among our enemies. The 24th, – Admirals and Generals consult together, and resolve upon nothing between them but to hold a council of war. The 25th, – this famous council sat from morning till late at night, and the result of the debates was unanimously not to attack the place they were ordered to attack, and for reasons that no soldier will allow to be sufficient.[47] The 26th, – the Admiral sends a message to the Generals intimating that if they do not determine to do something there, he would go to another place. The 27th, – the Generals and the Admirals view the land with their glasses, and agree upon a second council of war, having by this time discovered their mistake. The 28th, – they deliberate, and resolve to land that night. Orders are issued out accordingly, but the wind springing up after the troops had been two or three hours in the boats, the officers of the navy declare it difficult and dangerous to attempt the landing. The true state of the case is that our sea-officers do not care to be engaged in any business of this sort, where little is to be had but blows and reputation; and the officers of the infantry are so profoundly ignorant, that an enterprise of any vigour astonishes them to that degree that they have not strength of mind nor confidence to carry it through.

Shortly after relating this sorry catalogue of vacillation and incapacity, Wolfe also penned a deservedly well-known critique to his old friend Rickson, and in a curious foretaste of Wellington's remark that, in Flanders in 1794, he at least learned what not to do, he prefaced it with the observation that "I am not sorry that I went, notwithstanding what has happened; one may always pick up something useful from amongst the most fatal errors."[48]

> I have found out that an admiral should endeavour to run into an enemy's port immediately after he appears before it; that he should anchor the transport ships and frigates as close as can be to the land; that he should reconnoitre and observe it as quick as possible, and

lose no time in getting the troops on shore; that previous directions should be given in respect to landing the troops, and a proper disposition made for the boats of all sorts, appointing leaders and fit persons for conducting the different divisions. On the other hand, experience shows me that, in an affair depending upon vigour and dispatch, the generals should settle their plan of operations, so that no time may be lost in idle debate and consultations when the sword should be drawn; that pushing on smartly is the road to success, and more particularly so in an affair of this nature; that nothing is to be reckoned an obstacle to your undertaking which is not found really so upon *tryal*; that in war something must be allowed to chance and fortune, seeing it is in its nature hazardous, and an option of difficulties; that the greatness of an object should come under consideration, opposed to the impediments that lie in the way; that the honour of one's country is to have some weight, and that, in particular circumstances and times the loss of 1,000 men is rather an advantage to a nation than otherwise, seeing that gallant attempts raise its reputation and make it respectable; whereas the contrary appearances sink the credit of a country, ruin the troops, and create infinite uneasiness and discontent at home.

In this particular case, that uneasiness and discontent rightly brought the generals before a board of inquiry and afterwards brought Sir John Mordaunt to a court martial. Wolfe, rather unwillingly, attended as a witness but in marked contrast to his private and often violent effusions about the "three bad Generals" Mordaunt, Conway and Edward Cornwallis, he declined to publicly damn his old friend and patron. In the end, Mordaunt was acquitted but by then Wolfe had others matters to concern him.

Returning from Rochefort in a decidedly black mood, Wolfe had immediately resolved to give up his Irish appointment as Quartermaster General. Initially he may even have thought of resigning from the Army as well, but eventually he concluded that "I can't part with my other employment, because I have nothing else to trust to; nor do I think it consistent with honour to sneak off in the middle of a war."[49] This was just as well, for four days later he had the pleasure of writing to his father "that the King has been pleased to give me the rank of Colonel, which at this time is more to be prized than any other, because it carries with it a favourable appearance as to my conduct upon this late expedition."[50] He went on to ascribe this to the recommendation of Admiral Hawke, but it is undoubtedly of some significance that it followed close on the effective dismissal of Cumberland on 14 October and came on the day after Sir John Ligonier succeeded the Duke as Commander-in-Chief.

The colonelcy was still only brevet rank, but it brought with it command of the 2/20th, which was eventually to be redesignated the 67th Foot. Buoyed up by this change in his fortunes, James delayed resigning his Irish post, no doubt because the salary and emoluments attaching to it were extremely useful to him – or at least might have been, were they not so much in arrears. Nevertheless, his conscience continued to prick him and when he eventually did resign on 26 January 1758, he apologetically confessed to Bedford that "It is a mortification to have been so long in that office, and so useless, and more especially as under your Grace's government such reformations are more likely to be brought about which are most necessary."[51]

It is tempting to speculate what Wolfe might have achieved had he actually tried to reform the notoriously corrupt and inefficient Irish staff, but talented as he undoubtedly was, the task of cleaning that particular Augean stable would almost certainly have been too much for his patience. Instead, he was destined for greater things and his letter of resignation was actually prompted by the grant of a local commission, dated 23 January 1758, appointing him a Brigadier-General in North America.

4
America

Although the abortive raid on Rochefort may very properly be considered a part of the Seven Years War, that particular conflict really only began in 1756 and the coastal expeditions aside – breaking windows with guineas – was very largely confined to Central Europe. While the 20th Foot would certainly find glory (and Lord George Sackville meet undeserved infamy) at Minden in 1759, the real war, as far as Britain was concerned, actually began in the Ohio valley in 1754 – and began badly at that.

By the mid-point of the 18th century, British colonies occupied the whole of the eastern seaboard of North America from Georgia to Nova Scotia. Although prosperous and comparatively well-populated, these colonies stretched inland only as far as the Allegheny Mountains, and such was the impenetrable nature of this great barrier that at only two points did the British settlements and the neighbouring French colonies in Canada actually meet. The first was at the narrow isthmus connecting Nova Scotia with the Canadian mainland, and the other was in Upper New York in the disputed area about the head of Lake Champlain, which marked the watershed of the Hudson and Richelieu rivers.

Climate and geography conspired to effectively confine the French settlements to the banks of the mighty St. Lawrence river and at the same time ensure that they were self-sufficient in neither population, foodstuffs, nor material goods. All three had to be shipped across the Atlantic and in through the Gulf of St. Lawrence, and the vulnerability of this supply route was all too clearly demonstrated by Sir William Pepperell's surprising seizure of Louisburg in 1745. This substantial European-style fortress on Cape Breton Island was intended to guard the entrance to the river, but it fell almost at once to his enthusiastic rabble of New Englanders. Although it was soon returned in exchange for Madras, after the Treaty of Aix-la-Chapelle (Aachen) in 1748, its easy capture impelled the French to look for an alternative lifeline.

New France actually comprised two distinct elements: the Canadas and Louisiana. It had long been possible to travel between the two by way of the Ohio and Mississippi rivers, but now moves to reduce Canada's vulnerability and consolidate this rather tenuous trail by building forts at various points along its length coincided with expansionist moves across the mountain divide. The original royal charters granted to the Virginian and Pennsylvanian colonists had airily allowed them land rights as far west as the Pacific Ocean. In time these rights would become enshrined as the independent United States' "Manifest Destiny", but for the present it was the formation of the Ohio Land Company in 1748 which placed Britain and France on a collision course.

The Company's traders attracted the attention of the French, who, in order to protect their own interests, and above all that vital route to Louisiana, despatched their own men into the area. Everything hinged on possession of the Forks of the Ohio – where the Allegheny and Monongahela rivers join. The French won the initial race to build a fort there – Fort Duquesne – in the summer of 1754, and in the process they defeated and forced the surrender of a rag-tag force of Virginians led by young George Washington.[52] Thereafter, events began to spiral out of control. As far as both the colonial governments of Virginia and Pennsylvania, and the King's government in London were concerned, the first priority was to establish control of the Ohio country. Consulted, in his capacity as Commander-in-Chief of the British Army, the Duke of Cumberland rightly decided that if the potentially provocative step of sending regular troops to North America was to be undertaken at all, military operations should not be limited to the Ohio alone. Instead they were to encompass a simultaneous resolution of the other outstanding territorial disputes in the region.

Unsurprisingly, this decision led to a dramatic military escalation on both sides. Initially the King suggested sending just the 42nd Highlanders and some specially raised Highland independent companies, since it was considered that they would be well suited to irregular warfare. Wolfe, in fact, had already cynically commented in a letter to 'Little Rickson' that Highlanders would do very well in Nova Scotia since "they are hardy, intrepid, accustomed to a rough country, and no great mischief if they fall."[53] Cumberland, on the other hand, far from considering the 42nd expendable, reacted to this proposal with some concern, since transferring the Army's only Highland regiment to a putative American Establishment "would be losing the corps were the men to remain in America."[54] Instead, he assigned two other regular regiments from the Irish Establishment, (Halkett's 44th and Dunbar's 48th) and appointed Edward Braddock as Commander-in-Chief North America, with the local rank of major general.[55]

In line with Cumberland's thinking, Braddock's mission (as set out in his written instructions) was not to be confined to the seizure of the disputed Ohio country. While that was indeed to be his primary objective, he was then required to move northwards and consolidate his conquest by securing the French fort on the Niagara as well. At the same time, provincial forces under Colonel William Johnson were to push forward across the watershed and capture Fort St. Frederic (otherwise known as Crown Point) on Lake Champlain, while a third expedition under Lieutenant Colonel Robert Monckton was to cross the Massaquash river, take Fort Beausejour at the head of the Bay of Fundy and so secure the isthmus joining Nova Scotia with the rest of the continent. It was an ambitious scheme but, incredibly enough, in carrying it out the British government thought it could avoid actually going to war with France. It was merely to be a matter of properly *re-establishing* legitimate and "natural" borders.

Unfortunately, this ham-fisted attempt at dissimulation only resulted in a total lack of operational security. (In fact, so open were the preparations for the expedition that Braddock himself, on holiday in Italy when the news of his appointment caught up with him, actually returned home by way of Paris!) Far from viewing these warlike preparations with equanimity, the French immediately despatched no fewer than six battalions of regulars to Canada, whereupon a suddenly alarmed British government ordered their interception, even at the hazard of starting a war – which was, of course, exactly what happened.

On 8 June 1755 a brief but inglorious battle off the Grand Banks ended in the capture of just two ships, little more than 300 French infantrymen and a state of open if undeclared war between Britain and France. From there it all went downhill. On 9 July 1755 Braddock was ambushed and killed in a battle on the Monongahela River, just a few miles short of Fort Duquesne. Initially there was better news from Nova Scotia – the passage of the Massaquash was forced without serious difficulty and Fort Beausejour fell after four days – but this petty triumph was marred by the subsequent deportation of the French or "Acadian" population from Nova Scotia.[56] As for William Johnson's expedition against Fort St. Frederic, it too ended in a victory of sorts at Wood Creek and the capture of the French commander, Baron Deiskau. However, it then came to a complete halt with the building of Fort William Henry on the shores of Lake George. And that was as good as it got: two years later a French army, led by Louis Joseph de St. Veran, Marquis de Montcalm, swept down from Canada, took the fort and to all appearances seemed poise to march on Albany, or even New York.

Fortunately, as it turned out, a shortage of supplies and the desertion of his Native American allies prevented Montcalm's advancing further, but the capture of Fort William Henry severely damaged confidence in Braddock's successor. This was Major General John Campbell, Earl of Loudoun. A good organiser who had served as Sir John Cope's Adjutant General in 1745 and afterwards raised and commanded an army of loyalist Highlanders, Loudoun's appointment as Commander-in-Chief North America probably stemmed from a perception that he was able to deal with reluctant local authorities and could handle militia. Unfortunately this was true only up to a point. Had he gone to North America as an adjutant general or quartermaster general under an officer of proven fighting ability, the Earl might have done very well indeed. Unfortunately, like many other staff officers, his undoubted organisational talents were not matched by a capacity for independent command. He rightly recognised that the French could only be effectively fought in the Ohio valley, on the Upper New York frontier, and at the mouth of the St. Lawrence. Accordingly, he set about raising the necessary troops, or at least trying to persuade the colonial authorities to raise, pay and provision them, but that was just about the limit of his achievements. In Scotland, during the rebellion, he had raised what might have been a formidable loyalist army, but then failed to employ it effectively or even mount a credible resistance when the Jacobite army turned up. In America it was a very similar story, and in fact, he was rather unkindly compared there to the figure of St. George on an inn sign – forever armed and mounted, but riding nowhere. Choosing to direct his principal effort at Louisburg, he found it too well defended and covered by that squadron which so exercised Admiral Hawke during the Rochefort fiasco. Consequently he and his men were still hanging around at Halifax – planting cabbages, as legend has it – when Fort William Henry fell. Initially it looked as if he might survive this reverse, but he was regarded very much as Cumberland's man and so the Prime Minister, William Pitt, sacked him in December 1757.

Pitt's choice of a replacement for Loudoun was another Scots professional, the solidly unimaginative Major General James Abercromby. Ligonier, however, had a rather shrewder appreciation of his limitations than Mr Pitt, and ensured first that Abercromby's instructions were precise; and secondly, that his actual responsibilities were confined to mounting an offensive against Fort Carillon (Ticonderoga) on the Upper New York frontier.

The key fortresses of Louisburg and, ultimately, the Canadian capital Quebec were to be taken by a quite independent force. When Billy Pitt asked Ligonier to nominate its commander, he chose one of his own old ADCs, Colonel Jeffrey Amherst, and proposed that he be given a local commission as Major General in North America. Amherst was to be assisted by three equally temporary local brigadiers: James Wolfe, Charles Lawrence and Edward Whitmore. The latter two were already serving in North America, but Amherst and Wolfe might have seemed a touch junior for such important appointments. In fact, Ligonier had to contend with strong opposition from the King himself, but in the end he carried the day because the all-important naval side of the expedition was to be handled by Admiral Edward Boscawen.

Unlike Hawke, who was an excellent sea-officer but temperamentally ill-suited to conducting combined operations, Boscawen understood the business perfectly. In 1748 he had commanded just such an operation against Pondicherry in southern India. Although the war ended before the town fell – thus necessitating the exchange of Louisburg for Madras instead – it had nevertheless been a considerable achievement on his part to embark twelve independent companies, largely comprised of Jacobite prisoners and other equally unpromising material, transport them halfway around the world, land them on a hostile shore and then besiege the town in due form. Wolfe, indeed, admiringly referred to him as a good *fantassin* (infantryman) during the siege of Louisburg. He was, in the language of the time, an "active stirring man". This was just as well, for Amherst's chief qualification for the command of the land forces appears to have been that Ligonier knew him to be slow and methodical – a safe pair of hands, in other words, who could be relied upon not to cock things up. In fact, he was so slow and methodical that the expedition actually sailed without him!

Wolfe's letters from this period betray an air of hurry and excitement, harassment and urgent activity, in the midst of which he nevertheless found time to intercede through Sackville for the confirmation of William Rickson's appointment as Deputy Quartermaster General in Scotland and the brevet lieutenant colonelcy which customarily went with it; to discuss the selection of officers for his own as yet un-numbered regiment; and to try and find himself a couple of ADCs.[57] Unsurprisingly, he also took some pains to acquaint himself as much as possible with conditions in North America. He already knew a fair bit about Nova Scotia through his earlier correspondence with Rickson, but now he questioned at least two American officers. Of one, Thomas Cheshyre, little is known since he sailed for the East Indies with Draper, but Wolfe evidently thought highly of another called John Carden, whom he referred to as a "Lieutenant of Shirleys's or Pepperell's, I know not which, and has but one threadbare uniform to cover an indefatigable body spurred on to action by a daring mind."[58]

Notwithstanding all this activity, Wolfe still found time to indulge in his favourite pastime of grumbling. He might have no cause for the present to complain of his promotion and employment prospects, but, as he observed to his mother, the Rochefort affair had cost him £200 and now the American adventure was likely to cost him upwards of £500-600 for his campaign equipage and private stock of provisions – all the greater since he would now be expected to keep an open table for his own officers. In the circumstances it was just as well that he obtained a letter of credit from his father, but he still gloomily reflected that "if we should miscarry, my condition will be desperate, and my finances exhausted. The ladies too, will despise a beaten lover, so that every way I must be undone. And yet I run readily, heartily, and cheerfully into the road of ruin."[59] He also grumbled about his colleagues and the quality of some of the forces allocated to the expedition. Thus we hear that one of his fellow brigadiers, Colonel Edward Whitmore of the 22nd Foot, "has no health nor con-stitution for such a business as we are going upon; he never was a soldier, but otherwise a very worthy gentlemen."[60] In condemning Whitmore, Wolfe was only passing on gossip from Captain Isaac Barre, who was to be his adjutant general at Quebec, but he was able to speak at first hand when he described some of the troops to his Uncle Walter as "five-or-six-and twenty hundred, two very good battalions we have and the rest is *la canaille* from the second battalions upon this establishment."[61] He also complained about Portsmouth ("a sink of the lowest and most abominable of vices"), its "diabolical citizens", and its garrison – "vagabonds who stroll about in dirty red clothes from one gin shop to another."[62] It was with some relief, therefore, that he eventually informed his father that he had sailed from Spithead on 15 February, only to then have to report in one of his periodic jeremiads that he did not arrive in Halifax, Nova Scotia, until 9 May.[63]

From Christopher Columbus' time to our days there perhaps has never been a more extraordinary voyage. The continual opposition of contrary winds, calms, or currents, baffled all our skill and wore out all our patience. A fleet of men of war well manned, unincumbered with transports, commanded by an officer of the first reputation, has been eleven weeks in its passage. We made the Madeira Islands, the Canaries, Bermudas, and lastly to crown all the Isle of Sable [on the Banks 150 miles due east of Halifax]. Two or three of the ships are sickly, the rest are in very good condition. The Admiral, who has omitted no care or precaution to advance the service, is labouring to fit the fleet for sea with all possible despatch.

We found Amherst's Regiment in the harbour in fine order and healthy. Fraser's and Brigadier Lawrence's Battalions were here, and both in good condition. The Highlanders are very useful serviceable soldiers, and commanded by the most manly corps of officers I ever saw. Webb's, Otway's, and part of Monckton's battalions from Philadelphia came in with us. The detachments from this garrison are not joined, so that these battalions are very weak, scarce exceeding 300 men a regiment. About 500 Rangers are come, which to appearance are little better than *canaille*.

Brigadier Whitmore is expected every day with the artillery and troops from New York and Boston, Bragg's from the Bay of Fundy, and Anstruther's from Ireland.

A great quantity of fascines and gabions are made and other preparations of that sort, and a kind of small wooden fort (that takes to pieces) to secure our communications, instead of redoubts, which it seems the ground does not admit of. I have recommended a provision of palisades that the troops may lie quiet in their camps and to fortify our different magazines. We are to expect opposition at our landing. It is supposed they have about 1,500 irregulars, and that their garrison is augmented because seven ships (three of which are said to be men of war of two decks) have got into the harbour. The battalions are in general healthy, and I dare say will do their duty well. They are irritated against the enemy and have a quarrel of their own to decide besides the public cause.[64] As I foresaw long ago we shall find work to do. We are preparing a body of Light Foot to join to the Rangers, and I believe the whole will be put under the command of Captain Scott[65] (Major of Brigade), who is an active officer and used to that kind of war. Captain Raess came in yesterday from Sir C. Hardy's squadron off Louisburg. They have had the severest weather imaginable, and the snow is still upon the ground of Cape Breton, though here the weather is fair dry and warm. We don't entertain a right notion of L'Isle Royale in England; it is not possible to encamp there early in the year and to preserve the army. I wouldn't be understood by that to mean that we are prevented by the season at this time. We only await the arrival of Brigadier Whitmore and the equipment of the squadron to set sail, and certainly we shall struggle against all difficulties and push the affair with vigour . . . PS. – General Hopson[66] delivers over the command of the troops this day to Brigadier Lawrence.

Perhaps the most intriguing feature of this letter is the complete omission of any reference to the expedition's cold and snobbish commander, Jeffrey Amherst. Not only had he still to arrive in Halifax, but it seems abundantly clear both from this and a subsequent letter that, given the opportunity, neither Wolfe nor any of the other senior officers present were going to have any qualms about going ahead and mounting the operation without him. If so, they were to be disappointed, for the refitting of the fleet and bad weather conspired to keep the army in Halifax until the end of the month. In the meantime, Wolfe had been casting an ever more critical eye over both the forces and the preparations. Engineers, in particular, were in short supply: "One of the engineers, Green, is sick upon the continent and instead of Matt. Clarke and Gordon, who I suppose were far off, we have got two boys, Montresor and Williamson, and to make up the 300 artillery we must carry off all that are here. Among the officers of the infantry we have picked six or seven assistant engineers, enough to make out three brigades, six in each, besides the active Bastide and Major Mackellar." Digging tools were also lacking and even the small-arms were deficient: "As there are no spare arms, nor no rifled barrel guns, the firelocks of these regiments will be so injured in the course of the siege that I doubt if they will be in any condition of service after it is over. Some of them are already bad." For some reason too salt meat was being served out to the troops instead of fresh, despite its being readily available at the same cost, but oddly enough there was no shortage of rum. He also rather predictably found fault with the drill, for "My Lord Loudoun, whose management in the conduct of affairs is by no means admired, did adhere so literally and strictly to the one-two and the firings by the impractical chequer, &c., that these regiments must necessarily be cut off one after another unless they fall into some method more suited to the country and the kind of enemy they have to deal with."[67]

Those regiments eventually amounted to no fewer than fifteen regular battalions: 2/1st (Royal), Amherst's 15th under Lieutenant Colonel James Murray (later to be one of Wolfe's brigadiers at Quebec), Forbes's 17th, Whitmore's 22nd, Bragg's 28th, Otway's 35th, Hopson's 40th, Kennedy's 43rd, Warburton's 45th, Lascelles' 47th, Webb's 48th, Anstruther's 58th, Robert Monckton's 2/60th (Royal Americans), Lawrence's 3/60th (Royal Americans) and Fraser's 63rd/78th Highlanders.[68] The latter regiment had just been augmented by three additional companies, and the expeditionary force was completed by 330 officers and men of the Royal Artillery, five companies of New England Rangers, and a party of carpenters.[69] Actually, the 43rd Foot and a 200 strong detachment of the 35th were to be left behind under Lieutenant Colonel Monckton to defend Nova Scotia, which in itself led to a further delay while the 28th were relieved by six companies of the 43rd and brought round from the Bay of Fundy. On 28 May they finally hove into view aboard no fewer than twelve small sloops and Admiral Boscawen immediately gave the order to sail. Unfortunately, just as the fleet worked its way out of Halifax, the expedition's commander finally turned up at like the Devil at prayers, and as he blandly recorded in his public journal: "I had the good fortune of meeting Admiral Boscawen with the Fleet and the Troops coming out of the Harbour of Halifax on the 28th."[70]

If Wolfe and Lawrence were disappointed by the appearance of their general they gave no outward sign of it, but they must have been dismayed by his orders. Four days earlier Wolfe had been discussing a number of alternative landing places in order to avoid the heavily defended beaches of Gabarus Bay, where Pepperell had landed in 1745. Now Amherst, in spite of recent local intelligence, wanted to go straight in there.

As the 28th Foot, commanded by Lieutenant Colonel Hunt Walsh, were already carried in their own little flotilla, they were sent ahead in order to attempt or at least go through the motions of a landing at L'Orembec, just to the north-east of Louisburg, by way of a diversion. The rest, however, organised in three divisions, were to land to the south-west, in Gabarus Bay, just after dawn on 8 June. The Right Division, commanded by Brigadier Edward Whitmore and comprising the Royals, 17th, 47th, 48th, 58th and 2/60th, was to land by White Point, while the Centre Division, commanded by Brigadier Charles Lawrence, and comprising the 15th, 22nd, 35th, 40th, 45th and 3/60th, was to go ashore at Freshwater Cove, but only after the Left Division, commanded by James Wolfe, had first secured a beachhead in what is now known as Kennington Cove. This division, Wolfe's first real combat command, was itself made up of four elements. First came a small *ad hoc* battalion formed from the four "eldest" companies of grenadiers, supported by the Light Infantry and Rangers under Major Scott; then came Simon Fraser's 63rd/78th Highlanders, and finally eight more companies of grenadiers.[71]

After all the delays, the French were waiting for them. When Cape Breton Island was handed back to France in 1748 it was provided with a garrison of twenty-four independent *Companies de la Marine*.[72] These colonial troops had been reinforced in May 1755 by two regular army battalions; 2/*Artois* and 2/*Bourgogne*, but now the present crisis had attracted a number of Canadian and Acadian volunteers, and two more regular units – 2/*Cambis* and the mercenary 2/*Volontaires Etrangers*[73] – arrived just before the commencement of the siege. In fact the former only slipped in as late as the night of 7 June. Now some of them were entrenched above the beaches and coves of Gabarus Bay.

The landing passed off a great deal more easily than might have been expected. Wolfe sourly observed afterwards to Sackville that he "wouldn't recommend the Bay of Gabarus for a descent, especially as we managed it" but there was undoubtedly as much pique as truth in this. The French held their fire until the leading boats came close inshore just after dawn on 8 June, and for a moment or two it looked as if the operation might have to be aborted. Much has been made of the storm of artillery fire, but the greatest danger actually came from the violence of the surf. A number of boats were certainly upset, and others broken up on the rocks. Wolfe is said to have been on the point of aborting the operation, but at the last moment a sheltered landing place was discovered by some of the Light Infantry. Seizing the opportunity, he got his men on to the beach and there formed them up without too much difficulty. In fact, at the end of the day Amherst was able to report his total losses amongst the regulars at three officers, four sergeants, a corporal and thirty-eight men killed, while five subalterns, two sergeants, a corporal and fifty-one men were wounded. These figures do not include the Rangers who had one ensign and three privates killed, one man wounded and another returned as missing, or any of the naval personnel in the boats but it is undoubtedly significant that Amherst noted that twenty-one of the men – half the casualties – came from the grenadier company of his own 15th Foot and that all but eight of those were drowned rather than shot.[74]

These comparatively light casualties are certainly consistent with the way the operation was conducted, for Wolfe, as soon as he had formed his leading division on the beach, proceeded to scale the twenty-foot cliff and storm the battery planted on it. As far as can be ascertained, he had in fact outflanked the entire French defensive line and, having stormed the battery, he proceeded to roll up the French line at the point of the bayonet. He thus cleared the way first for the rest of his division to land and then Lawrence's as well, and the French were chased all the way back to the gates of Louisburg. Judging by the very moderate casualty list and the speed of the operation, there can have been little if any real resistance once the first division was ashore and Wolfe is said to have led the assault armed with nothing more lethal than a cane.[75] As for the French, Amherst reported just two captains of grenadiers, two lieutenants and something in the region of seventy men taken prisoner, but he was tolerably vague as to the numbers of their killed and wounded.[76] It may safely be concluded, therefore, that, as usual, most of those being attacked with "the cold steel" simply ran away too quickly to be killed!

With the beachhead secured the 28th Foot were brought back from L'Orembec and the next few days employed in getting men and stores ashore. Siege operations, unless crowned by a dramatic assault with sword in hand, are by their very nature tedious affairs and Louisburg was to be no exception. To first appearances, the town was strong enough, for it was built upon a peninsula, flanked on the one side by the eastern extremities of Gabarus Bay, and on the other by a natural harbour, wherein lay the French fleet. The entrance to this harbour was itself sufficiently secured on one side by the guns of a battery on Goat Island, on the other by one at Lighthouse Point, and by a third "Grand Battery" or *Batterie Royal* on the shore at the back of the harbour, so situated as to fire directly down the entrance channel. Not surprisingly, therefore, Boscawen declined to take the fleet straight in, as numerous armchair strategists and "cabinet practitioners", both at the time and afterwards, have advocated he should have done. However, with the British ashore and quite literally at the gates of the town, the French commander, the Chevalier de Drucour, had little option but to abandon his more isolated outworks, including the *Batterie Royal* and the one on Lighthouse Point.

On the night of 12 June, 400 Light Infantry and Rangers were ordered to "take post in the woods round the upper part of the N.E. harbour, there lie in ambuscade, and cover the march of the detachment of the army, which will be ordered to take post at L'Orembec, at the end of the N.E. Harbour, and upon Lighthouse Point." This detachment, commanded by Wolfe, comprised four companies of grenadiers, three companies of Rangers, "some Light Infantry" and a number of detachments totalling 1,220 men drawn from all the regiments but the 28th.[77] Both objectives were seized without interference and a number of guns were then landed at L'Orembec. By the 19th Wolfe had succeeded in establishing a battery there which played first on the Goat Island battery, then upon the shipping within the harbour, and latterly, as he extended his works, fired into the town itself. There were occasional setbacks, of course; while writing a report to Amherst that day Wolfe mentioned that he could see "the smoke of L'Orembeck" and casually concluded that the fishing village was being burned in reprisal for some ill-judged partisan activity. In fact, the detachment set down there to guard the fishing boats had indeed been attacked, not by the inhabitants but by some Native American warriors and, worse still, this was while the detachment "were, as far as I can find, all drunk and asleep, – sentries, guards and all."[78] Drunk or not, Lieutenant Crosbie and his men succeeded in driving off their attackers – which only confirmed Wolfe in his low opinion of the local tribesmen: "I take them to be the most contemptible *canaille* upon earth. Those to the southward are much braver and better men; these are a dastardly set of bloody rascals. We cut them to pieces whenever we found them, in return for a thousand acts of cruelty and barbarity."[79] Rather more serious, though, was a French sortie from the town on 9 July which surprised the 17th's grenadiers, killing their commander Captain William, Earl of Dundonald, and a number of others before the grenadiers of Whitmore's 22nd and Bragg's 28th Foot put in a successful counter-attack.

Satisfied with the effect of his batteries on the French shipping, Wolfe led his grenadiers forward, on 16 July, to seize the high ground in front of the Dauphin Gate and began establishing a new battery there. This one required a great deal of effort in building corduroy roads over bogs, and with the help of the ever-forgotten women, dragging the guns into position despite fog and heavy rain. At last, however, he sent a report to Amherst dramatically headed "Trenches at daybreak, 25th July":[80]

> Dear Sir, – The five gun battery is finished, and the cannon in readiness to mount. We want platforms, artillery officers to take the direction, and ammunition. If these are sent early, we may batter in breach this afternoon. Holland has opened a new boyau,[81] has carried

on about 140 or 150 yards, and is now within fifty or sixty yards of the glacis. The enemy were apprehensive of a storm, and fired smartly for about half an hour, which drove the workmen in; but when the fire ceased they returned to their business, and did a great deal. You will be pleased to indulge me with six hours rest, that I may serve in the trenches at night.

Brief and to the point though this report might be, its tone (and those of his other reports) reveals that Wolfe for once was thoroughly enjoying himself and revelling in his semi-independent, and above all, active command. Gone for the moment is the chronic grumbling and complaining which characterises so much of his peacetime correspondence. He establishes routines, organises reliefs, raises battery after battery, and cheerfully bombards his commander with information and advice. It was probably at his suggestion that the various volunteers serving with the army were ordered "to serve with the light infantry . . . Major Scott is to dispose of them, so that they will have some command, and act as Officers".[82] There are setbacks and problems, to be sure, but all of them readily and even enthusiastically overcome. "Our earth and sod are so very bad that I am obliged to have recourse to sandbags, and our wood for pickets is extremely unfavourable," he wrote on 20 July, "notwithstanding such difficulties I shall persevere till we demolish these gentlemen."

And demolish them he did. Thanks to the notorious damp fogs and long winters so characteristic of Cape Breton, the lime mortar of the outwardly formidable stone walls had never set properly and even the strongest bastions crumbled quickly. Wolfe's guns, moreover, had already destroyed a number of the enemy ships, while others had been sunk by the French themselves to serve as blockships in the channel. Only two now remained, and on the night of 25 July, while Wolfe was battering away at the bastion by the Dauphin Gate and beginning to open what looked as if it might be a practicable breach, Boscawen moved at last. Two of his captains, Laforey and Balfour, went in with 600 men in boats and seized both ships. Next morning, with all hope gone, Drucour sent a message that he was ready to surrender. He asked for terms, but so hopeless was his position that none were granted and so the garrison marched out on the morning of 27 July and laid down their arms in front of "sleepy old Whitmore", who was then effectively pensioned off by being made governor.

The fall of Louisburg ought to have been a famous victory and Wolfe eagerly looked forward to completing the conquest with an attack on Quebec. He bombarded Amherst's ADC with suggestions, and reminders to secure any St. Lawrence pilots who might be in the town. He even pressed him to "hint to the General that the French flints are very good, and may be useful in his army". Instead, to his dismay, the days passed in inactivity. Boscawen declined to go into the St. Lawrence since, in his opinion, the season was too far advanced, and perhaps he was right. For a start there were no fewer than 5,637 French prisoners to be shipped out. It would obviously take some little time to settle the new garrison, to embark the disposable troops, guns and stores and then proceed into little-known and often fog-bound waters. The following year it would take Wolfe's own expedition twenty days simply to sail from Louisburg to within a few miles of Quebec. With the best will in the world, therefore, Boscawen could not reasonably expect to set Amherst down there before the beginning of September, with only six weeks' grace before the first winter ice would force his withdrawal.

It could perhaps have been done, given the will and the energy, for Quebec at this time was poorly defended, but on the day Louisburg surrendered the first vague reports arrived of another disaster. By the 31st it was known that Abercromby had launched a frontal assault on the French lines at Ticonderoga on 8 July and suffered a complete repulse. Amherst immediately departed for New York with six battalions, and Wolfe, discontented once more, began soliciting a command under Sackville back in Europe. In the event he was sent off on a pointless little expedition to the Peninsule de la Gaspe at the very mouth of the St. Lawrence, which achieved nothing beyond the burning of a few fishing villages and was scarcely dignified by the seizure of some arms belonging to the local militia. And then, in November, as he had threatened, he went home.

NOTES

1. Guy, A.J. (Ed), *Colonel Samuel Bagshawe and the Army of George II*, (1990), pp94-95.
2. Glasgow, 7 April 1749. Beckles Willson *Life and Letters of James Wolfe*, (1909), pp95-6.
3. This was Richard Phillips' 40th Foot. To all intents and purposes it was indeed at this period an American regiment, having been formed in Nova Scotia and Newfoundland in August 1717 and then stationed there ever since. Cornwallis had originally been sent out with some 4,000 "military settlers" – soldiers and their wives discharged in the usual reductions which followed the peace in 1748 – but as it soon became clear, Cumberland also intended him to succeed Richard Phillips as colonel and governor.
4. Perth, 23 March 1750. (Beckles Willson op.cit. p117.)
5. Mackesy, P., *The Coward of Minden*, (1979), p29.
6. Oddly enough, Bury (or rather Albemarle, as he was by then) would serve on Sackville's court martial after the Minden affair – see Macksey, op.cit.
7. For example, an entry in Captain Stewart's orderly book under 18 April 1759 records that the officers of the 42nd Highlanders were to appear at a forthcoming review with their hair "Albermar[d]."
8. Perth, 31 January 1750. (Beckles Willson op.cit. pp112-3.)
9. Inverness, 6 November 1751. (Ibid. p161.)
10. Perth, 6 April 1750. (Ibid. pp120-1.)

11. Perth, 1 September 1750. (Ibid. pp130-1.)
12. Banff, 9 June 1751. (Ibid. p144.)
13. Wolfe to William Rickson, Glasgow, 2 April 1749. (Ibid. p93.)
14. Banff, 12 June 1751. (Ibid. pp146-7.)
15. Unfortunately, like many another, despite receiving some kind of rebuff, he still maintained a certain infatuation and two years later he wrote from Paris (Ibid. p203) that "I had a letter from my friend Gage* last post, in answer to one that I writ him by Lord Albemarle's directions. He says the little Maid of Honour is as amiable, and alas! (as he expresses it, poor gentleman) as cold as ever. What can that lady mean by such obstinate self denial? . . . I writ a long letter to her uncle this post, and sent him some books that he desired. I touched upon the tender string some time ago, as I told you; his answer was, that he was sorry to find me so serious upon the old story; and there the matter rests for ever."
    * Captain Thomas Gage, afterwards colonel of the 90th Foot, and in 1775 CinC North America.
16. Banff, 9 June 1751. (Ibid. p144.)
17. Inverness, 6 March 1752.
18. Canterbury, 27 December 1755. (Ibid. p284.)
19. Albemarle had served in Flanders and was commander of the force shipped across to the Tyne in 1745. Afterwards he commanded a division in Scotland, and served for a time as CinC Scotland. He and Wolfe were therefore professionally acquainted.
20. Paris, 9 March 1753. (Beckles Willson, op.cit. p207.) Major Robert Hart died on 21 March 1753 and was eventually succeeded by Thomas Wilkinson from 1st Footguards.
21. Glasgow, 22 April 1753. (Ibid. p210.)
22. This was Captain Benjamin Clements. He resigned soon afterwards.
23. He had, from time to time, perhaps only half-seriously talked of going into the Austrian or the Prussian service himself, and in connection with loose women it is amusing to find him writing to his father from Paris, stating that "I can assure you upon my honour that in the articles of play and women (the most extravagant in Paris) have not amounted to 20 Louis d'ors" and making a half-admiring reference to the fact that "Marshal Saxe died in the arms of a little whore that plays upon the Italian stage – an ignominious end for a conqueror." (Beckles Willson, op.cit. pp201-2.)
24. As he explained to his mother, "The Marines . . . will be put into Companies of 100 men each, and not into regiments as the newspapers have proclaimed, and these Companies are to have a field officer to inspect them, and a Lieut.Col. or Major to every ten or twelve Companies. The whole body of Marines will be under the Lords of the Admiralty and entirely out of our way." (Ibid. pp258-9.) This was a significant move, for the earlier marine regiments had been under Army control and organised just as any other infantry battalions. Unfortunately, this set-up was incompatible with the demands of the sea-service, which required the men to be parcelled out between different ships to the detriment of good order and discipline and the total disarrangement of the regimental oeconomy. Although the Army's last marine regiments were disbanded in November 1748, their accounts were not cleared until October 1764!
25. Beckles Willson op.cit.
26. Southampton, 4 September 1755. (Ibid. p274.)
27. In view of his splenetic remarks on this occasion it is in fact ironic to find Wolfe writing in the 20th's orderly book that when his men were drafted into

Dunbar's 48th ". . . not a man declined the service, and all marched off with a resolution never to dishonour the corps they served in, and to do their utmost in his Majesty's service and the good of their country; such troops as these, men that may be depended upon in all changes and circumstances, deserve to be considered as real soldiers, and to be valued and esteemed accordingly." (*Wolfe's Instructions to Young Officers*, p38.)

28. Inverness(?), October 1751. (Beckles Willson op.cit. pp156-7.)
29. Canterbury, 5 November 1755. (Ibid. p286.)
30. Exeter, 7 March 1755. (Ibid. p254.)
31. Anon. *Advice to Officers of the British Army*, (1946), p27.
32. Wolfe to Sackville (Beckles Willson op.cit. p357.)
33. HMC *Bathurst* MSS, p681.
34. Cumberland to Barrington (Secretary at War), August 1757. Quoted in Houlding, J.A. *Fit for Service* (1981) p371.
35. Hastenbeck was one of those deeply embarrassing affairs in which at one point each side was running away from the other. Unfortunately, the French realised what was happening first. An excellent account of the campaign may be found in Lieutenant General Sir Reginald Savory, *His Brittanic Majesty's Army in Germany during the Seven Years War*, (1966).
36. The regiments in question were George Howard's 1/3rd (Buffs), Bentinck's 5th, Edward Wolfe's 8th (King's), Amherst's 15th, Kingsley's 1/20th, Cornwallis's 24th, Home's 25th, Hay's 33rd, Hodgson's 50th and Brudenell's 51st Foot. Three women per company were allowed to go and there were also to be 140 light dragoons.
37. Canterbury, 27 December 1755. (Beckles Willson, op.cit. p284.)
38. London, 21 July 1757. (Ibid. p321.)
39. Beckwith later succeeded Wolfe as Lieutenant Colonel of the 20th and led it during the war in Germany.
40. London(?), (Beckles Willson op.cit. p323.)
41. London, 21 July 1757 (Ibid.)
42. To his mother. HMS *Ramillies*, 17 September 1757. (ibid)
43. HMS *Ramillies*, 21-23 September 1757. (Beckles Willson, ibid. p330.)
44. This was Richard "Black Dick" Howe, the future admiral.
45. Wolfe was quite right, for while attention was supposedly fixed on Fouras, Vice Admiral Broderick was busily surveying the beaches around Chatelaillon – and initially keeping very quiet about having sighted what he took to be some French troops lurking behind the sandhills.
46. Blackheath, 18 October 1757. (Beckles Willson op.cit. p336.)
47. As he later told Rickson, "The whole affair turned upon the practicality of escalading Rochefort; and the two evidences brought to prove that the ditch was wet (in opposition to the assertions of the chief engineer, who had been in the place) are persons to whom, in my mind, very little credit should be given; without these evidences we should have landed, and must have marched on Rochefort, and it is my opinion that the place would have surrendered, or have been taken, in forty-eight hours." The ditch was indeed dry, but Wolfe was surely overly-sanguine in his expectations of victory, for Mordaunt's nerve had evidently failed him on the 23rd, if not long before, and the council of war merely provided him with the justification for abandoning the enterprise which he was looking for.
48. Blackheath, 5 November 1757. (Beckles Willson op.cit. pp339-40.)
49. To his mother. Blackheath, 17 October 1757. (Ibid. p335.)
50. Blackheath, 21 October 1757. (Ibid. p337.)

51. London, 26 January 1758. (Ibid. p352.)
52. Just to underline the fact, the French pointedly ensured that, before being released, Washington signed a confession that he had started the fighting and acknowledged that he and his men were trespassing on French territory.
53. Banff, 9 June 1751. (Beckles Willson op.cit. p141.)
54. Quoted in McCardle, L. *Ill-starred General; Braddock of the Coldstream Guards,* (1958), p124.
55. McCardle's biography (ibid) is both useful and readable, and it is worth remarking that whilst by no means a military genius, Braddock was not the stiff-necked martinet of popular legend.
56. Some Acadians went to Canada and took part in the defence of that colony, but the greater number were deported to Louisiana, where their name in time became corrupted to Cajuns. Some of their descendants had their revenge at the battle of New Orleans in 1815.
57. Beckles Willson op.cit. p360. In a postscript to a letter to Sackville, Wolfe speaks of Adam Livingstone of the 21st (Royal Scots Fusiliers) and William Delaune of the 20th as being particularly suited to service in North America, but there is no further mention of Livingstone and in a later letter he laments the absence of Delaune, although he was to be with him at Quebec the following year.
58. Ibid. John Carden was commissioned a lieutenant in Shirley's 50th Foot, 10 September 1754. Both Shirley's 50th and Pepperell's 51st were captured at Fort Oswego and disbanded in 1757.
59. To his mother. Blackheath, 17 January 1758. (Ibid. p349-350)
60. To Sackville. (Ibid. p358.) Whitmore's first commission went back to 30 March 1710. He was Colonel of the 22nd Foot from 11 July 1757 until his death in 1762. The other brigadier, Charles Lawrence, on the other hand, had received his ensign's commission in the 11th Foot on 26 December 1726 and still had some mileage in him.
61. Blackheath, 21 January 1758. (Ibid. p351) The two battalions in question were Amherst's 15th Foot from the British establishment, and Anstruther's 58th from Ireland. The remainder of the men were reinforcement drafts intended for the battalions already on the American station.
62. To Sackville. (Ibid. p357.) Wolfe went on to describe the worst offenders as "Disorderly soldiers of different Regiments . . . some from the ships, others from the hospital, some waiting to embark, dirty, drunken, insolent rascals, improved by the hellish nature of the place, where every kind of corruption, immorality and looseness is carried to excess."
63. To Sackville. Halifax 12 May 1758. (Ibid. p263-5.)
64. This is a reference to the massacre which followed the fall of Fort William Henry. The garrison, which included the 35th Foot and a large detachment of the 3/60th, had initially been paroled and Loudoun accordingly sent them back to Philadelphia. However, it was subsequently decided that since the French, for their part, had failed to protect the surrendered garrison when it marched out, that parole should no longer be recognised, and so both the 35th and 3/60th were now at Halifax.
65. Captain George Scott, Hopson's 40th Foot.
66. Peregrine Hopson had succeeded Edward Cornwallis as colonel of the 40th Foot and governor of Nova Scotia in March 1752. In a later letter to his father Wolfe noted that "The King has thought proper to recall him, on account, I suppose of his age, with which, and the assurance given him of a good reception at home, he is well pleased" – indeed he subsequently died in June 1759.

67. To Sackville. Halifax, 24 May 1758. (Beckles Willson op.cit. p366-9.) The last comment in this dismal litany is of considerable interest, for whatever his personal feelings, Amherst, like Mordaunt, recognised the virtues of Wolfe's alternate firing. By next summer he would be ordering its use by all the regiments serving in North America.

68. This last unit had a somewhat confusing gestation. Originally raised in 1757 as the 2nd Highland Battalion, it appears in the 1758 *Army List* as the 63rd Highlanders (2nd Highland Bn.), but ultimately became the 78th Highlanders, by which designation it is most familiarly known. This came about as a result of the "insertion" into the line of various second battalions, such as 2/20th, and their re-numbering as regiments in their own right.

69. Knox, John *Journal of the Campaigns in North America* Vol.I (1914), p165.

70. CO5/53. Amherst had not in fact sailed from Dublin until the middle of March, a month after Boscawen and Wolfe, and was seventy-two days in his passage.

71. Knox, op.cit. Vol.III. pp3-4. It will be noted that although there were fourteen regular battalions in the expeditionary force, Wolfe had only twelve grenadier companies. One of the missing companies was presumably the 28th's, still aboard the sloops providing the diversion at L'Orembec, while the grenadier company of Fraser's 63rd/78th Highlanders may have remained with its parent unit since it was in the same division. The four "eldest" companies making up the first wave would therefore have been those of the Royals, 15th, 17th and 22nd Foot.

72. Misidentified in Amherst's intelligence reports as *Royal Marine*. There was indeed a regiment of this name in the French Army, but the *Companies Franche de la Marine* were actually independent companies administered by the Ministry of Marine, which bore responsibility for colonial defence. The rank and file of these companies were recruited in metropolitan France (or sometimes further afield), but the officers were generally Canadiens.

73. In fact this largely German unit was so mercenary that a good many of its men went into the equally cosmopolitan 60th (Royal Americans) after the surrender. Some of them had already deserted to the British lines during the siege.

74. Amherst Journal (Knox op.cit.) p5. The dead included Captain Charles Baillie of the 63rd/78th Highlanders, Lieutenants Henry Nicholson of the 15th, John Cuthbert of the 63rd/78th and Ensign Francis Ceruthers of Captain James Rogers' Rangers, all killed on the day, and Lieutenants James Fenton of 2/1st (Royals) and Alexander Fraser of the 63rd/78th who both later died of their wounds.

75. This story is certainly consistent with later sketches by Hervey and Townshend, which often depict Wolfe carrying a fusil (and sometimes a bayonet) but never show him encumbered with a sword. Like subsequent generations of British infantry officers, he no doubt took the view that he had soldiers to do any killing for him that might be necessary.

76. Three 24lbr cannon, seven 9lbrs, seven 6lbrs, two mortars and fourteen swivel guns were also captured.

77. The grenadiers were those of the 35th, 40th, 45th and 47th Foot, all commanded by Lieutenant Colonel John Hale of the last-named corps. The 1,220 battalion company men were organised into three provisional battalions, commanded by Lieutenant Colonel Arthur Morris of the 17th Foot, Lieutenant Colonel Lord Rollo of the 22nd, and a Major Ross. The Rangers were commanded by Captain Joseph Goreham.

78. Beckles Willson, op.cit. p378. It turned out that the skipper of the sloop that

had carried them round there had very considerately sold them a quantity of raw New England rum.

79. To his uncle, Walter Wolfe. Louisburg, 27 July 1758. (Ibid. p385.)
80. Ibid. p381
81. A French term for a gut or narrow channel, and in this case obviously referring to a new trench, although its use appears to be colloquial since it does not appear in Muller's works on fortification.
82. Amherst's orders (Knox op.cit.) 12 June. Wolfe subsequently recommended to him (28 July) that "The corps of Light Infantry requires some regulation; they should have a captain to every 100 or 120, and exact numbers from every regiment, thirty per battalion. The volunteers should be again joined to that corps, with command of their respective regiments; by this method they will be formidable." (Beckles Willson op.cit. p387.)

CHAPTER V

The Hero of Quebec

James Wolfe had a pronounced ruthless streak which he cheerfully displayed in both Scotland and Canada, usually to the hand-wringing distress of his later admirers, but never was it more clearly demonstrated than in his securing of the "River" command.

When news of Abercromby's defeat at Ticonderoga first arrived at Louisburg, Wolfe had immediately offered to take a brigade to New York or Boston in order to reinforce him. Almost at once, however, he changed his mind, as he recounted to his father:[1]

> I am in a kind of doubt whether I go to the [American] continent or not. Abercromby is a heavy man, and Brigadier Prevost[2] the most detestable dog on earth, by everybody's account. These two officers hate one another. Now, to serve in an army so circumstanced is not a very pleasing business. If my Lord Howe[3] had lived, I should have been happy to have received his orders; or if I thought that I could be useful or serviceable, the ugly state of affairs there wouldn't discourage me from attempting it.

In the face of this flat refusal Amherst resolved to go to New York himself and there on 9 November he learned that Abercromby had been sacked and that he was now appointed Commander-in-Chief North America in his place. In the meantime Wolfe, deciding that he had no real employment at Louisburg worthy of his talents, relied on a supposed verbal agreement with Ligonier to justify his leaving the army there and returning home on HMS *Namur*. Initially, he does not appear to have anticipated returning to America again in the following year, for it is clear from his correspondence, with Sackville and others, that he seems to have had a notion that his old colonel was about to be given command of an expedition to retake Minorca, or at least to effect a large descent on the French coast. Consequently, he made it clear to Sackville that he was keen to serve under him in Europe in command of his own regiment, (which was about to be designated the 67th Foot), but in the event Sackville got the command of the British contingent serving in Germany under Prince Ferdinand of Brunswick. Consequently, Wolfe was no sooner landed at Portsmouth on 1 November than he was soliciting Ligonier for a job there too – perhaps even a cavalry command.[4]

1
Politicking and Preparations

Ligonier was initially unimpressed by Wolfe's sudden reappearance out of the blue and promptly informed him on 9 November that; "The King will not give leave for anyone to serve in Germany without an Employment and at present I know of no one that will suit you" but then he softened the blow by inviting him up to London as soon as "you have seen your Regiment, and put the Recruiting Service on the best and most expeditious footing".[5]

To all appearances there was no great urgency in the invitation and at first Ligonier may only have wanted Wolfe to give him a proper briefing on the situation in North America at first hand. However, by the time the interview actually took place Wolfe had decided to put himself forward for the chief command. He had already taken the opportunity, when he apologised to William Pitt for leaving Louisburg, to rather artlessly declare that "I have no objection to serving in America, and particularly in the river St. Lawrence, if any operations are to be carried on there."[6] Although, for his part, Ligonier may not have been quite so forthcoming, the old Field Marshal was actually quite receptive to this proposal, for he knew Amherst's limitations as well as his qualities. Afterwards James wrote his general a decidedly disingenuous letter:[7]

> Upon my arrival in England, I learnt that the command in America had devolved upon you and that an order was gone to keep me there.[8] I went immediately to the Marshal and told him that I had no objection to serving in that country and was ready to return upon the first order. We had some discourse upon the navigation of the River St. Lawrence and upon the project of besieging Quebec, and I found it was a settled plan to carry on two separate attacks, one on the side of Lake George and one up the river. This much passed at our first conversation with the addition that I expressed my desire to go up the River but to be excused from taking the chief direction of such a weighty enterprise.

Like Amherst, we may dismiss the professed reluctance of the last sentence as pure humbug, particularly as it was followed shortly afterwards by the announcement that Wolfe had indeed been nominated to the command; "and I find nothing encouraging in the undertaking," he continued, "but the warmest & most earnest desire to discharge so great a trust to your satisfaction as my General, and to his Majesty and the Publick. I shall spare no pains, and shou'd be happy if the sacrifice of my own health & constitution, or even my Life, cou'd any how contribute to bring this bloody war, to an honourable & speedy conclusion."

It was, if one may borrow Captain Caroline Scott's inimitable turn of phrase, "enough to make a dog spew." The reality of the matter is without doubt that Wolfe had absconded from Nova Scotia with the sole intention of obtaining a command more to his liking. Disappointingly, he found there were apparently no vacancies in Germany or anywhere else in Europe, but Quebec still remained to be taken in the next year's campaign, and he was now very conveniently on the spot in London when the crucial decisions about the operation were being made.

Common decency may have compelled his outward show of deference to Amherst, but Wolfe's eagerness for an independent command is all too clear from the speed with which he drew up his own projected plan of operations – a plan which proceeded from the first on the assumption that he and not Amherst would have the chief command of the river expedition. The Commander-in-Chief North America was to be relegated to a supporting role in the backwoods of Upper New York, while his notional subordinate was to have the glory of taking Quebec. In fact, by the time Wolfe protested his innocence to Amherst it was all over. He had "volunteered" for the job to Billy Pitt on 22 November and first spoke with Ligonier on 1 December. Immediately afterwards the Field Marshal and the Minister conferred and agreed upon the matter. No one bothered to speak to Amherst. Instead, Wolfe's name was put forward to the King and within the week James was summoned to a conference with "some of the principal officers of state" and there invited to set out his plans and requirements.

Once again, he found there was to be a three-pronged attack on Canada. In the west, the capture of Fort Duquesne and Colonel Bradstreet's surprise seizure of Fort Frontenac during the previous summer was now to be followed up by an expedition against Fort Niagara under Colonel Prideaux. Although this was to be the smallest of the three operations, it was a highly important one. Capture of Niagara would not only completely seal off the overland route between Canada and Louisiana, and thus prevent the retreat of the French Army in that direction, it would also turn the flank of the defensive positions along the Upper New York frontier. Here Amherst was destined to go where Abercromby had failed, take Ticonderoga and Fort St. Frederic (Crown Point) and then push northwards to Montreal. Wolfe, meanwhile, was to sail up the St. Lawrence and launch a direct assault on the Canadian capital, Quebec. It seems to have been envisaged that Wolfe would be able to do so in concert with Amherst, or at the very least he would draw off sufficient French troops from the Lake George frontier to make life easier for his chief. Indeed, in May 1759 Wolfe predicted to his Uncle Walter that "If I find that the enemy is strong, audacious, and well commanded, I shall proceed with the utmost caution and circumspection, giving Mr Amherst time to use his superiority. If they are timid, weak, and ignorant, we shall push them with more vivacity, that we may before the summer is gone go to assist the Commander-in-Chief."[9] In other words, if the French position at Quebec should prove too strong he would content himself with containing it until Amherst turned up. He was to reckon, however, without Amherst's foot-dragging; and it also proved to be the British, not the French, who were ignorant of what awaited them.

The biggest problem Wolfe faced at this stage was in fact a lack of hard information on his objective. Unlike comparable European fortresses, Quebec was virtually unknown to the outside world and intelligence concerning it was pretty well limited to a by-now outdated map which fortuitously happened to be contained in a 1744 *History of New France*, and to a report by an Engineer officer named Patrick Mackellar, who had been held in the city for a time after his capture at Fort Oswego in 1756. Unsurprisingly, Mackellar had not been allowed to see very much and the information which he was able to provide turned to be quite out of date – at least in detail – but the broad outlines were straightforward enough.

Quebec occupied a triangular position on a high rock on the north or left bank of the St. Lawrence River more or less at the point at which the river widens dramatically into a great estuary some 700 miles from the Atlantic. On one side was the broad cliff-girt river itself, and on another was a much smaller tributary called the St. Charles River. The only practicable avenue of approach was from the western or landward side, which was understood to be covered by a quite inadequate line of fortifications. The trick was to get there. From the very outset, as he explained to his uncle, Wolfe was alive to the possibilities of landing a substantial force above the city. However, it was by no means certain that it would be possible to get past Quebec and into the upper river in the first place. He therefore proceeded on the assumption that he would have to effect his initial landing somewhere on the Beauport Shore, just downstream from Quebec, then fight his way across the St. Charles river, before swinging around to attack the city from the west. It was unfortunate that a force of New Englanders had tried and failed to take the city by this route in 1690, but until he actually arrived on the spot and could have a proper look at his objective, and weigh up the possibilities, it was the only plan he had to work with.

In order to accomplish this great design Wolfe initially asked for "the following corps as a part of the army to act in the river viz. Bragg's (28th), Otway's (35th), Amherst's (15th), Kennedy's (43rd), Anstruther's (58th), two battalions of Americans (60th) and the three companies of Grenadiers in Louisburg".[10] Ligonier rightly considered this force insufficient, and discussed taking a battalion from Ireland and all the grenadier companies from the Gibraltar garrison, but in the end it was resolved to add three more complete battalions: Lascelles' 47th, Webb's 48th and Fraser's 78th Highlanders,[11] who were of course already in North America, besides a battalion of marines, and if possible to divert some troops previously earmarked for the West Indies as well.

This careful attention to his requirements must no doubt have been highly gratifying to the young general, but the question of commanding them turned out to be less straightforward. Wolfe rather pompously informed Ligonier that unless "he would give me the assistance of such officers as I should name to him he would do me a great kindness to appoint some other person to the chief direction. This I fear was not understood as it deserved to be . . ."[12] He should, of course, have known better, for while commanders were normally given a pretty free hand in appointing their own protégés and clients to junior staff positions, it was a different matter when it came to operational subordinates – in this case his three brigadiers. Wolfe wanted Robert Monckton, James Murray and Ralph Burton. The first had been in Nova Scotia since 1752, had taken Fort Beausejour in 1755 and since then served as lieutenant governor of the colony. He had not taken part in the Louisburg expedition, but he was generally regarded as a capable officer with considerable experience of North American conditions. Murray, a prickly character first com-missioned as a second lieutenant in Wynyard's 4th Marines on 2 February 1740, at first seems an odder choice, for he and Wolfe did not get on from the outset. Although Wolfe been impressed by his energy during the siege of Louisburg, he could not refrain from referring to him as "my old adversary" – apparently recalling a clash during the inquest into the Rochefort fiasco. However, Murray was also lieutenant colonel of Amherst's 15th Foot and while he was therefore likely to display more loyalty towards his colonel than to his general, his name probably went forward as a diplomatic sop to the displaced commander-in-chief. Per-haps because of this, for his third choice Wolfe wanted an undoubted friend, Ralph Burton of the 48th, but instead he had George Townshend forced on him.

Townshend's only discernible qualifications for the job were his political connections. Although he subsequently rose to high rank, he was certainly not a professional soldier. Born in 1724 he had joined the Army as a volunteer in 1742 and cheerfully occupied a succession of minor staff jobs. Latterly, he was one of Cumberland's ADCs and by 1748 was a captain and lieutenant colonel in the Footguards. At that point, however, he fell out with Cumberland, resigned from the Army and turned to politics until the Duke's fall re-opened the way to a military career. He returned to the Army with the brevet rank of colonel but no regimental commission and no job. On the other hand, Townshend was not only a nephew of the Duke of Newcastle but he had been Billy Pitt's closest ally in promoting and piloting an important Militia Bill through Parliament. He was thus in the happy situation of having powerful friends on both sides of the ruling coalition. Now he called in old favours and, as Horace

Walpole put it, "thrust himself again into the service."[13] Wolfe was unimpressed and gave way with bad grace and a letter of welcome that whilst polite and conventionally effusive, contained a barbed reference to his unwanted subordinate's lack of experience.[14] It was hardly a good start.

The brigadiers aside, Wolfe generally got his way in the nomination of the lesser appointments, for this was of course one of the traditional opportunities for the exercise of patronage granted to senior officers. As Francis Grose put it,

> If any appointments, such as extra-engineer, brigade-major, inspector of the works, or resident commissary, happen to fall within your disposal, be sure to give them all in your own regiment, and to persons who do not want them and are incapable of doing the business. The less they are qualified to act, the greater the obligation to you, and the more evident the demonstration of your power. It will show that your favour is sufficient to enable a man to hold and to discharge any office, however deficient his knowledge of the duties.[15]

In pursuance of this happy principle Wolfe wrote as early as 20 December to his childhood friend Colonel George Warde, at Squerries, offering him the post of either adjutant general or quartermaster general. As it happened, Warde had already secured a job in Germany, so instead Wolfe gave the adjutant general's job to another friend, Captain Isaac Barre. Guy Carleton became his quartermaster general despite some initial opposition from the King, while Patrick Mackellar was the obvious choice as engineer, since he was perhaps the only man on the expedition who had actually seen Quebec. Both Wolfe's Aides de Camp, Hervey Smith ("Little Smith") of the 15th and Tom Bell of the Marines, had worked for him at Louisburg and both, oddly enough, had been wounded there, which might have struck some as ominous.[16] On 28 January Wolfe was writing to Major Alexander Murray of the 45th Foot at Louisburg, offering him the command of the small provisional battalion to be formed from that garrison's grenadier companies and he was also able to employ both Delaune and Carden in command of light infantry companies, as he had wanted to do the year before.

Somehow, amidst all the bustle of patronage and preparation, James also found time to renew an earlier acquaintanceship at Bath with a Miss Katherine Lowther, and to propose and be accepted. It was no doubt a typically hurried pre-embarkation affair and none of their presumed correspondence survives, but there was little enough time for dalliance, for he sailed from Spithead on 14 February, arrived at Halifax on 30 April and was at Louisburg two weeks later.

There, his troubles began with the news that his father had died on 26

March, and the discovery that rather less troops than expected were waiting for him. A certain level of wastage had been anticipated, but the assumption that this could be made good through local recruiting in North America had proved, according to Amherst at least, to be a mistake. Nor had any reinforcements come from the West Indies. Instead of the projected 12,000 men, Wolfe was to have only 400-odd officers and just over 7,000 regular infantry, besides 300 gunners and a battalion of marines. Nevertheless, he still expected to pick up three companies of grenadiers and hoped to have at least one of the three companies of light infantry from the Louisburg garrison as well. Unfortunately, the orders which the governor, Brigadier Whitmore, had actually received from London directed him to give up the three grenadier companies, but made no mention of providing any other troops. Consequently, when Wolfe asked him on 19 May for the grenadiers, and for one or more of the companies of light infantry, "sleepy old Whitmore" very coldly advised him that the grenadiers were at his disposal whenever he wanted them, but that he had no orders concerning his light infantry. In short, he quite flatly refused to part with any of them, even although Wolfe offered him some of his New England Rangers in their place.[17] Wolfe had 546 of the latter, besides officers, and disparagingly dismissed them to his Uncle Walter as "six new raised companies of North American Rangers – not complete, and the worst soldiers in the universe."[18] This unkind remark has been held against him ever since, not least because only one of the companies, Benonie Dank's, had not been at Louisburg the year before. In fact Joseph Gorham's "Old Company" dated back to the first capture of the place in 1745. Wolfe, nevertheless, was no blinkered martinet. He knew well the Rangers' true quality and their capabilities, but he was about to conduct a regular operation for which he already had far fewer regular troops than he had counted on and was thoroughly disgusted by Whitmore's refusal to help. All he could do was to make sure that those men he took with him were up to the job.

Wolfe's orders for May of 1759 are taken up with instructions for his officers to check the condition of both men and arms, and to ensure that each soldier was provided with thirty-six rounds of ammunition, besides a good reserve packed in casks on each transport. They were also to take the rather elementary step of checking "the ammunition as is delivered to them, that they may be sure it fits their arms". So bad was this particular problem that the Board of Ordnance had been forced to reduce bullets in size from 14 to 14½ to the pound in order to ensure that they *would* fit. This was done only as recently as 1752 so it was inevitable that considerable quantities of the larger size would still have been in store. There was also a further complication in that some of the light infantry and rangers were armed with carbines, which took a yet smaller ball, as did the captured French fusils which Wolfe ordered issued to his officers. John Knox of the

43rd, for one, was particularly pleased with this last measure as he and his fellow officers had hitherto been doing duty with ordinary Land Pattern firelocks, after having been ordered to lay aside their impractical espontoons the year before.

Just as importantly, a large number of flat-bottom boats, whaleboats and cutters were also assembled and the troops then proceeded to practise landing from them, as Knox recorded on 30 May:

> The first brigade of the army, with the Louisbourg grenadiers, landed today for exercises; they performed several manoeuvres in presence of general officers, such as charging in line of battle, forming the line into columns and reducing them; dispersing, rallying and again forming in columns, and in line of battle alternately, with several other evolutions; which were all so well executed, as to afford the highest satisfaction to the generals . . . The troops have been daily engaged in these exercises, whenever the weather permitted.

Such rehearsals obviously made sense, but just as revealing is another passage in Knox's invaluable journal, in which he wrote:

> I flattered myself that I should have seen the Grenadier companies of the garrison reviewed by General Wolfe, but it was over before I could get there. I was told they went through all their manoeuvres and evolutions with great exactness and spirit, according to a new system of discipline; and his Excellency was highly pleased with their performance. Some commanding officers of corps, who expected also to be reviewed in their turn, told the General by way of apology, that by their regiments having long been cantoned, they had not in their power to learn or practise this new exercise; to which he answered 'Poh! poh! new exercise, – new fiddlestick! if they are otherwise well disciplined and will fight, that's all I require of them.'[19]

The new exercise was presumably the alternate firing, but whatever his personal views on the manifold shortcomings of the old-fashioned and impractical "chequer" still being practised by some of his battalions, Wolfe obviously knew better than to follow Grose's satirical advice and begin by "overturning their whole routine of discipline" on the very eve of embarkation.

That embarkation finally got underway at the beginning of June and all in all the senior naval officer, Vice Admiral Charles Saunders, initially had no fewer than 162 vessels under his command: twenty-one liners varying in size from the 50-gun *Sutherland* to his own *Neptune* (90), five frigates, fourteen sloops, two bomb vessels, a single cutter and no less than 119 transports of varying shapes and sizes.[20] All of them, moreover, were at

Wolfe's disposal for as long as he had occasion for them and on 27 June the first British troops were set ashore on the Isle de Orleans, in the very throat of the St. Lawrence estuary. Quebec lay just four miles away across the water.

2
The River War

Wolfe soon discovered that the French had anticipated him and were busily digging in above the Beauport Shore, in precisely the area where he had planned to effect his landing. That they were also there in some considerable strength is a sad indictment of Amherst. The Marquis de Montcalm had taken the calculated risk of switching five of his eight regular battalions away from the Upper New York frontier, which had hitherto been the principal theatre of war, in order to meet this new threat, and what was more he got away with it. It is true that both Fort Carillon at Ticonderoga and Fort St. Frederic on Lake Champlain had to be abandoned (and blown up) in July, and a retreat made up the lake to a more northerly defensive position at Isle aux Noix, but Amherst made no attempt to exploit his considerable numerical superiority. Far from mounting a powerful offensive aimed at breaking through this new position and moving on Montreal, he instead idled the summer away in constructing a new and quite unnecessary fort of his own on the site of Fort St. Frederic at Crown Point.

In the meantime, at Quebec, untroubled by a poorly executed attempt to destroy the fleet by means of fire ships on the night of 28 June, Wolfe started landing his army in earnest. The Isle de Orleans served as an admirable base-camp, but he needed to bring his men closer to their objective if they were to fight. Dalling's Light Infantry and the advance elements of Monckton's brigade were put ashore at Beaumont, on the undefended south shore of the St. Lawrence, on the evening of the 29th. The rest of the brigade, comprising the 15th, 43rd, 48th and 78th Foot, also landed there next morning and despite some harassment from Canadian militia in the woods, marched westwards to seize a useful position at Point Levis, nearly opposite Quebec itself.[21] Initially this landing was no more than a pre-emptive move aimed at denying the French the opportunity to place a battery on the promontory and so prevent Saunders' ships from moving past the city and into the upper river. However, on 2 July, despite complaining of a painful bladder, Wolfe carried out a reconnaissance along the south shore and made the happy discovery that it would be possible to establish a battery of his own at Pointe aux Peres (just to the west of Point Levis), which could fire directly into Quebec.

So far so good. But while Wolfe had been getting a feel for the lie of the land, Saunders had officers out charting the St. Lawrence and now had to advise the General of the previously unsuspected Beauport Bank. This was a wide expanse of rocky shallows in front of the Shore which would prevent his ships coming in close enough to provide naval gunnery support for a landing there. Without such fire-support that landing would probably have little chance of success and so Wolfe's attention naturally turned instead to the area above the city. Shortly after arriving at Louisburg in May, he had discussed the likely options for attacking Quebec in a letter to his Uncle Walter. Although proceeding from the assumption that he would initially be able to establish a beachhead on the Beauport Shore, he subsequently anticipated "a smart action at the passage of the river St. Charles, unless we can steal a detachment up the river St. Lawrence, and land them three, four, five miles, or more, above the town, and get time to entrench so strongly that they won't care to attack."[22] Now, apparently unable to land at Beauport, let alone get across the St. Charles, his projected landing in the upper river had to be brought forward.

Gorham's Rangers and 270 men detached from Murray's brigade (presumably his regimental light companies) were ordered to reconnoitre the north shore for a suitable landing place between Anse de Meres at the mouth of the river and St. Michel, about three miles further upstream. At the same time, Townshend's brigade was placed on standby to launch a diversionary attack on the eastern flank of the Beauport Lines at Montmorency.

Murray duly reported that a landing at St. Michel appeared practicable and so in the early hours of the morning of 9 July all the grenadier companies were landed a short distance below the falls at the mouth of the Montmorency River. As soon as the beachhead was secure, Townshend's brigade followed. The diversionary force was now in place, but the second phase of the operation had to be delayed. Saunders was for the moment unable to wrest control of the basin from the French gunboats and floating batteries, and so get his ships above the city. Wolfe was unimpressed, and in the meantime, therefore, two of Murray's battalions and the rest of the guns were also brought ashore at Montmorency.

Then on 15 July, two days after the bombardment of Quebec began, the grenadiers were concentrated again on the Isle de Orleans for "a particular Purpose". Next day Wolfe had had a conference with Saunders "concerning the projected Descent" and afterwards wrote an interesting letter to Monckton at Point Levis, discussing an attack to be launched straight across the basin.[23]

> . . . If the Rafts are found to answer, they will carry your attack directly across the River, opposite the right of the Enemy's encampment [as viewed from Monckton's position at Beaumont]. But

if the Rafts are defective, we must make the best shift we can, w^h. the long Boats of the Fleet. I only wait the naval preparations – everything is ready on our side; and I flatter myself, that the prodigious fire from hence [the batteries at Montmorency] will make the enterprise easy. There is a woody Gully upon the Right of the French Camp; The Highland Reg^t. might penetrate there & to the left of it & gain their Flank: the Redoubt must be vigorously attack'd & kept, it is out of Musquet shot from their lines, & cou'd not either be supported by them or retaken <u>when</u> in our possession. The Corps of Troops encamped above Beauport, will probably move towards the upper attack, or if they do not, the road is open to us, & we shall fall upon them behind . . .

It has generally been assumed that the "projected Descent" discussed with Saunders and Monckton's attack across the basin were to have been one and the same. Upon closer consideration, however, this interpretation is doubtful to say the least. For a start there is that casual reference to "the upper attack" and we also know that on that very same night, the 16th, the Admiral intended to run some of his ships past Quebec and into the upper river. It must, therefore, be *this* operation which Wolfe was referring to when he spoke in the letter of awaiting the completion of the "naval preparations". With the imminent prospect of being able to effect a landing at St. Michel within a day or two at the most, it is quite inconceivable that he could have been planning to mount a full dress frontal assault on the Beauport defences in the meantime. On the contrary, Wolfe actually seems to have intended that Monckton should only launch a very noisy diversionary attack against the Beauport position, in order to distract attention away from the "upper attack" at St. Michel. Wolfe assumed that the French reserve would be drawn away from above Beauport to deal with that attack, but in the event of Monckton's diversion being successful in fixing their attention, he would be able to march across and attack the rear of the French army.

It may well be, however, that Wolfe was going to be stretching himself too thinly with this cunning plan, but in the event the attempt to enter the river was not made until the night of the 18th. The *Diana* (36) went aground, but the *Sutherland* (50) and *Squirrel* (20) both ran safely past Quebec and into the upper river accompanied by two sloops and two transports. As Wolfe later reported to Pitt this "enabled me to reconnoitre the country above, where I found the same attention on the enemy's side, and great difficulties on ours, arising from the nature of the ground, and the obstacles to our communication with the fleet. But what I feared most, was, that if we should land between the town and the river Cape Rouge, the body first landed could not be reinforced before they were attacked by the enemy's whole army." [24]

Nevertheless, putting these concerns aside, Wolfe decided to seize the vital moment and proceed with the St. Michel landing. On the morning of 20 July the grenadier companies, still waiting patiently at the Isle de Orleans, were ordered to hold themselves in readiness while Saunders busied himself in preparing boats for the artillery. In the meantime, as time was obviously going to be of the essence, orders were also sent for Monckton to embark part of his brigade and all his light infantry immediately. Instead of mounting an elaborate, and perhaps futile, diversionary attack, they were to be rather more sensibly employed in securing the beachhead at St. Michel. Wolfe also stressed that "If you cou'd be here, a little before high Water, we should have time to fetch another load of Troops, before the Tide ebbs . . ."[25]

Then, just as suddenly, the operation was cancelled. That same afternoon Wolfe had to tell Monckton that "Particular circumstances make it necessary to delay our attempt for a few days . . ." It is not difficult to guess what these circumstances were, for in his subsequent despatch to Pitt Wolfe spoke of calling off the landing after finding the French moving guns into the area. The success of the operation would obviously hinge on his being able to establish a beachhead at St. Michel and then concentrate all or most of his forces there before Montcalm turned up. In theory it ought to have been possible to do just that without a diversionary attack at Beauport, just so long as Townshend's and Murray's brigades could be embarked and brought upstream on the tide faster than the French could march overland. The unwelcome appearance of those guns now suggested otherwise, for where there were guns there must presumably be troops as well. As Wolfe readily confessed, if the initial landing were to be seriously opposed or at least heavily counter-attacked before the rest of the army could be brought up then the whole operation would not only fail, but would probably result in such heavy losses as to require a retreat out of the St. Lawrence altogether. As it happened, there were in fact only a few militia in the area at the time, but Wolfe could not know that and indeed it is obvious that he was particularly uneasy about the lack of good intelligence on the French strength and dispositions.

Such was his concern on this particular point, that his next move was to send Lieutenant Colonel Carleton even further up the river with the grenadiers of Monckton's brigade and some rangers "for intelligence". Carleton duly landed at Pointe aux Trembles, some twenty miles above Quebec on the following day, and kidnapped a number of civilians – refugees from the city for the most part – who were questioned and subsequently returned to the city under a flag of truce. It is unlikely, however, that Carleton learned very much and after a planning conference on 23 July Wolfe's attention turned in earnest to the Beauport Lines. Nevertheless, he was far from sanguine. On the 25th he wrote to Monckton asking him to send two companies of Boisrond's Marines over to him at the Montmorency camp next day in order to "mask our real intentions", and also ordered "a Corps of Troops" to be ready to accompany him up the Montmorency river for a reconnaissance in force. If a crossing point could be discovered the army might thereby be able to get into the rear of the Beauport Lines and thus avoid having to mount a frontal attack. In the meantime, he reasoned that his "escort", comprising a composite light infantry battalion led by Lieutenant Colonel William Howe, and a part of Murray's brigade, ought to be strong enough to seize and hold the ford until Townshend brought the rest of the troops up. Unfortunately, once again Wolfe found himself anticipated and as he related to Pitt: "In reconnoitring the river Montmorenci, we found it fordable at a place about three miles up; but the opposite bank was entrenched, and so steep and so woody, that it was to no purpose to attempt a passage there."[26] Traditionally it is reckoned that a reconnaissance party has not probed far enough until it has been shot at, and this was certainly the case here, for Wolfe and his men were twice attacked:

Early in the morning a Party of Indians crossed the ford & were beat back by our People. About noon they came over in greater numbers – drove two comps. of foot, who retired in great confusion & disordered the Battalion. Coll. Howe's Light infantry attacked their flank & endeavoured to surround them, & Br. Murray detached two Comp's of Otway's to get upon their right flank. The Enemy put into Disorder & defeated & driven over the water. In these two Skirmishes we had near 40 killed & wounded – chiefly from the opposite Bank of the River, by the indiscreet pursuit of some of our people.[27]

Thus thwarted in his attempts to manoeuvre around the French army, both above and below Quebec, Wolfe was at last faced with the distinctly unpalatable prospect of tackling the Beauport defences head-on. For the most part the chain of redoubts and entrenchments was sited on top of the wooded cliffs overlooking the shore, but his attention was still drawn to that apparently isolated redoubt on the beach, which was to have been Brigadier Monckton's objective had his diversionary attack gone in on the 17th or 18th[28]. As Wolfe afterwards (and a touch disingenuously) explained to Pitt:

I proposed to make myself master of a detach'd redoubt near to the water's edge, and whose situation appeared to be out of musket shot of the intrenchment upon the hill; if the enemy supported this detached place, it would necessarily bring on an engagement, which we most wished for; and if not, I should have it in my power to examine their situation, so as to be able to determine where we could best attack them.

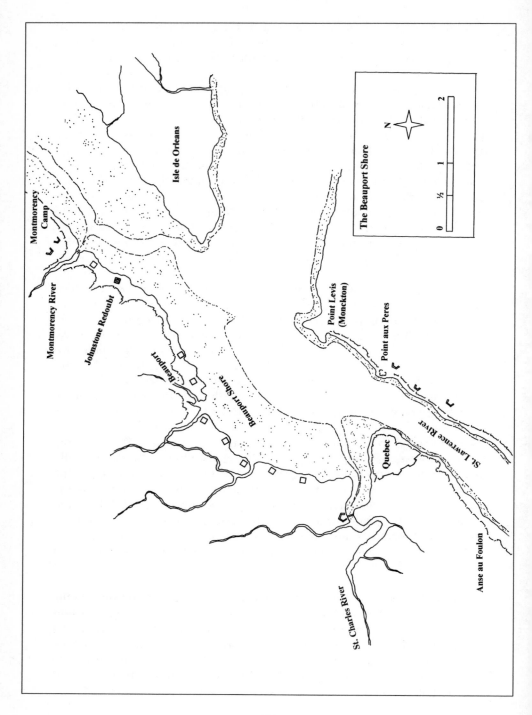

Admiral Saunders had already prepared two "cats" (Whitby colliers employed as transports) as landing vessels and now James Cook, the master or navigating officer of HMS *Pembroke* (60), "said he believed the cats could be carried within 40 or 50 yards of the redoubts. I told him at the time that I would readily compound for 150 or 200 yards, which would have been near enough had the upper redoubt been as far from the enemy's entrenchments as it appeared from our camp to be."[29] Wolfe's stated intention at first, therefore, was no more than to run the cats ashore with four companies of grenadiers aboard under the command of Lieutenant Colonel Ralph Burton, seize the redoubt and see what reaction this produced. At the same time, according to John Knox's account, on the night of 27 July "a verbal order was sent to each regiment to have an expert Officer, Serjeant, and twenty-five chosen men in readiness, at a moment's warning, for a very particular service . . . this duty fell to my lot."[30] Once again the "particular service" was never revealed, but Wolfe's more formal orders for the operation, issued on 29 July (just after another failed French attempt to destroy the fleet by means of fire-rafts), are not without interest, although as usual the drafting of them left something to be desired:[31]

Two hundred men of the Royal American battalion, with their blankets, and two days provision ready dressed, to be in readiness below the Cove at eight in the morning, to embark in four flat-bottom boats; this detachment is intended to reinforce the company of grenadiers, if there should be occasion: the boats are to row up with the flood, but out of cannon shot, till they are opposite the upper redoubt, when they must rest upon their arms, and wait for further orders.

Anstruther's regiment, the light infantry, and rangers, are to march at nine, under colonel Howe's command, about a mile into the woods, towards the ford where the Canadians and Indians are encamped; this body must skirt about within the wood from the camp of the light infantry to the road, but so as just to be seen from the opposite side of the river by the enemy. As major Hussey's corps[32] will have been up most of the night, they are to be left to guard the camp of the light infantry: colonel Howe will lengthen his line of march, so as to appear numerous; the remaining battalion[33] will get under arms when the water begins to ebb, in readiness to cross the ford, if there should be absolute necessity for so doing; in the mean time they will continue their work with all possible diligence and assiduity.

If ships can be brought near enough to operate, and the wind is fair, an attack will be made upon one of the enemy's most detached works, in aid of which attack the artillery from hence must be employed.

175

Brigadier general Townshend will be pleased to give such direction as he thinks most fit for service upon this head.

In general the cannon can't be fired, nor even be brought up to fire, till it is visible that the attack will be made.

If the day is over hot, and no wind, this operation can't take place.

If the battalions should march, colonel Howe must return to his camp in the most secret manner. The marines must be brought into the two redoubts where Lascelles's regiment takes post; the remaining part of the Americans into the great redoubt, Hessen's company[34] into the fortified house; Anstruther's and the light infantry will be ready to join the army.

For all his military virtues, Wolfe never did learn to draft a coherent dispatch or set of orders – or to employ a competent adjutant general or a military secretary to do it for him. Equally confusingly, these orders referred to two quite different fords. The first, where Howe was to mount his demonstration, was the one above the falls which Wolfe had reconnoitred on the 26th, while the second actually lay on the shore below the falls and was only usable at low tide. The latter was to assume some importance once the operation got underway, but Wolfe's penultimate paragraph proved prophetic, for a flat-calm next morning meant that the attack had to be delayed until the 31st.

Even then, it stalled almost at once. The grenadiers and 2/60th duly embarked at 9 a.m. and rendezvoused with Monckton's 15th and 78th from Point Levis about an hour later. After waiting in mid-stream for high water, the two cats were duly run ashore at 11 a.m. only for Burton to realise that his objective was much higher up the beach than expected and so far from being isolated was in fact adequately covered by the entrenchments above. Under a heavy fire Wolfe was duly summoned and as he afterwards told Saunders with a certain touch of pride, "I was no less than three times struck with the splinters in that ship, and had my stick knocked out of my hand with a cannon-ball while I was on board reconnoitring the position and movements of the enemy." Those movements appeared to indicate a certain disorder and confusion in the enemy ranks" and "remarking their situation much better than I ever could do before" he therefore took the fateful decision to mount a frontal assault. As he explained rather spikily to Pitt:

The place where the attack was intended, has these advantages. Our artillery could be brought into use. The greatest part, or even the whole of the troops, might act at once; and the retreat (in case of a repulse) was secure – at least for a certain time of the tide. Neither one nor other of these advantages can any where else be found. The Enemy were indeed posted upon a commanding Eminence – The beach upon which the troops were drawn up, was of deep mud, with holes, and cut by several gullies – The hill to be ascended very steep, and not every where practicable – The enemy numerous in their intrenchments, and their fire hot – If the attack had succeeded, our loss must certainly have been very great, and theirs inconsiderable, from the shelter which the neighbouring woods afforded them – The river of St. Charles still remained to be passed, before the town was invested. All these circumstances I considered; but the desire to act in conformity to the King's intentions, induced me to make this trial, persuaded that a victorious army finds no difficulties.

It seems unlikely that Wolfe actually took very much persuading to reach this decision, for as he also admitted in the letter to Saunders he had always "had it in view" and half of Monckton's brigade was already at hand in boats to support the initial landing. Unfortunately, he reckoned without the tide.

In order to run the cats as close inshore as possible the first phase of the operation had been launched at or just after high water. Now, in order to bring Townshend's and Murray's brigades across the Montmorency it was necessary to wait for the tide to fall far enough to uncover the lower ford on the beach below the falls. This delay, while both the grenadiers and Monckton's men waited offshore, compromised Billy Howe's demonstration against the upper ford and gave the French time to shift two battalions of regulars (*Guyenne* and *Royal-Roussillon*) across from there to support the men in the threatened trenches. Nevertheless, although the brigadiers had been decidedly unenthusiastic about the operation beforehand, there was a palpable air of excitement amongst the troops themselves, well captured by our friend John Knox of the 43rd Foot over at Point Levis. His journal records the steady escalation of the operation and the decision, when orders came at noon for the 43rd to stand by, that "the regiment should embark, land, and fight by companies under their own Officers, which afforded the highest satisfaction to the soldiers".[35]

It was all the more unfortunate, therefore, that when the grenadiers finally moved in at about 5 p.m. their boats promptly grounded on a previously unsuspected rocky ledge, and there was a further delay of about half an hour while Wolfe went off in a boat with some naval officers to find a way through. Once they finally made it to the shore, their orders were to form up in four bodies,[36] which, according to one of their officers they did as well as they could in waist-deep water. They were then supposed to wait for Monckton's brigade to land and for Townshend to bring the other two brigades across the Montmorency ford. HMS *Centurion*, meanwhile, had successfully suppressed the fire of the French battery above the Montmorency, but the "upper" battery was still very much in action. This was unfortunate for as soon as the grenadiers landed they came under fire from the battery and impetuously ran "like blockheads up to it" long before Monckton and his men could land.[37] Unsurprisingly, the French gunners took to their heels in the opposite direction, but such a storm of fire then came down on the grenadiers from the trenches above that they themselves were forced to take shelter in or behind the redoubt. Moreover, according to Knox, they now discovered that the hillside to their front was not only very steep, but the lower slopes were covered with an abattis – a precursor of barbed wire entanglements made up of felled trees and shrubs laid with their branches in the direction of an attacker. Unable to get forward and unwilling to fall back, the grenadiers started to take heavy casualties, especially amongst the officers. Providentially, however, at this point a sudden and extremely violent thunderstorm burst over the battlefield, reducing visibility to a few yards and stopping all the firing.

It has sometimes been suggested that had they not been so disorganised and poorly controlled by this time, the grenadiers might have been able to take advantage of this downpour to get up the cliffs and take the French position with the bayonet. Instead, Wolfe very sensibly and not a little courageously seized the opportunity to shut down the operation. He had already sent orders for the grenadiers to fall back on Monckton's battalions, which had finally landed, but being uneasily aware that the tide had already turned, "I thought it most advisable, not to persevere in so difficult an attack, lest (in case of a repulse) the retreat of Brigadier Townshend's corps might be hazardous and uncertain." Under cover of the torrential rain, therefore, the available boats were hastily loaded with as many wounded and unwounded men as they could stow and sent off, while Wolfe and the greater part of the 78th Highlanders marched along the beach and crossed to safety by the Montmorency ford.

It had been an expensive exercise which Wolfe reckoned had cost 210 killed and 230 wounded (or 443 killed and wounded according to Knox), including four officers killed on the spot and twenty-nine wounded.[38] Next day he minced few of his words in an order which managed to rebuke the grenadiers and yet at the same time encourage both them and the rest of the army to do better next time:

> The check which the grenadiers met with yesterday will, it is hoped, be a lesson to them for the future. They ought to know that such impetuous, irregular, and unsoldier-like proceeding destroys all order, and makes it impossible for the commander to form any disposition for an attack, and puts it out of the general's power to execute his plan. The grenadiers could not suppose that they alone could beat the French army, and therefore it was necessary that the corps under brigadiers Monckton and Townshend should have time

to join, that the attack might be general. The very first fire of the enemy was sufficient to repulse men who had lost all sense of order and military discipline. Amherst's and the Highland regiment alone, by the soldier-like and cool manner in which they formed, would undoubtedly have beat back the whole Canadian army, if they had ventured to attack them; the loss however is inconsiderable; and may, if the men shew a proper attention to their officers, be easily repaired when a favourable opportunity offers.[39]

3
Above the Town Again

Wolfe, as usual, displayed a less certain touch in dealing with his higher-ranking colleagues in the recriminations that followed. It is unlikely that he had ever got on with Townshend and there is evidence of their having clashed on at least two occasions since landing. Wolfe's journal for 7 July, for example, records "Some difference of opinion upon a point termed slight & insignificant & the Commander in Chief is threatened wth Parliamentary Inquiry into his Conduct for not consulting an inferior Officer & seeming to disregard his Sentiments!" Just what this refers to remains obscure, but it most likely had something to do with the arrangements for landing Townshend's brigade below the Montmorency, for the aristocratic amateur was the most likely of the brigadiers to have recourse to threats of Parliamentary action. Townshend himself records another difference of opinion on the 13th, but the most ominous sign of growing tension again appears in Wolfe's journal, this time in a note concerning the Montmorency operation in which he mentions: "Dislike of the Gen[l]. Officers and others to this Business – but nothing better propos'd by them."

In the meantime the business of the siege had to go on. Burton's grenadier companies were for the moment returned to their parent units and the 78th shipped back across to Point Levis. Then on 3 August Murray went back up the river with the 3/60th, and some rangers – the rest of his brigade being left at Montmorency in charge of the senior officer, Lieutenant Colonel Harry Fletcher of the 35th. Murray's primary mission on this occasion was to assist Rear Admiral Holmes in destroying the remaining French warships, which had taken refuge there, and above all to try and open a line of communication with General Amherst. Like Carleton, Murray attempted a landing at Pointe aux Trembles on 8 August, but by this time the French had moved some regular troops into the area. A Colonel de Bougainville had been put in charge of a flying column comprising picquets[40] drawn from all five of Montcalm's regular battalions, together with the blue-coated *Corps de Cavallerie* and some of the ubiquitous Canadian militia. Consequently, when Murray attempted to land he met with a rather hotter reception than Carleton had done and drew off again in short order. At least one report put his losses at 140 killed and wounded, including thirty seamen, but this seems far too high, particularly since the 3/60th only lost a total of two killed and twenty-nine wounded of all ranks in the period up to 2 September.[41]

Next day Murray landed instead on the south shore at St. Antoine and from there reported to Wolfe that the river was too low for the Navy to penetrate high enough to find the French ships. Nevertheless, on the 18th he had his men rowed further upstream under cover of darkness to Deschambault, where he successfully landed and destroyed a depot containing the spare kit of Montcalm's regular battalions. Some of Bougainville's men eventually turned up as well but, perhaps realising it was too late to save anything, merely contented themselves with an ineffectual harassing fire until Murray re-embarked. By now Wolfe had grown impatient and not a little anxious about the large number of boats which Murray had taken off with him. Orders were therefore sent to recall him and, leaving the 3/60th and the ships above Quebec, he eventually returned to Point Levis on the 25th with decidedly mixed news. On the plus side, some prisoners had informed him of Colonel William Johnson's[42] capture of Fort Niagara on 25 July and of the abandonment of Forts Carillon and St. Frederic. Encouragingly, the French commander, Brigadier Bourlamaque, had apparently retired to Isle aux Noix with just 3,000 men, but otherwise there was no word from Amherst and certainly no sign of him breaking through.

Back in May, Wolfe had written to his Uncle Walter that "If I find that the enemy is strong, audacious, and well commanded, I shall proceed with the utmost caution and circumspection, giving Mr Amherst time to use his superiority." Thwarted in all his attempts to outmanoeuvre and to bludgeon his way through the French defences, Wolfe had indeed turned to a more cautious and circumspect policy in August. Unable to bring the French Army to battle in the open, he took on the civilian population instead. To his prolonged bombardment of the near-defenceless city was now added a series of destructive raids up and down the shores of the St. Lawrence, burning village after village. At the time Wolfe publicly justified this policy as being in retaliation for attacks on sentries and foraging parties by local militia, but he had already anticipated it in a letter to Amherst on 6 March:[43]

> If, by accident in the River, by the Enemy's resistance, by sickness, or slaughter in the Army, or, from any other cause, we find, that Quebec is not likely to fall into our hands (persevering however to the last moment), I propose to set the Town on fire with Shells, to destroy the Harvest, Houses, & Cattle both above and below, to send off as many Canadians as possible to Europe, & to leave famine and desolation

behind me; belle resolution, & tres chretienne! but we must teach these Scoundrels to make war in a more gentlemanlike manner.

He also justified the policy to Pitt as having in part been carried out in the hope that it might provoke Montcalm into coming out to fight, but in reality there can have been little hope of that. All that can be said in Wolfe's defence is that destroying the Canadian settlements did at least have some military justification, but it cannot disguise an abiding impression that these punitive raids were born of frustration as much as policy. Another pointer to this may be a temporary collapse in Wolfe's health at this time and his confinement to bed on 19 August. Throughout his life he complained constantly of the state of his health and he is often portrayed as a man strong in spirit but cursed with a weak and sickly constitution. Yet was this really so? Physically, there may not have been so very much wrong with him. Whilst the symptoms may well have been real enough, there must also be a very strong suspicion that the causes were psychological rather than pathological. It is certainly worth bearing in mind that the three best known of his recorded periods of illness coincided with periods of acute personal stress. As we have seen, he fell ill immediately after his first battle at Dettingen in 1743, which was undoubtedly a traumatic experience for him. Significantly, he was also ill in Scotland, not as a result of any one dramatic event this time but during a period of acute frustration when he felt himself an exile on a foreign shore. Now he was ill again, and just as his first battle may not have matched his youthful expectations, his first truly independent command was also going wrong.

Wolfe certainly had reason enough to be depressed. In his despatch to Pitt written at the end of the month he admitted to the loss of ten officers and 173 men killed and a further 43 officers and 603 men wounded since arriving in the river. Yet all that he had to show for these losses was a devastated countryside and the partial destruction of the city by constant bombardment. As he grumbled in his last letter to his mother, "My antagonist has wisely shut himself up in inaccessible entrenchments, so that I can't get at him without spilling a torrent of blood, and that perhaps to little purpose." Moreover, he was at odds with his brigadiers and increasingly, it seems, with individual members of his personal staff as well. In fact relations with some of them were so bad that he subsequently destroyed that part of his journal written after 16 August, which, according to Tom Bell, "contained a careful account of the officers' ignoble conduct towards him in case of a Parliamentary enquiry." He was now just as much alone as he had been in Scotland and perhaps even more so. In these circumstances it is perhaps not so very surprising that his physical health once more gave way under the strain, or that he should go on to refer to "my plan of quitting the service which I am determined to do the first opportunity."[44]

At any rate, notwithstanding the gloomy pessimism of both this letter and his formal report to Pitt drawn up two days later,[45] Wolfe was about to rouse himself for one more attack. He knew only too well that if Quebec was not taken before the end of September, the fleet and most (if not all) of the army would have to withdraw from the river before the advancing pack-ice sealed its mouth. He actually seems to have been turning the matter of another attack over in his mind as early as 11 August and a week later was impatient for Murray to return in order to put it into operation. Perhaps it may even have been his anxiety at Murray's non-appearance which finally triggered his collapse on the 19th if its real causes were indeed nervous rather than physical. Ordinarily Wolfe was a firm believer in the advice which would later be offered by Grose to General Officers, Commanding-in-Chief, that: "As no other person in your army is allowed to be possessed of a single idea, it would be ridiculous, on any occasion, to assemble a council of war, or, at least, to be guided by their opinion: for, in opposition to yours, they must not trust to the most evident perception of their senses. It would be equally absurd and unmilitary to consult their convenience; even when it may be done without any detriment to the service: that would be taking away the most effectual method of exercising their obedience . . ." Nevertheless, despite his unhappy experience of such councils at Rochefort, Wolfe (still bed-ridden) formally asked on 28 August for his brigadiers' written opinion on three different options:[46]

1st. – in dry Weather a large Detachment may march in a day & a night so as to arrive at Beauport (fording the Montmorency 8 or 9 miles up) before day in the morning – it is likely they wou'd be discovered upon their march on both sides the River – If such a Detach[t]. penetrates on their entrenchments & the rest of the Troops are ready, the consequence is plain.

2[d]. If the Troops encamped here pass'd the Ford n[r]. the falling Water, & in the night march on directly towards the Point of Beauport – the light infantry have a good chance to get up the woody Hill, trying different places; & moving quick to the right, wou'd soon discover a proper place for the rest: the upper redoubt must be attack'd, & kept by a Company of Grenad[r]. – Brig[r]. Monckton must be ready off the Point of Beauport, to land when our People have got up the Hill – for which Signals may be appointed.[47]

3[dy]. All the chosen Troops of the Army attack at the Beauport at Low Water – a Division across the Ford an hour before, the other attack.

NB for the first – it is enough if the Water begins to fall a little before day light or about it.

For the other two, it wou'd be best to have it low water – about half an hour before day – . . .

In his letter to Admiral Saunders, two days later, Wolfe observed that, "My ill state of health hinders me from executing my own plan; it is of too desperate a nature to order others to execute." Not surprisingly, there has been considerable speculation by historians as to just what Wolfe's own plan entailed, but there can be little doubt that it was the first of these options, for the other two were merely variations upon the plan which had gone so badly wrong on 31 July. Wolfe readily admitted to Saunders that both planning and execution had been at fault on that occasion, but while propositions 2 and 3 addressed those faults to some extent, neither of them required his personal leadership. On the other hand, leading a considerable detachment, presumably of at least brigade-strength, on a desperate night march through the woods was indeed an operation which only he personally could, in all conscience, undertake.

His brigadiers certainly thought so too. After conferring at some length they responded that "that part of the Army which is proposed to march through the Woods nine miles up the Montmorenci to surprize their Camp is exposed to certain discovery, and to the disadvantage of a continual Wood fight." No one, of course, needed any reminding what had happened to Braddock in the woods by the Monongahela River back in '55. Nor were they particularly keen on the idea of another attempt on the Lines, at dawn or at any other time, for even if they should win through, there was still the infinitely depressing prospect of then having to fight their way across the St. Charles. Instead, they respectfully advocated evacuating the Montmorency camp and effecting a landing somewhere above the city, for "When we establish ourselves on the North Shore, the French General must fight us on our own Terms; We shall be betwixt him and his provisions, and betwixt him and their Army opposing General Amherst."

This paper was presented to Wolfe on the 29th and next day, in his letter to Saunders, he conceded that "The generals seem to think alike as to the operations; I, therefore, join with them, and perhaps we may find some opportunity to strike a blow." He was not, it may be gathered, very optimistic about the outcome of the move, which may account at least in part for his declared intention to quit the service. If so, however, his spirits were about to lift dramatically once the operation actually got underway, which it did with surprising rapidity. In accordance with a plan drafted by the brigadiers, the guns were withdrawn from the Montmorency position on 1 September and most of the troops followed next day. A substantial rearguard remained in position until the 3rd in the vain hope that Montcalm might be tempted to come out and fight, but as usual he failed to oblige. Apart from a 600-strong detachment (comprising the 2/60th and a battalion of marines) left to guard the stores and hospitals on the Isle de Orleans, the army was then concentrated at Point Levis, on the south shore. Once that had been done, the batteries there were left in charge of Lieutenant Colonel Burton with his own 48th Foot and some more marines, while everybody else marched upstream as far as the Etchemin river and embarked on the ships waiting there.

Monckton's First Brigade was now to comprise the 15th, 43rd and 3/60th with a total of 1,009 rank and file, while Townshend's Second Brigade, comprising the 28th, 47th and 78th, mustered 1,028 men, and Murray ended up with the 918 bayonets of the 35th, 58th and Louisburg Grenadiers.

Although the ships were by that time anchored off Cap Rouge, some thirteen miles above Quebec, orders for a landing still further upriver, just a little below Pointe aux Trembles, were issued on 8 September. However, as it was raining heavily the operation was first deferred in the hope of an improvement in the weather, and then at half past one the following morning it was postponed indefinitely. Notwithstanding Saunders had steadily been passing more and more ships up the river, the troops were wretchedly overcrowded on the available transports and so about half of them were set ashore again. According to an ambiguous entry in Townshend's journal, Wolfe went down the river in the rain "reconnoitering". The journal appears to imply that he went off on the 8th, but if so he saw little if anything to encourage him, for next day, presumably just after calling off the landing, he wrote another despondent report, this time to the Earl of Holderness. In it he described the brigadiers' conference and the move upriver, but expressed considerable pessimism as to the outcome. It is unfortunate that we do not know more about the next few hours for this was the crucial point in the campaign. Sick and dispirited, Wolfe's role had lately been an entirely passive one – the brigadiers were very much in charge and they had prevailed upon him to adopt a plan in which he reposed no confidence.

Now, rather to the brigadiers' consternation, his old spirit suddenly reasserted itself. Having unburdened himself to Holderness, Wolfe went off down the river again later that day and finally pitched upon a suitable landing place at the Anse au Foulon, only a short distance away from his earlier objective, St. Michel. As he did not live to justify himself afterwards, all manner of speculation has grown up over the years as to why Wolfe picked the Foulon, but there is in reality no mystery at all, for it was in just the right place. A landing could certainly be effected further upstream, near Pointe aux Trembles, with much less difficulty and danger. After all, both Carleton and Murray had been sent up with raiding parties in July and August, but at no time did Wolfe ever contemplate taking the whole army there, for once ashore he would then be nearly twenty miles away from Quebec. With the best will in the world that would allow the French at least a day, and perhaps more like two in order to prepare for his arrival before the city, particularly if the local commander, Colonel de Bougainville, did his duty and imposed every possible delay upon the British advance. The consequences of this might easily have been fatal. Just a year before, Montcalm had required only twenty-four hours to construct the line of fortifications at Ticonderoga, on which Abercromby had obligingly wrecked his army. There was no reason to suppose that, with the resources of Quebec at his back, Montcalm should not be able to throw up an equally formidable line in front of the city. With little or no room for manoeuvre, Wolfe's only options would have been an ignominious retreat or a near suicidal frontal assault.

Conversely, landing at the Foulon would quite literally deposit the army on the enemy's doorstep with all the consequent advantages of surprise, and of inconvenience to the French – above all, Montcalm would be forced to fight the British in the open. At the same time Wolfe could also achieve a more effective concentration of his own forces by bringing the 48th and 2/60th across from Point Levis and the Isle de Orleans respectively. Moreover the Foulon also offered yet another, as it turned out, quite crucial advantage – there was a narrow road traversing the cliff. It was steep, and it was apparently at least partially blocked by an abbatis, but were this to be cleared it presented Wolfe with the means to pass his troops up from the river very quickly indeed, and to get his guns up as well!

Next day Wolfe went back downriver again, this time taking his senior officers (rather unconvincingly disguised in "grenadiers' coats" and "coloured [i.e. civilian] cloaths") to a little outpost known as Gorham's Post No.1, which lay approximately halfway between Point Levis and the mouth of the Etchemin river. From there he pointed out the salient features of his objective and announced his intention of landing the army there in the early hours of 13 September.

This abrupt turnaround in Wolfe's spirits and the fact that he was no longer willing to be "guided by their opinion" undoubtedly upset the brigadiers. Only a few hours before the operation was due to be launched they addressed a rather petulant letter to him, asking that he take them more fully into his confidence and requesting "as distinct orders as the nature of the thing will admit of, particularly to the place or places we are to attack; This circumstance, perhaps very decisive, we cannot learn from the publick orders . . ."

Wolfe's final set of orders issued on board the *Sutherland* on 12 September are indeed brief and uninformative, but as he rather caustically replied to Monckton; "It is not a usual thing to point out in the publick orders the direct spot of an attack, nor for any inferior officer not charg'd w^h: a particular duty to ask instructions upon that point." Here was the

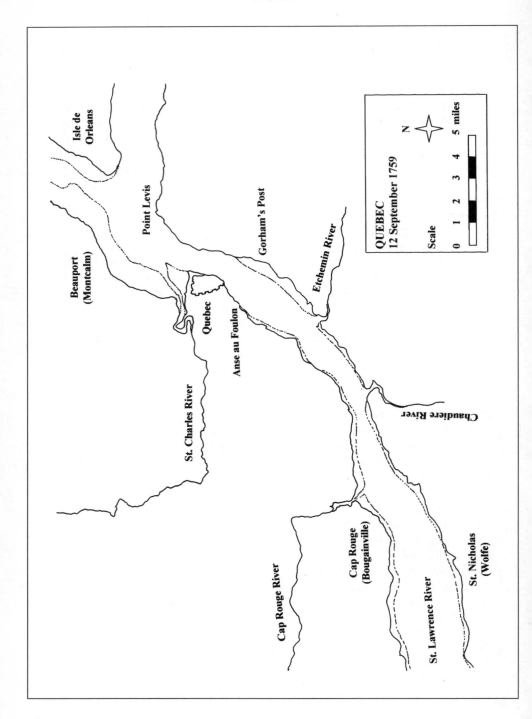

QUEBEC
12 September 1759

Scale

0 1 2 3 4 5 miles

N

Isle de Orleans

Point Levis

Gorham's Post

Etchemin River

Beauport (Montcalm)

Quebec

Anse au Foulon

St. Charles River

Chaudière River

Cap Rouge River

Cap Rouge (Bougainville)

St. Lawrence River

St. Nicholas (Wolfe)

old Wolfe speaking, and no one could have been in any doubt that he was very much in charge again as he condescended to explain.

> My reason for desiring the honour of your Company with me to Goreham's post yesterday, was to shew you, as well as the distance wou'd permit, the situation of the Enemy, & the place where I mean't they shou'd be attack'd; as you are charged with that duty, I should be glad to give you all further light, & assistance in my power – the Place is called the Foulon . . . where you remarked an encampment of 12 or 13 Tents & an Abbatis, below it – you mention'd today, that you had perceived a breast-work there, which made me imagine you as well acquainted w^h. the Place, as the nature of things will admit of. [48]

As to precisely what he intended to do after they actually landed, that would obviously depend on the French . . .

4
The Plains of Abraham

At the time the man ultimately responsible for ensuring the security of the Foulon, Colonel Louis-Antoine de Bougainville, was at Cap Rouge with the bulk of his flying column, which had now been reinforced by the grenadier companies belonging to Montcalm's regular battalions. He was supposedly watching the British ships, but at the critical moment was for some reason quite oblivious to the departure of the heavily laden boats which began dropping down the river with the tide at about 2 a.m. on the morning of 13 September. While de Bougainville slept, the unfortunate officer actually on the spot at the Foulon, a Canadian named Captain Louis de Vergor was dealing, as he thought, with an entirely different matter. The French had planned to run a convoy of supply boats down the river to Quebec that night, but although the operation was cancelled de Bougainville failed to inform de Vergor and his hundred-odd militia of the fact. Consequently, the Captain and some of his men stationed along the shore mistook the British boats for their own and were encouraged in this happy belief by a French-speaking officer, Captain Donald MacDonald of the 78th Highlanders.[49]

MacDonald was in one of the first of eight flat-bottomed boats allocated to Howe's light infantry. A total of thirty were available, each capable of loading fifty men, besides officers. Under the original arrangements for landing the army near Pointe aux Trembles, it had been intended that they should carry the three battalions of Murray's brigade and the 15th and 43rd from Monckton's. Instead, as Wolfe's orders issued on 11 September noted: "As the Leostoff [sic] and Squirrel frigates are ordered to follow the flat-bottom boats, the troops belonging to these ships are to remain on board, and the boats intended for these corps are to take in others . . ."[50] Consequently, the first eight boats carried Howe's light infantry, while the others carried the 28th, 43rd, 47th, 58th Foot and the Louisburg Grenadiers. In addition, some 350 men of the 78th Highlanders were packed into the ships' longboats. Half an hour behind them the remainder of the army came down on the transports, ready to be landed as soon as the boats had discharged the first lift or "flight".

Wolfe's intention, as he had explained to Monckton on the 12th, was to land just to the west of the Foulon. Once ashore, a forlorn hope of volunteers under Captain Delaune was tasked with seizing control of that vital road.[51] Although it was at least partially blocked by an abbatis, the French were evidently still using the road to relieve their piquets along the shore. It would certainly be guarded, but Wolfe was justified in anticipating that twenty-four determined regulars with fixed bayonets would be able to it seize it from a handful of militiamen. As he had written in 1757: "nothing is to be reckoned an obstacle to your undertaking which is not found really so upon *tryal*; that in war something must be allowed to chance and fortune, seeing it is in its nature hazardous, and an option of difficulties; that the greatness of an object should come under consideration, opposed to the impediments that lie in the way." What neither he, nor Captain Chads the Naval beachmaster, counted upon, however, was the strength of the ebbing tide which carried the boats much too far downstream.

When Billy Howe and his light infantry came ashore in the grey pre-dawn light, at about four in the morning, he very soon realised that he was in the wrong place. With every passing minute increasing the likelihood of the French discovering what was going on, he took a famous decision. Delaune and his forlorn hope were quickly sent off back along the beach to find the road, while Howe himself led three companies directly up the face of the cliff. This had formed no part of Wolfe's original plan, for it involved a hazardous climb as the men dragged themselves up the treacherous shale slope by tree roots and branches. On the other hand, it did at least have the merit of surprise, for they eventually scrambled to the top *behind* the French piquet posted at the head of the road. Equally fortunately, one of the first on the spot was the resourceful Captain MacDonald, and as Knox gratefully remembered:

> . . . as soon as he [MacDonald] and his men gained the height, he was challenged by a centry, and, with great presence of mind, from his knowledge of the French service, answered him according to their manner: it being yet dark, he came up to him, told him he was sent there, with a large command, to take post, and desired him to go with all speed to his guard, and to call off all the other men of his party who were ranged along the hill, for that he would take care to give a good

account of the B . . . Anglois, if they should persist; this *finesse* had the desired effect, and saved us many lives, &c. [52]

The French did not remain deceived for long, of course. In the growing light the British boats became clearly visible and a battery at Samos, a short way above the Foulon, briefly opened fire before being dealt with by Billy Howe's light infantry. In the meantime, Wolfe was pushing his men up the road as fast as they landed. Montcalm had earlier sworn that "100 men, well posted, could stop the whole army and give us time to wait for daylight",[53] which was perhaps true enough, but only up to a point. In the first place, Vergor's hundred men were scattered in small piquets up and down the shore, rather than concentrated at the Foulon; and secondly, Montcalm had certainly reckoned without the British seizing control of the road. Its capture was crucial to the success of the whole enterprise, for it enabled Wolfe to establish his army on top of the cliff far more quickly and easily than Montcalm, or anyone else, could ever have anticipated.

Initially, Wolfe formed his men with their backs to the river, in order to be able to deal with a French counter-attack from any direction, but finding no opposition he faced them to the right by files and marched out on to the Plains of Abraham. The weather was showery when he finally halted at about 6 a.m. and wheeled into a new position, admirably described by Knox:

> Quebec was then to the eastward of us in front, with the enemy under its walls. Our right flank was flanked by the declivity and the main river to the southward, and what is called the lower road leading (westward) from the town, with the river Charles and the north country, were on our left. If the reader will attend to this description, observing the cardinal points, he may thereby form as lively an idea of the field of battle as if a plan were laid before him . . .

While the area had originally been no more than grazing land, Knox mentions patches of corn and there also seems to have been a lot of scrub around its fringes. Nevertheless, it was to all intents and purposes an open field rising very gently towards the city, in which neither side could claim any advantage from the terrain.

On first taking up this position, Wolfe still only had the battalions which comprised the first flight drawn up in a single line, but once the rest of the army came up he redeployed his forces in a horseshoe formation. The brigade organisation having been abandoned, Monckton as senior brigadier was given charge of the right, while Murray had the notional centre. In fact, Murray actually commanded the left of the firing line, for Townshend's left wing (comprising the 15th and both battalions of the 60th) was refused in order to face northwards on a line parallel to the St. Foy

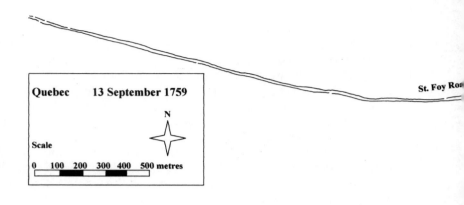

Quebec   13 September 1759

N

Scale

0   100   200   300   400   500 metres

St. Foy Road

Sillery Road

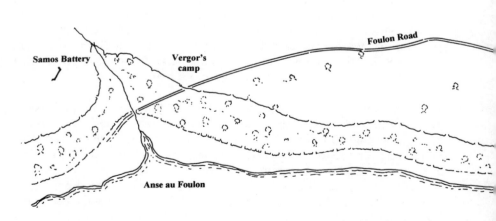

Samos Battery

Vergor's camp

Foulon Road

Anse au Foulon

River St. Lawrence

190

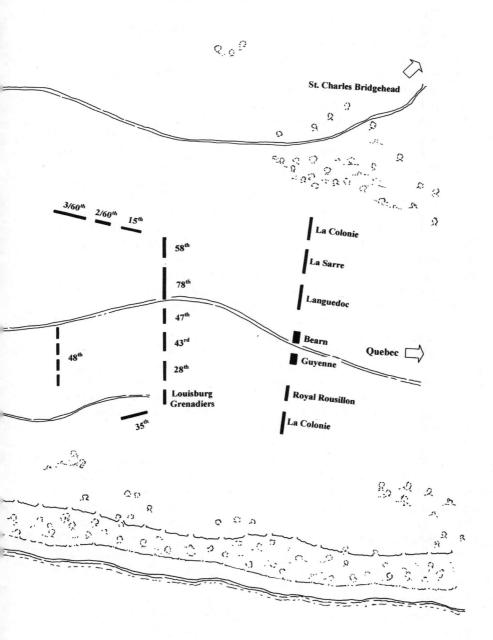

St. Charles Bridgehead

3/60ᵗʰ   2/60ᵗʰ   15ᵗʰ

58ᵗʰ   La Colonie

78ᵗʰ   La Sarre

47ᵗʰ   Languedoc

48ᵗʰ   43ʳᵈ   Bearn   Quebec

28ᵗʰ   Guyenne

Louisburg   Royal Rousillon
Grenadiers

35ᵗʰ   La Colonie

Road. This was primarily done to counter the growing numbers of Canadian militia assembling on that flank, but it may also have effectively denied the road to the French army. Similarly, the 35th, drawn up in what Knox describes as a semi-circular formation, were covering the right flank against more Canadian militia in the bushes lining the cliff-top. The main battle-line therefore comprised the Louisburg Grenadiers drawn up on the right, and then the 28th, 43rd, 47th, 78th and 58th Foot, while the 48th, under Lieutenant Colonel Burton, stood behind in reserve, "drawn up in four grand divisions, with large intervals."

A surprising number of men had been left on the transports or on the beach. All in all, according to the Morning State appended to the official report on the battle (see detailed discussion in Appendix I), there should have been a total of 3,826 soldiers present, besides officers and NCOs, and Mackellar's plan evidences 3,111 in what he called the "front line". This latter figure, however, is slightly misleading for while it is accurate in deducting those men known to have been left to guard the landing place, it also includes the men serving in the four units on the flanks as well as those in the main battle line proper. In fact, the six battalions forming that battle line mustered no more than 1,768 bayonets and may perhaps have had as few as 1,734. In addition there were at least two brass 6 lbrs, which had been dragged up the Foulon road by Williamson and his gunners, although the Morning State refers to there having been three.

The tactical formation adopted was interesting. Most accounts record that the battalions were drawn up only two ranks deep, rather than three, although Malcolm Fraser of the 78th refers to the line being "no more than three deep" which suggests that his own corps at least drew up in the usual manner. It is not clear whether this reduction in depth was done in conformity with a standing order to that effect, issued by Amherst in his capacity as CinC North America on 9 July 1759, or was simply an *ad hoc* expedient to cover the required frontage. Quartermaster Sergeant John Johnson of the 58th certainly thought it was down to the last reason, for he recalled that the files were drawn up "at least three feet asunder, and forty yards or more in the intervals between the Battalions."[54] Taken in conjunction with the figures contained in the Morning State, this would suggest the length of the main firing line must have been very close on 1,000 metres. If, on the other hand, the battalions were drawn up on the usual frontage of 24 inches (or 0.6 metres) per file, as laid down in the 1756 *Regulations*, they still ought to have covered around 800 metres in total, unless of course Johnson was also exaggerating as to the intervals between each battalion.

While they awaited Montcalm's arrival with his regulars, the already substantial numbers of Canadian militiamen already arrived on the Plains engaged in a fairly intensive skirmishing and eventually Wolfe ordered his men to lie down. He, on the other hand, is often accused by later writers of deliberately or at least recklessly exposing himself. Colonel Stacey, for example, in referring to Wolfe's death describes it as "a fate which he had done nothing to avoid and may even have deliberately courted." This is, of course, utter nonsense. In the first place, as we have seen, his spirits had dramatically improved since taking the decision to land at the Foulon; and secondly, his inconspicuously plain and shabby red frock coat was hardly calculated to attract an assassin's attention in the way that Lord Nelson's full dress uniform and decorations would do at Trafalgar. In any case, the real reason for his apparently "exposing" himself was altogether much more mundane. Wolfe had perforce to fight his battle on foot, and this imposed a number of constraints on just how he went about it. Conventionally, a general officer would sit on horseback behind the lines, surrounded by his staff and with a reasonably good view of the proceedings. His ADCs, also mounted, would ride about swiftly delivering orders and returning with situation reports. Wolfe and his staff, on the other hand, were not only restricted to a walking pace, but their visual range was also severely curtailed, not least by the fact that they were quite unable to see over the heads of their own troops. In order to see anything at all they not only had to be on the spot, but usually standing right in the front line as well. Unsurprisingly, in the circumstances, Wolfe also preferred to go and see things for himself rather than rely upon messengers. "The general moved about everywhere," wrote Mackellar, and shortly before the battle proper began he visited Townshend to reassure himself as to the security of the left flank. That done he passed along the line to take up a position on a low rising ground "from whence he had a view of the whole field."

In contrast to the determined efficiency being displayed that morning by Wolfe and his officers, the Marquis de Montcalm was panicking. Despite the earlier movement by most of the British troops to the ships some miles above Quebec, the French commander had remained convinced that Wolfe still intended, ultimately, to fight his way ashore at Beauport. He was certainly encouraged in this happy belief by a demonstration mounted in the basin by the boats of Admiral Knowles' ships on the night of 12 September. But having vainly stood to in expectation of a landing on the Beauport Shore until just after dawn, the Marquis was disagreeably surprised to receive reports of an *actual* landing at the Foulon.

It does not require any great exercise of hindsight to argue that Montcalm should have delayed attacking Wolfe for a few hours in order to first effect a proper concentration of his forces. Even if the British threat to the St. Foy road, whether actual or imagined, prevented a physical junction with the troops from Cap Rouge, Bougainville could still have been relied upon to provide a significant if not decisive diversion. Instead, having for some reason become convinced that the British were already digging in, the Marquis allowed himself to be drawn into battle without any coherent idea of what was going on. Not to put too fine a point on it, he and his men simply marched to the sound of the guns and pitched in almost as soon as they arrived, without adequate planning or preparation.

There were seven infantry battalions making up Montcalm's hastily formed line (all the cavalry were with Bougainville): on the right was a battalion of colonial militia, made up of men from Quebec and Montreal, and next came two regular battalions, *La Sarre* and *Languedoc*. All three, commanded by Colonel de Senezergues, were deployed in line formation – which would presumably have been three-deep as prescribed in 1754 – but by all accounts the two regular battalions forming the centre, belonging to the regiments *Bearn* and *Guyenne*, were deployed in column under Montcalm's personal command. The left wing, under Colonel de Fontbrune, was again deployed in line, and also comprised just two battalions, the regular *Royal Roussillon*, and a militia unit made up of men from Montreal and Trois Rivieres.

Lacking anything like a proper Morning State, it is difficult to establish with any certainty just how strong Montcalm's army actually was. Most British writers reckoned that they were outnumbered by the French, but Townshend appended a fairly detailed breakdown to his official report[55] which reckoned Montcalm's main battle-line to be 1,960-strong, with a further 1,500 militia infesting the bushes. Whilst this estimate sounds rather low it is probably not too far from the truth, especially if, as was conventional, he omitted officers and NCOs from the totals. In addition to the ordinary wastage to be expected in the course of the campaign, Montcalm's regular battalions had earlier been stripped not only of their grenadier companies (always kept up to strength at the expense of the ordinary fusilier companies), but of two piquets apiece, one serving with Bougainville's force, and another in the city garrison. Moreover, the slight advantage in numbers which Montcalm might have enjoyed in pitting his seven battalions directly against Monckton's and Murray's six was negated by the fact that he had only one gun to Wolfe's two (or three)[56] and by a crucial difference in tactical doctrine. In contrast to the British obsession with firepower, the French army, at this time, generally took a fairly relaxed attitude to discipline in general and musketry in particular. While British officers strove to control their men's fire, French officers actively encouraged what was called a *feu de billebaude*, which basically amounted to everyone blazing away in their own time. On the whole, moreover, the French favoured rapid offensive movements relying upon the bayonet, and for that a column formation was preferred.

Like Wolfe, Montcalm did not live to explain himself, but it is reasonable to suppose that, having no great confidence in the ability of his men to win a static firefight, he intended to pierce the British centre with a column attack. At about 10 a.m. he waved them forward and within a few minutes it was all over. As the French advanced, the battalions on each wing opened an ineffectual fire on the waiting British and by all accounts quickly fell into disorder. The ranks of the five regular units had been padded out with conscripted militiamen and there are suggestions that, having fired, these men promptly went to ground. The British battalions, on the other hand, waited until the French came within forty yards' range, whereupon they opened up with a steady platooning[57] described by Knox as "a well-timed, regular and heavy discharge of our small arms."

In the centre, however, the 43rd and 47th Foot momentarily held their fire, for in 1755 Wolfe had devised a patent method for demolishing French column attacks. In his instructions to the 20th Foot, issued on 15 December that year, he had written:

> If the center of the battalion is attacked by a column, the wings must be extremely careful to fire obliquely. That part of the battalion against which the column marches, must reserve their fire, and if they have time to put two or three bullets in their pieces, it must be done. When the column is within about twenty yards they must fire with a good aim, which will necessarily stop them a little. This body may then open from the center, and retire by files towards the wings of the regiment, while the neighbouring platoons wheel to the right and left, and either fire, if they are loaded, or close up and charge with their bayonets.

Wolfe had indeed ordered his men to load two balls that morning and now Knox of the 43rd described how his own regiment and the 47th, unaffected by the musketry on either side, gave the oncoming columns "with great calmness, as remarkable a close and heavy discharge, as I ever I saw . . . and, indeed well might the French Officers say, that they never opposed such a shock as they received from the center of our line, for that they believed every ball took place."[58] The 43rd and 47th Foot mustered a total of 452 men in the firing line that morning. If an optimistic 20% of shots went home, at close range, the effect will indeed have been devastating and even a 10% hit-rate will have sufficed to drop the leading rank of both columns. Either way, as the smoke thinned all the way along the line it revealed the French army broken and in flight.

Wolfe, unfortunately did not live to see his victory. As Mackellar noted, just before the French advanced the General took post on a low rising ground on the right of the line. A few minutes earlier he had ordered a volunteer named James Henderson, serving with the Louisburg Grenadiers, to secure it with a few men and "Maintain it to the Last Extremety." Now, as the battle began, Wolfe stood beside Henderson, but as the volunteer rather illiterately recounted, the General

Was Scarce A Moment With me till he Receved his Fatal Wound . . . When the Genr^l Receved the Shot I Caut Hold of him And Carried him of the Feild, he Walked About one Hundred yards And then Beged I Would Let Sit Down, Which I Did. Then I Opened his Breast, And found his Shirt full of Blood At Which he smiled And When he Seen the Distress I was In, My Dear, Said he, Dont Grive for me, I Shall Be Happy In a Few Minutes, take Care of your Self As I see your Wounded. But Tell me O tell me How Goes the Battle their, Just then Came some Officers Who told him that the French had given Ground & Our troops Was pursuing Them to the Walls of the town, he Was then Lying in my Arms Just Expirin That Great Man Whos Sole Ambition Was his Country Glory Raised himself up on this News And Smiled in my Face. Now, Said he I Die Contented, from that Instant the smile never Left his Face till he Deided.[59]

Traditionally Wolfe is held to have been shot by a Canadian marksman ensconced in the bushes lining the top of the cliff. Although a deserter from the 60th supposedly confessed to the deed on the scaffold,[60] it is unlikely that any one individual could claim the credit, for he was actually hit three times! Be that as it may, he fell in gallant company, for Monckton, (standing between the 43rd and 47th) was shot and wounded at about the same time, as were Carleton, Barre, Spital and Smyth. While Wolfe's death at the very moment of victory undoubtedly put a suitably dramatic period to his career, there is no denying that it also came at an extremely inconvenient time. With Monckton down as well, command devolved upon Townshend, but with so many other staff officers also wounded it took some time for the Brigadier to learn of the fact. In the meantime, it fell to Brigadier Murray and Lieutenant Colonel Hunt Walsh of the 28th to initiate what turned into a fairly disorderly pursuit of the fleeing French and Malcolm Fraser of the 78th wrote

> . . . when the fire slackening, and the smoke of the powder vanishing, we observed the main body of the Enemy retreating in great confusion towards the Town, and the rest towards the River St. Charles. Our Regiment were then ordered by Brigadier General Murray to draw their swords and pursue them, which I dare say increased their pannic but saved many of their lives, whereas if the artillery had been allowed to play, and the army advanced regularly there would have been many more of the enemy killed and wounded, as we never came up with the main body.[61]

As it was, the French casualties were quite heavy enough in all conscience. An officer named La Pause reckoned that the regulars lost about 150 killed on the spot and another 370 (presumably wounded for the most part) were captured.[62] As in the British Army, a significant number of senior officers went down. The most prominent amongst them was Montcalm himself, badly wounded by a canister round and dead by the following morning, and both his brigadiers, Senezergues and Fontbrune, were also killed.

Nevertheless the British victory was by no means as complete as it might have been. Another contemporary version of Wolfe's final moments, recounted by Knox, tells how

> ... being asked if he would have a Surgeon? He replied, 'it is needless; it is all over with me.' One of them then cried out, 'they run, see how they run.' 'Who runs?' demanded our hero, with great earnestness, like a person roused from sleep. The Officer answered, 'The enemy, Sir; Egad they give way every-where.' Thereupon the General rejoined, 'Go one of you, my lads, to Colonel Burton-; tell him to march Webb's regiment with all speed down to Charles's River, to cut off the retreat of the fugitives from the bridge.' Then turning on his side, he added, 'Now, God be praised, I will die in peace.' And thus expired.

Whether, in all the confusion, Ralph Burton ever received the message is not known, but as Malcolm Fraser recounted, Brigadier Murray placed himself at the head of the 78th and having pursued the French as far as the city, then tried, on his own initiative, to seize the bridge. Unfortunately, the attempt foundered when he and the Highlanders came under heavy fire, first from the floating batteries covering the bridge, and then from a large body of Canadian Militia still hanging on in the scrub outside the St. John's Gate. In fact, as a direct result of this abortive attempt to cut off the French retreat, the 78th afterwards returned more casualties than any other British unit – eighteen killed and 148 wounded before being extricated. By that time, a minor crisis was developing behind them. Finding that he was now in command, Townshend "immediately repaired to ye center, & finding that ye pursuit had put part of ye troops in great disorder I formed them as soon as possible. Scarce was this effected when Monsr. de Boncainville wth about 2000 men, ye corps from Cap rouge & that neighbourhood, appeared in our rear."[63]

Just before the main battle began, Wolfe had taken the precaution of ordering the 3/60th back to cover the head of the Foulon Road and now Townshend marched the rest of the army back there to confront Bougainville, who took the hint and drew off again without engaging. In the meantime, with the St. Charles bridge still in their hands, the rest of the French were enabled to escape.

The rest of the story is quickly told. Despite Bougainville's desperate efforts to throw supplies and reinforcements into the city, Quebec surrendered to Townshend on 18 September, and almost immediately afterwards the prospect of ice closing the mouth of the St. Lawrence forced the Royal Navy to withdraw from the river. With the ships went Wolfe's corpse, the wounded Monckton, and, with rather less excuse, Townshend as well. Quebec was entrusted to a perilously weak garrison under Murray, while further upstream the Chevalier de Levis rallied the remnants of Montcalm's beaten army for one last gallant offensive to retake the city. They came in early Spring, before the winter snows had melted and in a dramatic reversal of roles Murray sallied out to fight him, only to be badly defeated in the battle of St. Foy on 28 April 1760. Ironically, the battle, fought on the same ground as Wolfe's victory in September, was unnecessary for Levis was desperately short of ammunition for his big guns and could only go through the motions of mounting a formal siege. All now depended on whether the Royal Navy or French reinforcements would be the first through the ice and into the river, but on 9 May HMS *Lowestoft* turned up and Wolfe's legacy to the British Empire was secured.

5

James Wolfe and King George's Army

There were probably only four men with Wolfe when he died: James Henderson, of course, and Lieutenant Henry Browne, also of the Louisburg Grenadiers (who may have been the officer charged with taking Wolfe's last orders to Burton), a surgeon's mate named Hewit and an unknown private soldier. However, when the artist Benjamin West came to paint his magnificent *Death of Wolfe* in 1770 he not only grouped most of the General's sorrowing staff and subordinates around him but also depicted him in an attitude of martyrdom, deliberately alluding to religious images of Christ brought down from the cross. It is easy to mock the painting's pretentious anachronisms, but there can be no doubting that it adequately reflects Wolfe's popular status as the Hero of Quebec.

It is, of course, much more difficult to assess his professional status, solely on the basis of his first (and last) campaign. Wolfe's critics are certainly prone to dwelling upon his apparent dithering before Quebec, without properly considering the scale of the problems which he faced. It is axiomatic that unless a commander intending to besiege a fortress enjoys an overwhelming superiority in numbers, he must first destroy or defeat the field army covering it. Yet at Quebec, Wolfe found that army strongly entrenched in a near impregnable position, which was so situated as to virtually preclude his manoeuvring around it. He was, in short, faced with just three unsatisfactory alternatives: he could mount a costly frontal assault on the Beauport Lines, he could take the army upstream to Point aux Trembles and then march on the city, with the expectation of finding Montcalm just as solidly entrenched when he arrived, or he could take a gamble on getting his men ashore just above Quebec and then fight Montcalm in the open. He had, from the very start, contemplated the latter and is still criticised by some for the fearful risk which he eventually took in carrying it out, but it is generally his conduct up until that point which attracts most adverse comment.

Amongst the more recent critics, Colonel Stacey tells us in his rather muddled monograph, that Wolfe originally planned to land at Beauport, then planned to land at St. Michel on 5 July, turned again to Beauport on 16 July, changed his mind and essayed a second attempt at St. Michel on 20 July, before trying to turn the flank of the Beauport position on 26 July and then mounting an actual assault on the 31st. All in all, by interpreting every cough, wheeze and visit to the privy as another plan, Stacey credits Wolfe with devising no fewer than seven different ones before finally settling on the successful landing at the Foulon, but this is grossly unfair. In reality, as we have seen, his initial surmise (for it was no more) that a landing could be effected at Beauport was laid aside as soon as he arrived there and found the French already digging in. Thereafter, until his failure of nerve on 20 July, his attention was very firmly fixed on the upper river. The disastrous Beauport operation on the 31st was certainly Wolfe's responsibility alone and its uncharacteristic lack of proper planning betrays his frustration, which may in turn have led to the physical collapse which followed – and eventually to his initial acceptance of the brigadiers' plan of landing at Point aux Trembles. Although outwardly attended with much less risk than the subsequent landing at the Foulon, their plan was a bad one which handed the initiative to the French and was almost bound to end in failure. The only realistic chance of victory lay in Wolfe's own resolution to land at the Foulon. If he had held off from doing so earlier, it was surely only because of the considerable risks involved, and he did so at the last only because all the other alternatives had been exhausted. It is said that even then, there was also a contingency plan to re-embark the troops and sail home if a proper lodgement could not be made on the top, but if true (and there is no reason to doubt it) this only reflects careful planning, not despair at the operation's chances of success. His ultimate triumph at Quebec was not merely a matter of luck, though that certainly played a part, but of sound judgement, resolution in the face of considerable adversity, and thorough preparation.

His more uncritical admirers, such as Beckles Willson, have been in no doubt that, with Wolfe at its head, rather than Billy Howe, the British army would have performed very differently in the subsequent American Revolutionary War. Conversely his surprisingly numerous detractors, including Sir Garnet Wolsey, have dismissed him as no more than a good regimental officer who was patently out of his depth at Quebec. The best that can be said for either view is that we simply do not know and cannot know how he may subsequently have matured as a commander, any more than it would have been possible to predict the ultimate greatness of a certain Major General Arthur Wellesley had *he* been killed – as he might so very easily have been – when his horse went down in the mêlée at Assaye in 1803.

Even if Wolfe is admitted to have reached his operational ceiling at Quebec, his reputation should not rest upon that one battle alone, for his eventual influence in shaping the character of the British Army was immense. As a member of the mafia which formed the backbone of the 18th-century army he actively encouraged volunteers and made most of his appointments on the grounds of ability and merit, rather than birth or property. Moreover, Wolfe was also an innovator. During his own lifetime his teachings were enthusiastically spread by numerous disciples including the officers of the 20th, his own 67th and the Duke of Richmond's 72nd. In 1768 a useful compilation of his regimental orders was anonymously published as *General Wolfe's INSTRUCTIONS to Young Officers*. It was popular enough to go through a second edition and was no doubt read with profit by more than one generation of soldiers. He was also responsible for introducing the Prussian-style alternate firing and a new bayonet drill in the face of the express opposition of the then commander-in-chief. In the immediate term he can therefore bear actual, if unacknowledged, responsibility for the 1764 *Regulations* and the influential *Norfolk Discipline*. In the longer term it was Wolfe's volley and bayonet tactics, first described in December 1755, which formed the cornerstone of British infantry tactics in the Peninsular War and at Waterloo. He is and will be remembered, above all, for that brief battle on the Plains of Abraham but his influence on the development of the British Army, and in particular on its infantry tactics, was perhaps his real legacy.

NOTES

1. Camp near Louisburg, 7 August 1758. (Beckles Willson, *Life and Letters of James Wolfe*, p393.)
2. Jacques Prevost, a Swiss mercenary and lieutenant colonel commandant of the 4/60th.
3. By all accounts a very talented officer, Howe was shot dead in an ambush during the final approach to Ticonderoga on 6 July 1758.
4. In a letter written to Rickson on 1 December, Wolfe was still keen on this idea and said: "If I followed my own taste, it would lead me into Germany; and if my poor talent was consulted, they would place me in the cavalry, because nature has given me good eyes, and a warmth of temper to follow the first impressions." (Beckles Willson, op.cit. p403)
5. Quoted in Whitworth, Rex, *Field Marshal Lord Ligonier* (1958), p275.
6. Wolfe to William Pitt, 22 November 1758. (Beckles Willson, op.cit. p400.)
7. Wolfe to Amherst, 29 December 1758. (WO 34/46b – not in Beckles Willson.)
8. He was intended by Ligonier to have taken a brigade to New York – precisely the job he had already turned down before leaving Louisburg.

9. Wolfe to Major Walter Wolfe, 19 May 1759. (Beckles Willson, op.cit. p427.)
10. Wolfe to Amherst, 29 December 1758. (WO34/46b.)
11. This was the same regiment which had fought at Louisburg as the 63rd Highlanders. It was redesignated the 78th as a result of the embodiment of the 67th and other former 2nd Battalions, but nevertheless some of its officers, including Malcolm Fraser, continued to use the old designation at Quebec.
12. Wolfe to Amherst, 29 December 1758. (WO34/46b.)
13. Quoted in Stacey, C.P., *Quebec 1759* (1973) p88.
14. Wolfe to Townshend, 6 January 1759. (Beckles Willson, op.cit. p414.) Strictly speaking, Townshend might reasonably claim to have been shot at nearly as often as Wolfe, but he had no command experience whatsoever. Moreover, the basic premise of Townshend's recent Militia Bill was that a standing army was an unnecessary expense and that a county militia (commanded by members of the nobility and gentry, whose military rank would depend entirely upon their social one) would be sufficient for the defence of the realm. Such an attitude was anathema to professionals such as Wolfe, and this difference in outlook alone would have been cause enough for friction between the two men.
15. Anon. *Advice to the Officers of the British Army* (1946), p18.
16. The brevet and local commissions granted to Wolfe's staff appointments were mostly dated 30 December 1758. John Carden's precise status is unclear. He appears in the 1758 *Army List* as a lieutenant in the reduced Shirley's 50th, but cannot be found in the 1759 edition. In 1760 he is listed as a Captain in the 60th and was eventually killed at Ticonderoga during the American Revolutionary War.
17. CO5/51.
18. Louisburg, 19 May 1759. (Beckles Willson, op.cit. p427.) Whitmore also proved uncooperative in bringing the Ranger companies up to strength, as Wolfe complained on 6 June (CO5/51): "There are a thousand of the Boston Militia at Louisbourg; I desired Brig. Whitmore to compleat our Companies of Rangers from them, and to give me a hundred Labourers, solely as Pioniers, the Men were ask'd if they chose to go, and as it seldom happens, that a new-England Man prefers service to a lazy life, none of them seem'd to approve of the proposal".
19. Knox, John, *Historical Journal of the Campaigns in North America,* Vol.I (1914) pp348-9, 353.
20. CO5/51 f32.
21. According to Wolfe's orders of 4 May 1759, the 48th were originally assigned to Murray's brigade and the 58th were to have served in Monckton's, but they had evidently been exchanged by the time the army got into the river, for the 48th went ashore with Monckton at Point Levis and the 58th with Murray at Montmorency.
22. Halifax, 19 May 1759. (Beckles Willson, op.cit. pp427-9.)
23. Quoted in Stacey, op.cit. pp68-9.
24. CO5/51. (Montmorency, 2 September 1759.) Confusingly, Wolfe preceded his account of the abortive St. Michel landing on 20 July with a paragraph describing the bloody reconnaissance up the Montmorency on the 26th, which may well have encouraged later suggestions that he originally planned to attack the Beauport Lines on or about the 17th.
25. Quoted in Stacey, op.cit. p71.
26. CO5/51. (Montmorency, 2 September 1759). Stacey, op.cit. p74, rather perversely suggests that the "real intentions" which the marines were to mask may have been the aborted St. Michel landing, but there is no reason to

doubt that they were to cover the projected move on the Montmorency ford. Throughout the campaign the marines were used only as labourers or to man static fortifications. The standard of their musketry was probably as good as that of the "land forces", and they may even have had a fair idea of platooning, but they were not normally trained in "evolutions" and their ability to manoeuvre was therefore limited.

27. Wolfe Journal, 26 July 1759. The known casualties included Captain George Fletcher of the 35th, who was killed, and one of Wolfe's ADCs, Tom Bell, who had his arm "broke by the rascals". Although he was evidently fit for "light duties", Bell had to be replaced as a full-time ADC by Major Thomas Gwillim of the 7th Fusiliers, who had incidentally succeeded to a regimental majority in his own corps (who were still in Gibraltar) on 1 May 1759. The 26th was a busy day: Colonel Simon Fraser and Captain James MacPherson of the 78th were both wounded in a skirmish at Beaumont (by the same bullet, according to Knox) and Captain John Carden of Dalling's Light Infantry was injured near Pointe aux Peres.

28. This was the "Johnstone" redoubt, named after a Scots Jacobite serving on Montcalm's staff. All the British accounts refer to it as the "upper" redoubt by way of distinguishing it from the "Sault" redoubt at the bottom end of the Lines.

29. Wolfe to Saunders, 30 August 1759. Text from *Gentleman's Magazine,* June 1801 (quoted in Knox op.cit. p456-8).

30. Knox, ibid. p444.

31. Anon: *General Wolfe's Instructions to Young Officers,* (1780) pp90-1.

32. Major John Hussey of the 47th Foot was 2IC of Howe's light infantry battalion.

33. Presumably a mistake for "battalions".

34. Captain Moses Hazen, a ranger officer who subsequently commanded a Canadian regiment – "Congress's Own" – during the Revolutionary War.

35. Knox, op.cit. p451 – i.e. the men were not to be told off into Bland's "chequer".

36. One of them obviously being the Louisburg Grenadiers, while the other companies were presumably to be grouped together according to their parent brigades.

37. Wolfe to Saunders and Pitt (Knox, op.cit. pp456-8.) According to Knox, Monckton had the 15th and 78th ready to go immediately. The 43rd and 48th were to be in the second lift. The camp and batteries at Point Levis were left in charge of small detachments from each corps, together with Dalling's Light Infantry and the marines,

38. Knox op.cit., Vol.II, p454 – the reason why the proportion of dead to wounded was so high was that not all of the latter could be recovered before the Indians came down to scalp and murder them.

39. *Wolfe's Instructions,* pp91-2.

40. Picquets were the standard form of provisional unit employed in the French Army when small detachments were required – especially for hazardous operations. The 1750 Regulations laid down that they were to comprise a captain, lieutenant, two sergeants, a drummer and 47 men drawn from all the fusilier or battalion companies. The practice originally arose in order to avoid the danger of complete companies being lost, with all the practical and above all financial consequences this would entail, but since they were picked men they were also in effect an elite. The practice passed over to the British service and the light companies which Amherst ordered to be formed on 14 April 1759 were in effect picquets and sometimes referred to as such.

41. CO5/51 f86. Murray's brigade major, Captain Richard Maitland, was wounded however.

42. The original British commander, Brigadier General John Prideaux of the 55th, had been killed when he accidentally walked in front of a mortar just as it was being fired!
43. HMS *Neptune,* 6 March 1759. (WO34/46b – not in Beckles Willson.)
44. 31 August 1759. (Public Archives of Canada – photographic facsimile in Stacey op.cit.)
45. Although it was dated from Montmorency Camp on 2 September, the despatch was originally composed some time earlier, and Wolfe's equally useful letter to Saunders of 30 August was largely written to reassure the Admiral that certain passages critical of the Navy in the original draft were to be omitted from the final version.
46. Townshend Papers – quoted in Stacey, op.cit. pp182-3.
47. A comprehensive selection of signals had earlier been issued by either Wolfe or Saunders for the Montmorency operation. These included "A red flag upon the main top-gallant mast head of one of the cats is a signal for Brigadier Monckton to join. A blue and white stripped flag at the top, for Brigadier Townshend to pass the Ford." (Knox, op.cit. Vol.I pp450-1.)
48. Quoted in Stacey, op.cit. pp113-4.
49. Townshend names him as Captain Fraser, but this must be a mistake for "a Captain of Fraser's", since, in describing what must be the same officer's part in a later incident, Knox rather more convincingly calls him Captain Donald MacDonald and refers to "his knowledge of the French service." Stewart of Garth, in his monumental *Sketches of the Highlanders of Scotland*, states that MacDonald, who came from Benbecula, was a brother of Clanranald. He can thus be identified as the officer of that name who served in the French Army from 1742 to 1746, first as a cadet in the Irish regiment *Rooth,* and latterly as a lieutenant in the *Royal Eccossois*. MacDonald was taken prisoner after Culloden, but was released in 1748 and lived at home until joining Fraser's 63rd/78th Highlanders in 1757. He was subsequently killed at the battle of St. Foy in April 1760.
50. *Wolfe's Instructions*, p101.
51. An anonymous light infantryman recorded in his journal that Howe called for the volunteers of the light infantry (i.e. the aspirant officers) "signifying to them, that the General intends that a few men may land before the Light Infantry and army, and scramble up the rock when ordered by Capt Delaune, who is to be in the first boat along us . . . He observing our number consisted only of eight men, viz,: Fitz-Gerald, Robertson, Stewart, McAllester, Makenzie [sic], McPherson, Cameron, Bell. Ordered we should take 2 men each of our own choice from three companys of Lt. Infantry, which in all made 24 men." (Quoted in Knox, op.cit. Vol.II, p95.) Although Captain Delaune was present, it seems likely that he too was in fact serving as a volunteer and that Dalling's Light Infantry had been left at Point Levis.
52. Knox, op.cit. Vol.II, p96.
53. Undated. Quoted in Stacey, op.cit. p119.
54. Quoted in Knox, op.cit. Vol.II, p99.
55. CO5/51 f101: Right: La Colonie [i.e. Colonial troops] 350, La Sarre 340, Languedoc 320 Column: Bearn 200, La Guienne 200 Left: Royal Roussillon 230, La Colonie 320 Militia in the Bushes and along the face of the Bank 1500
56. Some accounts suggest that Montcalm had at least four guns, but Townshend (ibid.) notes only one 12 lbr in front of the right wing. Another was intended to be on the left "but not placed". Since, in the circumstances, any guns brought onto the field by the French will have been left there, Townshend is probably correct.

57. Sir John Fortescue in his monumental but overrated *History of the British Army* famously describes all of Wolfe's men firing one single shattering volley, "the most perfect volley ever fired on battlefield", but this appears to rest on a misreading of Knox.
58. Knox, op.cit. Vol.II, p101.
59. *English Historical Review,* Vol.12 (1897), pp762-3. Henderson, whose presence is confirmed by other sources, was subsequently commissioned in the 28th.
60. As the deserter in question was supposed to have confessed to the deed at Crown Point, he is probably the Jonathan Barns executed there as a traitor on 6 April 1761. (Stewart Orderly Book)
61. *Journal of the Society for Army Historical Research,* Vol.XVIII, (1939), p156.
62. Chartrand, Rene, *Quebec 1759* (1999), p93. These figures do not, of course, include the militia, although some 110 were captured.
63. CO5/51.

Appendix I

Wolfe's Army

Halifax, 30 April 1759

Staff:
Commander-in-Chief: Major General James Wolfe

Aides de Camp:
Captain Hervey Smith: Captain, 15th Foot 8 November 1756
Captain Thomas Bell: 1st Lieutenant, Marines 21 March 1757

Quartermaster General:
Lieutenant Colonel Guy
   Carleton   (72nd Foot)

AQMG:
Captain Matthew Leslie: Lieutenant, 48th Foot 4 November 1755
Captain Henry Caldwell: Lieutenant, 69th Foot 7 October 1757

Adjutant General:
Major Isaac Barre: Captain, 32nd Foot 1 October 1755

Engineers:
Major Patrick Mackellar   (Subdirector and Chief Engineer)
Captain Lieutenant Hugh
   Debbeig   (37th Foot)
Captain Lieutenant Adam
   Williamson   (40th Foot)
Lieutenant John Montresor

Acting Engineers:
Captain Lieutenant Samuel
   Jan Hollandt   (60th Foot)
Lieutenant Tonge
Lieutenant Goddard
Lieutenant Adolphus Benzell   (1st Foot)

Lieutenant Joseph Frederick
   Wallet des Barres   (60th Foot)
Captain Derecuine   Captain of Miners

Royal Artillery:
Lieutenant Colonel George
   Williamson
Three companies: 21 Officers
                          309 R&F

Brigade Structure

The organisation set out below is largely as described in Wolfe's orders of 4 May 1759. Under those orders, the 48th were originally assigned to Murray's Brigade and the 58th were to have served in Monckton's, but they had evidently been exchanged by the time the army got into the river for the 48th went ashore with Monckton at Point Levis and the 58th with Murray at Montmorency. Regimental strengths are as per the embarkation return of 6 June 1759 (CO5/51 f67) – the figures are apparently exclusive of officers serving on the staff, and drummers.

Brigadier General Robert Monckton
Major of Brigade: Captain John Spital (47th Foot)

15th (Amherst's)	34 officers 560 R&F
43rd (Kennedy's)	29 officers 686 R&F
48th (Webb's)	36 officers 816 R&F
78th (Fraser's)	50 officers 1,219 R&F

Brigadier General George Townshend
Major of Brigade: Captain Thomas Gwillim (7th Foot)

28th (Bragg's)	26 officers 565 R&F
47th (Lascelles')	36 officers 643 R&F
2/60th (Monckton's)	27 officers 554 R&F

Brigadier General James Murray
Major of Brigade: Captain Hon. Richard Maitland (43rd Foot)

35th (Otway's)	36 officers 863 R&F
58th (Anstruther's)	27 officers 589 R&F
3/60th (Lawrence's)	29 officers 578 R&F

NB: Lieutenant Henry Dobson of Lascelles' 47th Foot was appointed a major of brigade by Amherst on 17 May. This meant that for a time there were four brigade majors, though it is not clear how the extra man was employed. However, Gwillim was subsequently appointed ADC to Wolfe after Tom Bell was wounded in a skirmish on the Montmorency on 26 July.

Marines:
Lieutenant Colonel Hector Boisrond

Provisional Battalion from Portsmouth Division – 25 Officers 577 R&F

In addition to Boisrond's battalion, a considerable number of marines were landed from the ships. In theory as many as 1,945 R&F would have been carried as part of the various ships' complements at Quebec, although not all of them will have been available for service on land and none will have been commanded by anyone senior to Boisrond since field officers of marines did not serve afloat.

Grenadiers
On 28 June Wolfe ordered that "The grenadiers of Louisburg, and Major Dalling's light infantry are to receive orders from Colonel Carleton."

Louisburg Grenadiers: Lieutenant Colonel Alexander Murray

Three companies of grenadiers taken
from the garrison of
Louisburg, viz.   22nd (Whitmore's)
                  40th (Hopson's)
                  45th (Warburton's)
Total: 13 officers 313 R&F

Grenadiers of the line:

Wolfe's orders of 28 June 1759 stated that "When the ten companies of the grenadiers of the line are collected as one corps, they are to be commanded by Colonel Burton[1], and Major Morris[2] to assist him."

---

1. Lieutenant Colonel Ralph Burton, 48th Foot
2. Major Roger Morris, 35th Foot

Light Infantry

Light Infantry Battalion:	Major John Dalling	(28th Foot)
	Captain William Delaune	(67th Foot)
	Captain John Carden	(60th Foot?)
	approx 200 R&F	

Light Infantry of the line:

Considerable confusion has arisen from the mistaken assumption that Dalling's little battalion was the only regular light infantry corps serving with the army. However, Amherst had ordered on 14 April 1759 that each regular battalion serving in North America should form its own light company comprising one captain, one lieutenant, one ensign and 70 rank & file. Wolfe's own orders of 28 June therefore directed that "When the light infantry of the line are formed in one corps, they are to receive their orders from Colonel Howe[1], who has Major Hussey[2] to assist him."

Knox noted in his journal on 16 May (Vol.I, p209) that Wolfe also confirmed Amherst's orders concerning their dress:

> . . .the sleeves of the coat are put on the waistcoat, and instead of coat-sleeves, he has two wings like the grenadiers, but fuller; and a round slope reaching about halfway down his arm; which makes his coat of no incumbrance to him, but can be slipt off with pleasure; he has no lace, but the lapels remain; besides the usual pockets he has two, not quite so high as his breast, made of leather, for ball and flints; and a flap of red cloth on the inside, which secures the ball from rolling out, if he should fall.
>
> His knapsack is carried very high between his shoulders, as the Indians carry their pack. His cartouch-box hangs under his arm on the left side, slung with a leathern strap; and his horn under the other arm on the right, hanging by a narrower web than that used by his knapsack; his canteen down his back, under his knapack, and covered with cloth; he has a rough case for his tomahock, with a button; and it hangs in a leathern sling down his side, like a hanger, between his coat and waistcoat. No bayonet; his leggings have leathern straps under his shoes, like spatterdashes; his hat is made into a cap, with a flap and button, and with as much black cloth added as will come under his chin, and keep him warm, when he lies down; it hooks in the front, and is made like the old velvet caps in England.

Subsequently, Wolfe rather sensibly modified these orders by ruling that "The light infantry of this army are to have their bayonets, as the want of

---

1. Lieutenant Colonel William Howe, 58th Foot
2. Major John Hussey, 47th Foot

ammunition may at some times be supplied by that weapon, and because no man should leave his post, under pretence that all his cartridges were fired. In most attacks of the night it must be remembered that bayonets are preferable to fire."

Rangers:

Major George Scott   (40th Foot):

Captain Jonathan Brewer	3 officers 82 R&F
Captain Benonie Dank	3 officers 90 R&F
Captain Joseph Gorham	7 officers 88 R&F
Captain Moses Hazen	3 officers 86 R&F
Captain James Rogers	4 officers 108 R&F
Captain William Stark	3 officers 92 R&F

The additional officers in Gorham's company are presumably staff appointments such as adjutant, quartermaster and surgeon. He was the senior ranger officer present and had commanded the "battalion" during the Louisburg campaign in the year before.

Knox of the 43rd noted in his journal for 5 May 1759 (Vol.I, p307):

> The rangers have got a new uniform clothing; the ground is of black ratteen or frieze, lapelled and cuffed with blue; here follows a description of their dress; a waistcoat with sleeves; a short jacket without sleeves; only armholes and wings to the shoulders (in like manner as the Grenadiers and Drummers of the army) white metal buttons, linen or canvas drawers, with a blue skirt or petticoat of stuff, made with a waistband and one button; this is open before and does not quite extend to the knees; a pair of leggins of the same colour with their coat, which reach up to the middle of the thighs (without flaps) and from the calf of the leg downwards they button like spatter-dashes; and this active dress they wear blue bonnets, and, I think, in great measure like our Highlanders.

The Morning State figures in CO5/51 differ considerably from the oft-quoted printed return included in Knox's *Journal* (Vol.I p104) which evidences no fewer than 4,816 officers and men, exclusive of staff and artillery. For the purposes of comparison Knox's figures for the rank and file only appear in the additional right-hand column.

The explanation is provided by Malcolm Fraser of the 78th Highlanders, who noted in his journal (*JSAHR* XVIII, p159) that:

> The detachment of our Regiment consisted, at our marching from

Morning State, 13 September 1759 (CO5/51 f102)

Regt.	Field Officers	Capts	Lieuts.	Ensigns	Sgts.	Drums	R&F. CO5/51	R&F. Knox
15th (Amherst's)	1	3	14	3	20	2	279	352
28th (Bragg's)	1	5	7	7	18	7	300	362
35th (Otway's)	2	5	11	10	28	-	406	456
43rd (Kennedy's)	1	6	6	5	19	11	256	280
47th (Lascelles')	1	5	8	8	21	7	196	305
48th (Webb's)	1	5	15	8	33	14	649	605
58th (Anstruther's)	1	4	7	6	19	2	300	296
2/60th (Monckton's)	0	2	6	6	21	10	218	266
3/60th (Lawrence's)	1	4	11	11	28	14	474	474
78th (Fraser's)	0	6	11	5	23	12	532	603
Louisburg Grenadiers	1	2	9	-	9	4	216	216
Total	10	47	104	69	239	83	3826	4215
Artillery	1	1	4				40	

3 x 6 pounders

Point Levi, of six hundred men, besides commissioned and non-commissioned Officers; but of these, two officers and about sixty men were left on board for want of boats, and an officer and about thirty men left at the landing place: besides a few sick left on board, so that we had about five hundred men in the action.

Knox's figure of 603 rank and file agrees with the reported strength of the 78th at Point Levis, at the outset of the operation, and pretty well with the subsequent embarkation orders which assumed a strength of about 600 for this particular unit. On the other hand, the Morning State figure of 532 is explicitly confirmed by Fraser's statement that 500 were "in the action" and 30 more left on the beach.

Both returns may, therefore, be correct, with Knox's one giving the number of men embarked off Cap Rouge on 12 September and the Morning State enumerating those who actually landed at the Foulon on 13 September. Judging by Fraser's account, neither set of figures includes the light infantry serving in Billy Howe's battalion, and this is confirmed by Mackellar's plan which evidences just 3,111 rank and file actually present in the ten battalions making up the front line. However, it is possible to estimate from their allocation of eight flat-bottom boats in the embarkation orders that there may have been as many as 400 under his immediate command and another 200 following aboard the transports, under Major Hussey, making as many as 600 in all, exclusive of officers.

Commanding Officers, 13 September:

15th Foot:	Major Paulus Aemilius Irving

15th Foot: Major Paulus Aemilius Irving
28th Foot: Lieutenant Colonel Hunt Walsh
35th Foot: Lieutenant Colonel Harry Fletcher
43rd Foot: Major Robert Elliot
47th Foot: Lieutenant Colonel John Hale
48th Foot: Lieutenant Colonel Ralph Burton
58th Foot: Major James Agnew
2/60th Foot: Captain Ralph Harding
3/60th Foot: Lieutenant Colonel Sir John St. Clair
78th Foot: Captain James Campbell
Louisburg Grens: Lieutenant Colonel Alexander Murray
Light Infantry: Lieutenant Colonel William Howe

Casualties at Quebec, 13 September: (CO5/51 f97)

Regiment	Killed			Wounded		
	Officers	Sergeants	R&F	Officers	Sergeants	R&F.
15th (Amherst's	0	0	2	4	5	52
28th (Bragg's)	1	1	3	5	4	40
35th (Otway's)	1	0	6	6	1	28
43rd (Kennedy's)	0	0	3	3	2	18
47th (Lascelles')	1	0	1	8	1	28
48th (Webb's)	0	0	0	0	0	3
58th (Anstruther's)	1	1	8	4	3	80
2/60th (Monckton's)	0	0	5	6	2	81
3/60th (Lawrence's)	0	0	2	0	0	2
78th (Fraser's)	3	1	14	10	7	131
Louisburg Grenadiers	1	0	3	5	0	47
Royal Artillery	0	0	2	0	1	5

Appendix II

Wolfe's Commissions

2nd Lieutenant, 1st Marines	3 November 1741
Ensign, 12th Foot	27 March 1742
Adjutant, 12th Foot	13 July 1743
Lieutenant, 12th Foot	14 July 1743
Captain, 4th Foot	23 June 1744
Major of Brigade (Flanders)	12 June 1745
Major, 33rd Foot	5 February 1747 (abortive)
Major, 20th Foot	5 January 1749
Lieutenant Colonel, 20th Foot	20 March 1750
QMG Ireland	29 March 1757 – 26 January 1758
Colonel (brevet)	21 October 1757
Brigadier General (North America)	23 January 1758
Colonel, 67th Foot	21 April 1758
Major General (North America)	30 December 1758

Select bibliography

Anon.   *Advice to the Officers of the British Army* (2nd
                             Edition, London 1946)
Atkinson, C.T.   "Jenkins' Ear, The Austrian Succession War
                             and the Fortyfive" *Journal of the Society for Army
                             Historical Research* Vol.22 1943-44)
Bland, Humphrey   *Treatise of Military Discipline* (1727 etc.)
Boatner, Mark   *Biographical Dictionary of the American War of
                             Independence* (London, 1966)
Brown, I.G. & Cheape, H. *Witness to Rebellion* (East Linton, 1996)
Bruce, Anthony   *The Purchase System in the British Army*
                             (London, 1980)
Callaghan, R.   *The East India Company and Army Reform 1783-
                             1798* (1972)
Chartrand, Rene   *The French Soldier in Colonial America* (Ottawa
                             1984)
                             Quebec 1759 (Oxford 1999)
Clode, C.M.   *The Military Forces of the Crown, their
                             Administration and Government* (London, 1869)
Forbes, Rev. Robert   *The Lyon in Mourning, or, a Collection of Speeches,
                             Letters, Journals etc. Relative to the Affairs of
                             Prince Charles Edward Stuart* (Scottish History
                             Society, 1895)
Gruber, Ira (ed.)   *John Peebles' American War 1776-1782* (1997)
Guy, A.J.   *Oeconomy and Discipline: Officership and
                             Administration in the British Army 1714-1763*
                             (Manchester, 1985)
                             *Colonel Samuel Bagshawe and the Army of
                             George II* (London 1990)
Hayter, Tony   *An Eighteenth-Century Secretary at War: The
                             Papers of William, Viscount Barrington* (London,
                             1988)
Houlding, Dr. J.A.   *Fit for Service: The Training of the British Army
                             1715-1795* (Oxford 1981)

	French Arms Drill of the 18th Century (Bloomfield Ont., 1988)
Katcher, Philip	*Armies of the American Wars 1755-1815* (London, 1975)
Knox, Capt. John	*An Historical Journal of the Campaigns in North America* (ed. Doughty, A.G. – Champlain Society, 1914-1916)
	A List of the Colonels, Lieutenant Colonels, Majors, Captains, Lieutenants and Ensigns of His Majesty's Forces (1740)
McCardle, Lee	*Ill-starred General: Braddock of the Coldstream Guards* (Pittsburg, 1958)
May, Robin & Embleton, Gerry	*Wolfe's Army* (Revised edition, London, 1997)
Peterkin, Ernest	*The Exercise of Arms in the Continental Infantry.* (Bloomfield Ontario, 1989)
Prebble, John	*Mutiny: Highland Regiments in Revolt* (London, 1975)

Public Record Office (Kew):
CO5/51	Correspondence etc. relating to operations in North America
WO1	In-Letters, Secretary at War
WO4	Out-Letters, Secretary at War
WO25	Commission Registers and Notification Books
WO34	Amherst Papers
WO64	Manuscript Army Lists
Reid, Stuart	*Like Hungry Wolves: Culloden Moor 1746* (London, 1995)
	1745: A Military History (Staplehurst, 1996)
Rodger, N.A.M.	*The Wooden World: An Anatomy of the Georgian Navy* (London, 1986)
Savory, Sir Reginald	*His Britannic Majesty's Army in Germany During the Seven Years War* (Oxford, 1966)
Simes, (Capt) Thos.	*The Military Medley* (1768)
Stacey, C.P.	*Quebec 1759: The Siege and the Battle* (2nd Edn. London, 1973)
Steele, I.K.	*Betrayals; Fort William Henry and the "Massacre"* (Oxford, 1990)
Stewart, David	*Sketches of the Highlanders of Scotland* (Edinburgh, 1822)
Western, J.R.	*The English Militia in the Enighteenth Century* (London, 1965)
Whitworth, Rex	*Field Marshal Lord Ligonier: A Story of the British*

	Army (Oxford, 1958)
	William Augustus, Duke of Cumberland (London, 1992)
Willson, Beckles	*The Life and Letters of James Wolfe* (London, 1909)
Windham, William	*A Plan of Discipline composed for the Use of the MILITIA of the County of Norfolk* (1759)
Wolfe, James	*General Wolfe's INSTRUCTIONS to Young Officers* (2nd Edition, 1780)

Index

217